Against

the

Unspeakable

Cultural Frames, Framing Culture

Robert Newman, Editor

Complicity,
the Holocaust,
and Slavery
in America

AGAINST THE UNSPEAKABLE

Naomi | Mandel
University of Virginia Press | Charlottesville and London

University of Virginia Press
© 2006 by the Rector and Visitors of the University of Virginia
All rights reserved
Printed in the United States of America on acid-free paper

First published 2006

1 3 5 7 9 8 6 4 2

Library of Congress Cataloging-in-Publication Data

Mandel, Naomi, 1969–

Against the unspeakable : complicity, the Holocaust, and slavery in America / Naomi Mandel.

p. cm. — (Cultural frames, framing cultures)

Includes bibliographical references and index.

ISBN-13: 978-0-8139-2580-6 (cloth : acid-free paper)

ISBN-13: 978-0-8139-2581-3 (pbk. : acid-free paper)

1. American fiction—20th century—History and criticism. 2. Holocaust, Jewish (1939–1945), in literature. 3. Holocaust, Jewish (1939–1945), in motion pictures. 4. Slavery in literature. 5. Suffering in literature. 6. Suffering in motion pictures. 7. Styron, William, 1925– —Criticism and interpretation. 8. Morrison, Toni. Beloved. 9. Schindler's list (Motion picture) I. Title.

PS374.H56M36 2006

813'.609358—dc22

2006025465

for my mother and father
who raised me in Israel
and taught me to read

Contents

Acknowledgments

Against the Unspeakable owes much to the faith, generosity, and imagination of many, and it is my pleasure to thank them here for their role in this book and in my life. Gabriele Schwab, whose enthusiasm for this project is matched only by her faith in its author, foresaw this book long before I did and was instrumental in making it a reality. Michael Clark has been unstinting with his time, his acumen, and his compassion; for good or ill, he is my implied reader. At the early stages of this project, Rey Chow inspired me to ask difficult questions and not to settle for easy answers. And although I can no longer thank him in person, Jacques Derrida introduced me to the terrain of the unspeakable and encouraged me to think critically about it. His loss is keenly felt.

The faculty and graduate students at the Department of English and Comparative Literature at the University of California at Irvine provided an intellectual environment that was ceaselessly challenging, exciting, and supportive of the kinds of work this book attempts to do. Robert Folkenflik and Steve Mailloux were instrumental in making my time there possible. Brian Crawford, Bernadette Meyler, Carrie Etter, Stacy Hinthorne, Helen Osterheld, John Schwetman, Krista Twu, Chris Weaver, and Vicki Silver clothed me, fed me, let me crash on their floor, and otherwise helped me feel at home in what was, at the time, a very foreign country. Nimisha Ladva and Richard House heard the most awkward versions of my ideas and graciously navigated my most turgid prose; their good sense and stalwart friendship continue to sustain me.

At the University of Rhode Island I have had the great good fortune to encounter creative, quirky, and edgy scholars who have contributed to this book in a myriad of ways. Jean Walton and Mary Cappello are the best colleagues, kindest neighbors, and most exciting interlocutors imaginable. Valerie Karno, Carolyn Betensky, Matt Frankel, and Ryan Trimm read versions of the chapters and provided critical insight and moral support. Katherine and Andy Scheil and Alain-Philippe Durand have been unfailingly encouraging. My students, whose encounters with this subject helped these chapters find their final form, deserve special thanks. In a class of his own is Stephen Barber, who challenges me to think on levels I never knew existed and who has helped me, in so many ways, to find my voice.

I want to thank Margot Norris for directing me to the University of Virginia Press, and Robert Newman and Cathie Brettschneider for welcoming this project and helping it on the road to completion. I am especially grateful to the press's anonymous reader, whose intellectual rigor and professional generosity raised the argument to another level. Ruth Melville banished as many inaccuracies as a careful copy editor can, and was infinitely patient with my first-book jitters. The University of Rhode Island provided a Faculty Development grant that gave me time to write. I am grateful to the editors of *Modern Fiction Studies* for their careful readings of an earlier version of my essay on *Beloved,* and to the Johns Hopkins University Press for permission to reprint material that originally appeared in that journal under the title "I made the Ink: Identity, Complicity, 60 Million, and More" (*Modern Fiction Studies* 48.3 [2002]: 581–613). I am grateful to Duke University Press for permission to reprint material that originally appeared, under the title "Rethinking 'After Auschwitz,'" in the journal *boundary 2* 28 (2001): 203–28. Sections of chapter 3 originally appeared in *Dialectical Anthropology* 24.3–4 (1999): 357–76 and are reprinted here with kind permission of Springer Science and Business Media.

The subject of this book is a difficult one to live with, and I am grateful to those whose friendship and care sustained me through its challenges. Scott Schaffer talked me off ledges and away from the edges of cliffs. John

Dyer, Stacy Lieberman, Christian Molstrom, and Mary-Beth O'Sullivan all helped me write this book, in some cases by enticing me away from it. Seth Yurdin and Aaron Stern understood why it needed to be written and kept me going in the final stages. Fred Gottlieb and Barry Wall helped keep my compos mentis. In Israel, Evie Goldfarb, Ohad Flinker, Sharon Tour, and my sister Jessica provided unflagging encouragement. And Erik Sklar has been a perpetual source of support for my work and a loving haven from it.

Though their primary contribution to this book is stated in its dedication, Jerome Mandel and Miriam B. Mandel actively participated at every stage. They are academics and understand the rigors of research, the solace of writing, the looming of deadlines, and the bittersweet glee of conclusion. Together and separately, and in very different ways, they illuminated every step of this road with their humor, their courage, and their spirit.

Against

the

Unspeakable

Against
the
Unspeakable

Meditating on the aftermath of the events of September 11, 2001, Art Spiegelman's monumental *In the Shadow of No Towers* refers back to *Maus*, his critically acclaimed account of how his father survived the Holocaust. In muted blues and grays, reminiscent of *Maus's* stark black-and-white, the familiar humanoid figure with mouse head and ubiquitous Cremo cigarette reflects on how one experience evokes another. "I remember my father trying to describe what the smoke in Auschwitz smelled like," he says. ". . . The closest he got was telling me it was . . . 'indescribable.'" A panel of silence follows, as Art gazes off into space. In the final panel he faces the reader: "That's exactly what the air in Lower Manhattan smelled like after Sept. 11!" (3).

Spiegelman's unique, compressed, and thoughtful style enables these four panels to do a great deal. As "indescribable" is mobilized to evoke the smell of burning bodies in Auschwitz and in Lower Manhattan, the limits of language take on special force, eloquently conveying what words cannot.[1] But "indescribable" also constructs an analogy that invites the reader to consider the terror attacks of September 11, 2001, in terms of another, earlier

From *In the Shadow of No Towers* by Art Spiegelman. (Copyright © 2004 by Art Spiegelman.
Used by permission of Pantheon Books, a division of Random House, Inc., and the Wylie Agency)

atrocity: Nazi Germany's policy of extermination in the first half of the twentieth century. Here, the limits of language serve as a bridge linking two very different historical events, aligning Al Qaeda terrorism with Nazi genocide. But in the context of this analogy, the Holocaust and September 11, 2001, are also subtly distinguished: while "indescribable" is the word that comes *closest* to Auschwitz, it is *exactly* the smell in Lower Manhattan. Holocaust horror, then, is posed as offering the terms with which to describe the events of September 11, but the former's challenge to description is slightly, but significantly, privileged over that of the latter. All horrors are indescribable, Spiegelman seems to be saying, but some horrors are more indescribable than others.

Here it is worth noting that the humanoid figure with the mouse head revives the visual iconography of *Maus* in order to mark Art's body as specifically *Jewish*. In *Maus*, the animal motif worked to perform—and to trouble—racial designations; similarly, "indescribable" is less an accurate description of empirical reality than it is a reflection on the extent to which that reality can be adequately represented or conveyed. What the father cannot quite put into words becomes, for the son, an effective means of expression, one depicted both as an affirmation (the triumphant "exactly," the exclamation mark) and as an address: establishing September 11, 2001, as a horror beyond words, the mouse persona gazes directly at the reader, inviting her to participate in this work of naming the unnameable as such, of assuming the burden of language's limits, and of reading the terror attacks of September 11 through the dark lens of the Holocaust.

Faced by this figure, I find myself at a loss. Part of me wants to explore the analogy, to address its implications, to delve into its emotional effects, and to

Against the Unspeakable

extract the cultural assumptions that enable it to operate. Part of me wants to step back from the analogy, granting its legitimacy as a personal, subjective response, one that says more about Art's relationship with his father and with his own oeuvre than about the air in Lower Manhattan. Caught between the intimacy of critical engagement on the one hand and respectful distance on the other, invited and repelled by the mouse figure's gaze, my attention shifts back to the third panel in the sequence, where Art, reflecting on his father's experience to make sense of his own, stares silently into space. The content of this silent space and the form of this space of silence enact a subtle alchemy, producing the impossibility of expression as the expression of impossibility. This alchemy—what makes it possible, what makes it work, what it invites, what it prohibits—is the subject of this book.

I open with these four panels of *In the Shadow of No Towers* because the context in which this alchemy is performed calls so clearly for the kind of debate in which the impossibility of expression as the expression of impossibility plays a crucial role. Could anyone but Spiegelman, one might ask, produce an analogy between September 11 and the Holocaust? Does this analogy—even from Spiegelman—do some kind of violence, and if so, to whom? Does the subtle privileging of the Holocaust's challenge to description over that of September 11 render this analogy more compelling or less? Does the authority of Art's father's experience grant Art's appropriation of his terminology some legitimacy, or does it render this appropriation more problematic? Does it matter that Art's father really did survive Auschwitz? Could Spiegelman have spoken these words in the guise of one of his other comic alter egos that populate *In the Shadow of No Towers,* or only as the visually Jewish Art from *Maus?* Does my own flight to the space of silence in the third panel engage these issues or elide them? These questions are familiar: they emerge from a tradition of rigorous scholarship about the Holocaust in particular, representations of atrocity in general, the politics of identity in multicultural America, the polarized atmosphere of the United States after September 11, and the effects of trauma. But they are circumscribed by these assumptions: atrocity challenges description, representation, comprehension, and speech; the cognitive categories marshaled to make sense of horror inevitably misrepresent it; this misrepresentation can do violence, cause harm, or perpetuate injury—effects that call for critical intervention and redress.

These assumptions constitute *the unspeakable:* the rhetorical invocation of the limits of language, comprehension, representation, and thought on the one hand, and a deferential gesture toward atrocity, horror, trauma, and pain on the other. Stemming from a long and illustrious history of representation's limits, the unspeakable has taken on a range of guises, from the sacred to the sublime to what some poststructuralists term "the real." Its most recent and perhaps most compelling form is in the unique challenge to language, coherence, and imagination posited by the atrocities and exterminations that have come to characterize the twentieth century and continue to inform the twenty-first. This challenge has its own seductive eloquence and has generated a formidable body of writing in literature, philosophy, history, psychoanalysis, critical theory, and ethnic and cultural studies. Repeatedly, we encounter questions like these: Now that the unthinkable, the unimaginable, has occurred, how do we think of or imagine ourselves? How can we remember a traumatic past? How do we understand what exceeds comprehension? And the question that seems to stand for them all: *How do we speak about the unspeakable?*

But this is perhaps the wrong question to ask. It assumes that "the unspeakable" has already happened and is somehow "out there," an independent if amorphous presence, somewhat detached from the culture that produced it and that posits itself in its wake. After all, "the unspeakable" is not merely an entity toward which we can gesture, with compelling injunctions to speak, witness, testify, or remember; it is, moreover, a discursive production that is re-created and reinforced whenever the limits of language, of comprehension, and of thought are evoked, be it in a space as narrow as a single comics panel frame or as expansive as the historical and political constellation of events to which the frame refers. The question; how do we speak

4

about the unspeakable? posits the unspeakable as something that must be responded to, reacted to, addressed. But the unspeakable is itself such a response, a reaction, an address, and the agendas and motivations that inform its evocations have yet to receive critical attention.

Why "unspeakable"? I choose the term for two reasons: first, the conjunction of physical articulation, language, and community in the term "to speak"; second, the extent to which this conjunction, and each of its elements, are both evoked and erased by the determined negation of "unspeakable." By "speaking" I refer not merely to physical articulation (with the concomitant assumption of the presence of a body and the capacity of such a body for comprehensible speech) but also to the work of representation in its various forms: historical, philosophical, and cultural as well as in narrative, art, literature, and film. Further, "speaking" evokes more abstract conceptual criteria: imagination, reification, rendering commensurable, communicating. What holds these terms together is the extent to which they all imply an inevitable reduction of infinite complexity to a limited concept, while retaining the term "speaking" reminds us of a necessarily material component of this reduction. The speaking body—Art's Jewish body—and the problematic implications of its necessarily reductive work of representation are, then, united in a position as privileged (speech is a privilege) as it is problematic. What is unspeakable evokes the privileges and problems inherent in speech while actively distancing itself from them, performing a rhetorical sleight of hand that simultaneously gestures toward and away from the complex ethical negotiations that representing atrocity entails.

The Holocaust is unspeakable, evoked, as it so often is, as the epitome of atrocity, horror, trauma, and pain; emblematizing the limits of language, of representation, and of thought; or figuring as a crucial presence that necessitates the rethinking of these terms. While the Holocaust's challenge to comprehension and cognition might sit uneasily with the proliferation of works on the topic, much Holocaust scholarship tends to affirm this challenge rather than dispel it. Two very different collections of writings about the Holocaust introduce their subject by gesturing toward this challenge. Roger S. Gottlieb prefaces *Thinking the Unthinkable* (1990)—a collection of essays in which Jewish theology figures prominently along with writings by Elie Wiesel, Primo Levi, Terrence Des Pres, and Jean-Paul Sartre—by emphasizing the belief that "the Holocaust possesses terribly important meanings for us" (1), but he proceeds to evoke the limits of meaning: "[w]e cannot master the Holocaust with our thinking. . . . Even if all our intellectual questions were answered, we would still cry: 'But how can this be?'" (2). In their introduction to *The Holocaust: Theoretical Readings* (2003), where critical theorists and philosophers like Walter Benjamin, Theodor Adorno, Emmanuel Levinas, Giorgio Agamben, Jean-François Lyotard, and Jacques Derrida are the prominent voices, Neil Levi and Michael Rothberg describe the Holocaust as a "limit case" that "illuminates the places where understanding breaks down" (2). Both collections demonstrate the extent to which the work of comprehension in this context almost inevitably invites a gesture toward comprehension's limits. Whether or not the Holocaust is indeed "unthinkable" (as per Gottlieb), a "limit case" (for Levi and Rothberg), or, as Paul Gilroy bluntly puts it in *Against Race,* "the most profound moral and temporal rupture in the history of the twentieth century" (25) is less to the point than the role such rhetorical moves, however inadvertently, perform, since scholars who may not subscribe to the assumption of the Holocaust's unspeakability tend nonetheless to gesture respectfully toward it. This gesture describes an arc that includes that which is gestured away from as well as that which is gestured toward, suggesting—however implicitly—the validity of both.

But the Holocaust's challenge to language, representation, and thought is not merely the province of conceptual limits in the face of a vast and violent historical event. When "experience" is suffering, trauma, horror, and pain, and when the extent and clout of these are especially compelling, evoking language's limits is often invested with an ethical injunction that prohibits "speaking the unspeakable" with the argument that to do so is to perpetrate a violence that may further wrong the victim. In the context of the Holocaust, this reverence toward the victim's subjective experience is wedded to an analogous reverence toward history's objective fact in the injunction against forgetting, or concerns about Holocaust denial, a conflation that propels scholars to carefully distinguish analyses of the Holocaust's representation, production, and presence in contemporary culture from the events of the Holocaust in general and from the experience of the victim in particular. In the face of such horror, analysis or critique is treated as a potential contaminant of historical truth or subjective experience and must be carefully distinguished from the historical record's validity and from the validity of the victim's suffering and pain: the first is perceived as too objective, the

Against the Unspeakable

second too subjective, to be the object of such work.[2] The negation performed by the "un" in "unspeakable" can be more accurately described as a prohibition, a kind of taboo, itself untouchable, around which discourse and culture are structured but which also embodies the disturbing potential of violence and contamination. Hence careful delineation of the parameters of the study at hand, an implicit acknowledgment of the kinds of misunderstandings that arise in this emotionally laden context. "I wish to make it clear," writes Amy Hungerford in her introduction to *The Holocaust of Texts*, "that I am not, in reading these texts [that engage with genocide], producing a reading of those historical events . . . while my subject is discourse about genocide of various kinds, my subject is not the discourse of those who experience the Holocaust . . . I do not produce an analysis, much less a critique of such things" (21).

That the Holocaust, as a historical event, is available to comprehension, to representation, to cultural construction and revision I do not doubt; that it *should* not be thus available is my focus here. *Against the Unspeakable*, taking as its starting point Peter Novick's suggestion, in *The Holocaust in American Life*, that the discourse "of uniqueness and incomparability surrounding the Holocaust in the United States . . . promotes *evasion* of moral and historical responsibility" (15), focuses on the forms and functions of this discourse, the implications of the evasions it promotes, the source of its appeal, and the possibilities opened up by its eschewal. Like Novick, I am interested in how the historical event of the Holocaust has been constructed and in how that construct reverberates in U.S. national and international politics. Also like Novick's, my argument is propelled by skepticism about assumptions of the Holocaust's uniqueness and inviolability—assumptions that importantly contribute to what I call "the unspeakable." But I differ from Novick in context and approach: Novick's book offers an account of how the Holocaust is constructed and produced in the United States (he pays special attention to the national and international political contexts of the postwar years to which this construction responded). *Against the Unspeakable*, on the other hand, reads a range of cultural productions (critical theory, literature, testimony, and film) that the unspeakable, directly or indirectly, informs, with an eye toward the interrelation of ethics and aesthetics (or, more precisely, the ethics of evoking the limits of aesthetics) in their analysis and reception. What, I ask, does evoking the unspeakable in the context of atrocity enable writers, artists, and critics *to do*? What does it make possible? What does it prohibit? What does it construct? What does it dismantle? These questions trace another distinction between my argument and Novick's, for when Novick frames his discussion as "the question of how we present ourselves to, how we wish to be thought of by, that vast majority of Americans who are not Jewish" (11) and emphasizes that "I ask about our centering of the Holocaust in how we understand ourselves and how we invite others to understand us" (11), his "we" and "our," like his "I," all refer to Jews; specifically, to American Jews. When I refer to "we," I attempt to evoke a broader community for whom the pervasive designation of "after Auschwitz" reflects both a rigorous interrogation into modern assumptions about coherence, certainty, and finitude *and* a insidious ethnic and cultural centrism.

In this broader context, the Holocaust, that paradigmatic challenge to representation, functions as a crucial but volatile tool for *political* representation, specifically for the articulation of identities that define their histories in terms of *other* atrocities. Phrasing a historical event in terms associated with the Holocaust (ghettos, concentration camps) works as a compelling strategy to draw international attention to the plight of suffering people.[3] Gary Weissman notes that "[t]erms such as 'the Cambodian holocaust,' 'the black Holocaust,' and 'the American Holocaust' . . . gain their rhetorical power by invoking the extermination of the European Jews" (24). However laudable their purpose—and drawing attention to suffering is, indeed, a laudable purpose—such strategies, when deemed "Holocaust appropriation," are condemned as inappropriate, unethical, or malevolent. Appropriations, like representations, vary, and while some reside relatively comfortably in their rhetorical contexts and are rarely challenged, others may rankle: Hilene Flanzbaum notes that "most Americans generally accept public officials comparing atrocities in Serbia or Rwanda with the Holocaust" but cites O. J. Simpson's lawyer Johnnie Cochran's use of the term "Nazis" to refer to the Los Angeles Police Department as an example of the inflammatory implications of "such easy metaphor-making" (7). As these examples demonstrate, claiming history as Holocaust is an identity game. Who gets to call whom a "Nazi"? Who can play the far more popular role of "Jew"? Who gets to participate in a collective psyche that represses the Holocaust or is traumatized by it? Whose history is so horrific that it is, like the Holocaust, unspeakable?

In the course of this book I will argue that the unspeakable—the limits of language, of representation, of comprehension, and of thought—is wielded

Against the Unspeakable

to simultaneously assert the compelling fact of historical victimization and to safeguard the inviolability of the victim's (or victims') pain, simultaneously articulating the *presence* of suffering and the *absence* of its voice. This conflation of rhetorical production with personal experience bears some similarity to the phenomenon of "personification" that Hungerford identifies in *The Holocaust of Texts*. Personification, Hungerford argues, conflates person with text and imagines the destruction of the former through the latter. Through "this tendency to imagine the literary text as if it bore significant characteristics of persons" (4), language becomes "a site where one can locate . . . ethnic or racial identities" (5). Through this phenomenon, the absence or disappearance of languages is perceived as genocide: it is this "rhetoric of personification that makes cultural change the same as personal death" (156). Arguing against this rhetoric, Hungerford concludes that distinguishing person from text enables more productive engagement with otherness and offers more hope for the alleviation of suffering. But if we consider the force of the *un*speakable, if we focus on the evocation of language's *limits* (both within texts and outside them) as a crucial space for the articulation of identity, something else happens: the claim of unrepresentability informs a subtle hierarchy similar to the distinction Spiegelman made between Auschwitz and September 11's claim to "indescribable," a hierarchy that extends from the event to its victims, its survivors, or those who, like Spiegelman's self-portrait as Art from *Maus,* align themselves with both. Thus the Holocaust, ostensibly mobilized in the service of articulating the experience of atrocity, effectively silences it—a practice that, Novick points out, is "deeply offensive. What else can all this possibly mean except 'your catastrophe, unlike ours, is ordinary; unlike ours is comprehensible; unlike ours is representable'" (9).

In this transformation from the absence of adequate words to the presence of human suffering, the critical eye, oddly, tends to focus on the former. Discussing the prevalence of references to "holocaust" in American discourse, Flanzbaum notes that there is a "slippery slope that comparison produces and analogy leads to. . . . Once we concede that some comparisons are appropriate, as in the case of the devastation in Serbia, for instance, how do you adjudicate the use of other comparisons that seem less appropriate? In short, if the Holocaust as metaphor is part of our common language, who can control who speaks it? No one, of course," she concludes, calling instead for "responsible evaluation and interpretation" (8). In the absence of "control"—which, as Flanzbaum notes, is impossible, even if it were desirable—morality moves to center stage as the arbiter of what is appropriate: as these metaphors proliferate, one feels, as Flanzbaum puts it, "morally obligated to respond" (8). Concern with this moral obligation informs critical work as different as Flanzbaum's balanced collection of investigations into "the Americanization of the Holocaust," Norman Finkelstein's polemical denunciation of "the Holocaust industry," and Berel Lang's concern with the limits of "Holocaust representation." Flanzbaum takes as a given that "the Holocaust as metaphor is part of our common language," concluding that its presence requires "responsible" criticism (8); Finkelstein's response to that presence is to attack it, work which, he posits, will enable the critic's noble gesture to reflect the victim's moral status. For Finkelstein, "The Holocaust" is an ideological structure, evoked to secure status in a culture in which moral (and material) capital accrues to the position of "victim," and he advocates abandoning this ideological structure in favor of what he calls the "Nazi holocaust," which is his referent for "the actual historical event" (3 n. 1). Doing so, he argues, is "the noblest gesture" toward the victims (150), one that will restore their "moral stature of . . . martyrdom" and expand the event's "moral dimension" (8). In his concern with the "actual event" over and above its ideological construction and his injection of the former with moral import, Finkelstein is very similar to Lang, whose *Holocaust Representation*—a more considered and coherent argument—argues for the Holocaust to be "registered and understood in empirical and historical terms" (142), assuming a "moral *presence* for matters of fact" (66) and situating "the historian as moral agent" (149).[4]

My point is that as the Holocaust, that paradigm of the unspeakable, becomes a key player in U.S.—and global—identity politics, concerns around its presence in this arena express less an investment in its *accuracy* as a designation for a range of atrocities than an investment in the *ethics* of this designation and, more importantly, of those who evoke and evaluate it: the critic, for Flanzbaum; the historian, for Lang; the polemicist, for Finkelstein. Perhaps, as Weissman suggests in *Fantasies of Witnessing*, it is not the Holocaust's pervading *presence* in contemporary life but its *absence* that facilitates this subtle translation from an investment in accuracy (wrong as an adjective) to a denunciation of evil (wrong as a noun). Weissman describes an overwhelming sense that "the Holocaust is not enough with us, the popularity of Holocaust museums and Holocaust movies notwithstanding"

(22), a sense that precipitates a "hierarchy of suffering" in which scholars and critics who did *not* witness the Holocaust construct a "fantasy of witnessing" in order to "occupy a privileged position in relation to the event" (21). In this hierarchy, Weissman notes, moral capital accrues to the ability to "feel the horror" (21). The result is a righteous clamor around the ethics of Holocaust appropriation, around responsible and irresponsible representations of atrocity. But what has thus far eluded critical scrutiny is the underlying social, cultural, and political context in which these evaluations operate and from which they receive their rhetorical, ethical, and political clout.[5] Given the prominence of "after Auschwitz" as a designation of the contemporary, the outrage generated by what are deemed unacceptable appropriations seems somewhat excessive until we remember that attempts to safeguard the Holocaust from such appropriations are really attempts to safeguard atrocity from language, redirecting the issue away from the fact of suffering and toward the terms in which it is couched.

To be "against" the unspeakable is not, then, to dismiss the existence of very real suffering. Nor is it to deny language's limits, the constraints of communication, the compelling choice of silence over speech, or the equally compelling—though in a different way—imposition of silence through illiteracy, disenfranchisement, and physical exhaustion, not to mention trauma, terror, torture, and the literal excision of the tongue. *Against the Unspeakable* does not quarrel with the presence of these silences but chooses rather to investigate their strategic evocation, setting these silences against (the preposition signals both opposition and relationality) the ideological context into which they enter and from which they emerge. There is, after all, a distinction between the inability of language to adequately convey experience—an inability which pertains to any experience, but which is rendered exceptionally poignant when "experience" is suffering, horror, trauma, and pain—and the rhetorical evocation of that inability, and that distinction cannot but become politicized when what lies beyond language's limits is "Auschwitz."[6] Such evocations of language's limits are not unique to the Holocaust, but their prevalence in the context of Holocaust studies, as well as in writing about atrocity in general, merits our attention.

I am, in other words, sympathetic both to the impetus to appropriate the Holocaust, or Holocaust-related terms, and to the outrage that such appropriation produces. I am invested both in explicit representations of atrocity and in representations that produce atrocity as *unrepresentable*. My concern is not with appropriation or representation in particular, or even with the Holocaust as such, but with the role played by the unspeakable in this context and the significance accorded to it. My argument here is twofold: First, phrasing an event in terms of the Holocaust or calling a specific atrocity a "holocaust" (or even a "Holocaust") does not appropriate a specific historical event; it appropriates (the assumption of) this event's *unspeakability*. By doing so, though, this appropriation situates itself in a hierarchy (pre)determined by the Holocaust. As the Spiegelman example demonstrates, there is a subtle distinction between Auschwitz's and post–9/11 Manhattan's claim to "indescribable," and this distinction privileges Auschwitz. Second, given the centrality of morality as an instrument that legislates between responsible and irresponsible representation, and the concurrent assumption that proper use of this instrument reflects on the moral stature of the critic, the historian, and the artist, "Holocaust" proscriptively informs the identity politics in which it functions.

In this context, representation, comprehension, aesthetics, and speech—each is expected to gesture modestly and deferentially toward its own limits, and the presence or the absence of such gestures are invoked to justify or condemn the object of such work on ethical grounds. It should go without saying, but too often does not, that such gestures are read into or out of the representation by this critical invocation, work that is itself dictated by a wide range of assumptions and agendas that are too easily rendered transparent in the context of the ethical urgency such work assumes when suffering is its subject. Here, it is not the experience of victimhood that claims a moral status but, rather, critical work that presumes, as Finkelstein does, to maintain the primacy of the victims' suffering over and above that suffering's representation. The rhetorical performance of evoking the unspeakable—identifying the limits of representation, comprehension, aesthetics, and speech—masquerades as ethical practice, and if I advocate "speaking the unspeakable," I do not mean, merely, transforming the silenced into speech. I am attempting to undo this masquerade, an unmasking that would reveal the critical and cultural apparatuses that wrote the script and set the stage, and the actor who dons the mask for her own purposes. When the unspeakable is spoken, I will argue, this collaboration is undone, and the actor's body, her *corporeality*, moves to center stage.

Against the Unspeakable argues that its strategic designation as beyond the limits of language facilitates a certain safe distance of the object of study from the study itself, paradoxically reinforcing atrocity's inaccessibility to knowledge in the context of knowledge's production and practice. Such designation reifies the limits of language and of representation and facilitates the evocation of these limits and their wielding in a variety of spheres: political, critical, and aesthetic. Further, this ethical investment in the limits of representation engenders a kind of myopia that focuses the critic's gaze on the object of representation rather than on representation as practice. Finally, the unspeakable's implicit privileging of the semantic (*language*'s limits) facilitates a certain dissociation from the speaker's *physical* presence and from her *act* of articulation. This dissociation weds epistemology and ontology, designating the limits of our language as the limits of our world, and implicitly evades the complexities of physical action as material differences are consigned to the unspeakable's immaterial realm. This is why, after exploring the evocation of the unspeakable in cultural productions (both in the United States and outside it) that bear directly on the Holocaust (in graphic, cinematic, and literary representations), I then turn to evocations of the unspeakable in literature about slavery in the United States by both black and white Americans: William Styron's *Confessions of Nat Turner* and Toni Morrison's *Beloved*. Both authors have been accused of appropriating another's history in order to articulate their own, and in keeping with my image of the masquerade, both novels have been described (justly or unjustly) as "blackface."[7]

In its conjunction of texts about the Holocaust with texts about American slavery, *Against the Unspeakable* participates in the work of Emily Miller Budick, Adam Zachary Newton, and Walter Benn Michaels, all of whom juxtapose literary works by African and Jewish Americans in order to explore the relations between the two. Budick's work focuses on how African and Jewish Americans employ images of each other to articulate themselves; she assumes that racism and anti-Semitism are not the causes but rather the (occasional) effects of "the embeddedness of language and culture within histories no one can forget or disavow" (2). Discussing Stanley Elkins's notorious analogy of American slavery with concentration camps, for example, Budick wonders "whether thinking about Jewish history produces the examples by which Elkins understands black history or, vice versa, whether thinking through African American history inevitably, irresistibly, provides the perspective on the Jewish experience" (83). *Against the Unspeakable* is predicated on a similar rethinking of cause and effect—a rhetoric of the unspeakable is not, I argue, the effect of atrocity's inherent challenge to representation, comprehension, and thought but, rather, its cause—and hopes to produce similarly productive readings of such (by now) fossilized antagonisms.

The unspeakable is my vehicle for such work, much as the metaphor of facing is a vehicle for Adam Zachary Newton's exploration of "the Black/Jewish relationship" in *Facing Black and Jew*. "Facing," for Newton, "is a strategy that underscores the varieties and vicissitudes of recognition, intertextual, interspatial, intercultural, which happen in language" (156). Structured as a dialogue between texts written by African and Jewish Americans (Ellison and Roth, Himes and Bellow, Wideman and Malamud), *Facing Black and Jew* pursues a vision of cultural engagement informed by Emmanuel Levinas's theory of ethics, a theory predicated on the figure of the face.[8] "Blacks and Jews share a history of otherness caricatured and defiled," writes Newton (12). In the context of "the story of competitive scar and wound"—that "commonly exploited narrative slot for Black Jewish Relations"—a history of atrocity is not just a serviceable schema but, most significantly, "a serviceable *American* schema" (6; emphasis in the original).

Unlike *Facing Black and Jew*, and unlike Budick's *Blacks and Jews in Literary Conversation*, *Against the Unspeakable* does not attempt to structure a dialogue between two groups; nor does it provide an account of the similarities and differences between African American and Jewish American articulations of a history of suffering. I do not offer a comparative analysis of two historical events but rather an interrogation of how a rhetoric of the unspeakable operates in narratives about each. Indeed, I want to trouble the Black/Jew dichotomy that informs Budick's and Newton's work, since it is this dichotomy that, in part, facilitates concerns about "Holocaust appropriation." This concern, I argue, is misguided: it is the rhetorical power of the unspeakable that is appropriated, not the historical event of the Holocaust. Indeed, the focus of this study is not the Holocaust, or slavery in the United States, or the atomic bombing of Hiroshima and Nagasaki (which I will discuss briefly in the following pages), but the implications of imparting a quality of "unspeakability" to atrocity and the concurrent political, cultural, and intellectual effects of such work. Though the Holocaust does play a more prominent role in this study than slavery does, the reason for this prominence does not reflect an implicit privileging of the Holocaust as *the* paradigmatic atrocity that defines contemporary life (chap. 1, "Rethinking 'After Auschwitz,'" explicitly dismantles this assumption). The prominence of the Holocaust in this study reflects its prominence in the rhetoric of the unspeakable, and the narratives of slavery that I address (only one of which is written by an African American) are here, not because slavery is more or less as unspeakable as the Holocaust, and not because the suffering of African Americans under slavery is more or less unspeakable than that of Jews during the Holocaust, but because the unspeakable plays such a crucial role not only in the narratives themselves but in their critical and cultural reception.

In "'You who never was there': Slavery and the New Historicism—Deconstruction and the Holocaust," Walter Benn Michaels offers a thoughtful investigation into the differences between how slavery and the Holocaust function in American memory and national identity. Starting with the questions, Do Americans believe their myths? and What myths do Americans believe? Michaels proffers this distinction between knowledge and experience, learning and remembering: "We learn about other people's history; we remember our own" (183). Morrison's *Beloved,* Michaels concludes, "redescribes something we have never known as something we have forgotten and thus makes the historical past a part of our own experience" (187), producing history as memory and enabling Americans—white as well as black—who did not experience slavery to claim it as their heritage. Moving to the Holocaust, Michaels identifies the performative—that Austinian speech act that, as Michaels puts it, "'transmits' rather than represents the events to which it testifies" (193)—as the site of a similar transformation that enables "people who did not live through the Holocaust to survive it" (194). Returning to the question, What myths do Americans believe? Michaels concludes: "Americans, especially American academics, believe in the myth of culture" (196).

The subtle transition from "Americans" to "American academics" masks other, subtler transitions from race to language and from Americans to Jews. For Morrison, Michaels argues, race (which Michaels aligns with "blood") provides "the mechanism for as well as the meaning of the conversion of history into memory" (186). Language, on the other hand, is aligned with the performative's eschewal of representation (since the performative transmits rather than represents). The transition from race to language, then, is also a movement from history, memory, and meaning on the one hand to the unspeakable on the other. Thus, while *Beloved*'s mechanism of race enables Americans to remember what they did not experience, for Jews (who, Michaels assumes, cannot claim race as a touchstone of identity) the memory of "our own" history of slavery is replaced by the unspeakable Holocaust, which stands in for Jewish culture generally. "Jews," writes Michaels, "can give up the belief in Jewish blood and give up the belief in a Jewish God; what they can't give up is Jewish culture. Hence the significance of the Holocaust and of the widespread insistence that *Jews* remember it" (195; emphasis mine). As "we" remember slavery and "Jews" remember the Holocaust, the role of race in Jewish identity is replaced by "culture," a move that enables, for Michaels, the production and maintenance of a new kind of survival, one predicated not on memory but on experience, an experience constituted by the performative's renunciation of reference (196).[9] Only at the point of replacing the body with culture as the locus of Jewish identity does Michaels clarify that by "Jews" he means "American Jews" for whom cultural assimilation is the equation of genocide. These then morph quickly (all this happens in the course of a few sentences) into "Americans, especially American academics" (196).

Michaels's point here is to evoke the possibilities that inhere in relocating identity from the body to culture.[10] Behind this point, though, lurks another: the limitation of these possibilities to a specifically *American* context. I discuss his argument at such length in order to make two additional points about the prominence of the Holocaust in this project: the Holocaust allows *Against the Unspeakable* both to extend its investigation beyond the national confines of the United States and to explore the possibilities opened up by considering the presence of the body in the articulation of identity. Hence my insistence that speaking implicates discourse with corporeality in a way that *un*speakable works to elide.[11]

In his conclusion to *The Black Atlantic,* Paul Gilroy asks: "What would be the consequences [for my argument] if this book had tried to set the Holocaust of European Jews in a provocative relationship with the modern history of racial slavery and terror in the western hemisphere?" (217). For Gilroy the question is rhetorical, but *Against the Unspeakable* gladly treads on this dangerous ground, taking seriously the issues of identity politics, of different histories of different suffering, and of the possibilities opened up in the appropriation of one by another. It is the presence of the unspeakable that makes this ground so dangerous, a presence with which Gilroy has yet to grapple.[12] But if we eschew the unspeakable (which Gilroy calls the "ineffable") we can productively engage with a range of representations of atrocity, with the concern about appropriation and about the presence of the body as a constituent of identity, and with the rush for a "moral high ground" that so strongly informs critical work in this context.

To demonstrate the previous point, to trouble the Black/Jew dichotomy, and to focus on the complex role that the unspeakable plays in representations of atrocity and in the identity politics that a history of atrocity informs, I return to Spiegelman's *In the Shadow of No Towers,* and to the return of "Auschwitz"—accompanied now by an atrocity I have not yet discussed, the atomic bombings of Nagasaki and Hiroshima. Moving from the personal account of his experience of September 11, 2001, to a broader, post-9/11, political context, Spiegelman writes: "The killer apes learned NOTHING from the twin towers of Auschwitz and Hiroshima . . . and NOTHING changed on 9/11. His 'president' wages his wars and wars on wages—same old deadly business as usual" (8). With the movement from the first to the third person, from the personal to the political, from his father's experience of World War II to his own perceptions of the Second Gulf War, Hiroshima enters the scene to join, with Auschwitz, in the analogy between September 11 and the Holocaust—now expanded to *nuclear* holocaust. What happens when Hiroshima joins Auschwitz in the realm of "Holocaust"? What is articulated, what is silenced?

As a rule, the tendency to add Hiroshima to Auschwitz and/or "Holocaust" reflects a concern with the developments of technology and culture and the impact of such developments on the contemporary. After Auschwitz and Hiroshima, the logic goes, what had been commonly perceived as "bettering the human condition" is now quite likely to worsen it. But in this global context it is important to recall that Auschwitz remains the signifier of something that happened to (technically) white, monotheistic, primarily European people, the producers and the products of Western culture and technology. Defining contemporary culture as "after Auschwitz," then, implicitly reinforces contemporary culture's identity and history as exclusively Western and European. As Darrell Fasching puts it, the "demonic narrative theme" that dominated Auschwitz "became globalized when it was incorporated into the Janus-faced technological mythos that emerged out of

Hiroshima" (3); Elie Wiesel prophesies that "if the human race should perish by the nuclear bomb, this will be the punishment for Auschwitz" ("A Plea" 141). Positing one Western atrocity as the globalization of another, as Fasching does, or as divine retribution for another, as Wiesel suggests, privileges Western atrocity in a global context, implying that to participate in this context is to possess Western culture and technology and—the logic follows—to imitate the United States and Nazi Germany in their use. Thus, both "Auschwitz" and "Hiroshima" work to cement Western hubris, within the ostensibly laudable context of evoking a global community unified by the threat of nuclear annihilation.[13]

Focusing on crucial distinctions between Hiroshima and the Holocaust complicates this context in important ways. Lisa Yoneyama points out that the impact of the Holocaust on Western thought required Western intellectuals "to place the memories of Nazism and the Holocaust in their ironic and inextricable relation to the liberal European traditions of republicanism, Enlightenment thought, and modernity" (10), leading to a postwar cultural agenda defined as "post-Holocaust" and "postmodern" (26). On the other hand, she writes, "the politics of memory in late-twentieth century Japan circulate around different 'posts': the post-nuclear, the postcolonial, and the post–cold war" (26). Ignoring these distinctions, Yoneyama continues, facilitates a strategic forgetting of such crucial points as the definition of Nazi war crimes, but not Japanese imperialism, as "crimes against humanity," or the Tokyo War Crimes Tribunal's failure to consider that using atomic bombs against civilian populations might constitute a crime against humanity as well.[14] As a result, she concludes, "Hiroshima" is remembered both in a universal discourse as the product of atomic warfare, and in the nationalism of postwar Japan as a traumatic event inflicted on a unilaterally innocent, civilian, Japanese population. Such a memory produces what Yoneyama calls a "phantasmatic innocence" according to which the bomb is remembered as a specifically Japanese experience, a construction of a victimized community that does not include the experiences and histories of the non-Japanese victims or the political reality of Imperial, wartime, and postwar Japan. As Kenzaburo Oe writes, the atomic bomb "has a positive significance for the Japanese people: it signifies a new sense of nationalism that has emerged from the dedicated twenty-year struggle to survive all that Hiroshima means" (148).[15]

My objective, like Yoneyama's, is not to blame the victims of the atomic bombing of Hiroshima and Nagasaki but rather to underscore the dangers of predicating identity—national, racial, religious—on a narrative of unspeakable suffering. Such evocations of the unspeakable play a dual role. On the one hand, they work as a crucial mode of empowerment, enabling and facilitating attention and relief to suffering communities. By evoking a history of unspeakable atrocity these communities legitimize themselves, their suffering, and their history. On the other hand, they do so at a price: silencing the specificity of experience. Important, interesting, and productive differences between atrocities like the Holocaust and Hiroshima, and the very different manifestations of suffering in the lives and bodies of those who are affected by each—all are rendered inaccessible in the context of the challenge to language, sense, and knowledge that the Holocaust and Hiroshima are assumed to pose. The question, how can one speak about the unspeakable? so often the starting point for discussions of atrocity, needs to be revised to account for the role the unspeakable plays in identity and in competing narratives about suffering. *Who* can speak? Or, more precisely: *Who can speak about not being able to speak?* And what agendas and assumptions are in operation in the claiming of identity as the heritage of unspeakable atrocity?

In *Writing Ground Zero: Japanese Literature and the Atomic Bomb*, John Whittier Treat eloquently demonstrates how the unspeakable functions for an identity that defines itself in terms of atrocity. "All the voices protesting the efficacy of language in expressing Hiroshima and Nagasaki belong to the hibakusha [a Japanese term literally meaning "explosion-affected person"] and to those who identify with their fate," writes Treat. "It is they, after all, who must fear that if a literature composed of such language were possible, the intimate links between themselves and the bombings would be severed and their existences violated even further" (28).[16] As the unspeakable is evoked to safeguard the "intimate links" between the hibakusha and those who identify with their fate (an expansion from physical identity to psychic affinity that I will discuss below), enter the Holocaust: "It is one of the hallmarks of atomic-bomb literature—indeed, lest this be mistaken as a peculiarly 'Japanese' trait, of Holocaust literature, too—that it depends to an uncommon degree on implication and insinuation. It is in the words of Lawrence Langer 'a literature of innuendo,' 'as if the author were conspiring with his readers to recapture an atmosphere of insane misery which they somehow shared, without wishing to name or describe it in detail'" (28).

What does the presence of the Holocaust at this juncture—the link between identity and unspeakable atrocity—do for Treat's discussion? Perhaps it mitigates the implicit essentialism behind the reference to a "peculiarly 'Japanese' trait." Perhaps it reflects the extent to which the unspeakable is presumed to be the property of the Holocaust, requiring other atrocities to be posited in the context of the Holocaust in order to be legitimized as themselves unspeakable. Given the extent to which "speaking" implicates discourse with corporeality, and given the role that Holocaust writers (including Berel Lang, George Steiner, Hannah Arendt, Primo Levi, Bruno Bettelheim, Terrence Des Pres, and Elie Wiesel) play in Treat's argument, we may assume that both possibilities are in effect. Ultimately, Treat's conflation of atomic-bomb literature with Holocaust literature (a conflation that occurs in the deliberately vague referent for the pronoun "it" in "it is a literature of innuendo") demonstrates how the unspeakable, precisely by virtue of its exteriority to language, can be wielded to efface significant differences and distinctions in the historical and political occasions that precipitate its presence and in the identities that define themselves by it: note Treat's casual expansion of "the hibakusha" to "those who identify with their fate."[17]

I want to expand on this final point by looking more closely at the term *hibakusha* itself. Robert J. Lifton notes that the official Japanese definition of hibakusha privileges physical presence at the site of atomic disaster.[18] The term, Lifton writes, refers to "possible exposure to significant amounts of radiation" (7) and is predicated on physical proximity to the bomb; he distinguishes between hibakusha, which literally means "explosion-affected person," and *seizonsha,* which means "survivor" and which is rarely used in this context (7).[19] In the conclusion to *Death in Life,* Lifton expands the scope of his discussion, replacing the crucial role accorded to physical presence with an emphasis on psychic reverberations, a move accompanied by the replacement of hibakusha with "survivor": "We are all survivors of Hiroshima and, *in our imaginations,* of future nuclear holocaust," he states, adding that in the case of atrocity of this magnitude "we are dealing with universal psychological tendencies; the survivor becomes Everyman" (479; emphasis mine). The expansion from hibakusha to survivor enables, again, the evocation of Holocaust suffering to articulate Hiroshima. Discussing the difference between Holocaust and Hiroshima survivors, Lifton identifies the "death imprint" of the former as psychic, of the latter as physical: while "concentration camp survivors . . . are likely to retain more diffuse and severe psychic impairment . . . Hiroshima survivors experienced this grotesqueness through a sense of monstrous alteration of the body substance" (480), but he quotes Elie Wiesel, that paradigmatic Holocaust survivor, as an example of both.

Like Treat's casual reference to "hibakusha and those who identify with their fate," Lifton's expansion of "hibakusha" from a physical identity to a psychic affinity is driven by the laudable agenda of constructing an international community with the common heritage of atrocity. I say this agenda is laudable because, though we cannot ignore how the authority to perform such an extension resides in institutions that are themselves implicated in postcolonial, postwar geopolitics, we should also keep in mind its more sympathetic motives: atomic bombs can, of course, pose a significant threat to the survival of the human species. The term "omnicide" is often used to describe such a threat. But this term, too, requires a closer look. "Omnicide" replaces "genos" in "genocide," effacing the specific role played by *identity* in the crime. When we say "omnicide," we evoke the connotations of a crime without negotiating the politics of naming its victims or its perpetrators. Further: if we take into account the extent to which hibakusha identity resides in the *physical* reverberations of the disaster—traces of radiation in their *bodies* and, most significantly, in their *blood*—we cannot ignore the prominence of the body in this context, or the implications of its erasure.[20] Thus, like Michaels's discussion of slavery and the Holocaust, the eschewal of reference in the expansion of "hibakusha" from a physical identity to a psychic affinity divests identity of the very corporeality that the initial violence was leveled against.

Treat's and Lifton's vision of a contemporary community haunted by atomic devastation, however sympathetic its motivation, is driven by an unspoken mandate to dissociate identity from the body, a mandate that receives its ethical clout from the disturbing conceptual realm of essentialism and that is weighted with the historical baggage of biological racism. Like Michaels's definition of "American," Treat's and Lifton's definition of contemporary global identity replaces the body with culture under the presumably ethical aegis of eschewing biological racism.[21] I will argue in the course of this book that this ethical aegis of eschewing racism is aligned with the ethical imperative of eschewing reference, according to which the unspeakable becomes a morally comfortable space for identity's articulation, a speech without the (racialized, politicized body of the) speaker. When identity is articulated in terms of atrocity imagined as unspeakable, the presence of the body in this identity is erased, and *speaking* the unspeakable propels the speaker into complicity with this presence and with the ideological implications of its history.

The entrance of "complicity" into my discussion of atrocity and its representation requires some important clarifications and distinctions. In the course of this book, I will touch on a number of manifestations of complicity, from acknowledging the participation of European culture in mechanisms of persecution to articulating the painful manifestations of these mechanisms in, and by, the persecuted. In these contexts complicity is often conflated with culpability or with collaboration.[22] But like Christopher Kutz in *Complicity: Ethics and Law for a Collective Age* and Mark Sanders in *Complicities: The Intellectual and Apartheid,* my concept of "complicity" borrows from Karl Jaspers's articulation of a community defined by those for whose actions we are "co-responsible." As a "folded-together-ness" (Sanders 5) or a series of "cultural and legal practices, surrounding relations of an agent to a harm that are mediated by other agents" (Kutz 2), complicity *precedes* the charge of collaboration or the conclusion of culpability; complicity is, in fact, *the condition of possibility* for the articulation of these charges. Further, as I will demonstrate in the final section of this book, complicity is a structure by which identity constitutes itself vis-à-vis the unspeakable; it is, finally, the condition of possibility for ethical engagement with the violence of such constitution.[23]

Against the Unspeakable, then, extends the aesthetic, ideological, and political implications of evoking representation's limits from the specific realm of Holocaust representation to the broader realms of U.S. and international identity politics. Further, by identifying the political and ethical implications of evoking the unspeakable, this book situates literary theory at the crossroads of language and materiality and, more specifically, poststructuralism and politics. I agree with the contention—an axiom for most poststructuralists—that representation is inevitably complicit in some form of hegemony. Given this complicity, to delineate the unspeakable is, for critical theorists like Lyotard, Agamben, Blanchot, and Derrida, an ethical gesture that itself embodies poststructuralism's engagement with politics; what is commonly called Derrida's "turn to the political," for example, attempts to posit critical reading as an ethical intervention in a political (or politicized) realm. What is significant about this moment—this gesture that embodies—is the imagery of spectrality that informs this turn, and this imagery, I claim, returns us to the disturbing materiality that the unspeakable, by positing suffering beyond the limits of language, excluded from the human community of speech. It is this spectrality that can, I submit, contribute to the by now familiar tension between poststructuralism and cultural studies, a tension beautifully articulated in Gilroy's brief critique of Foucault in *Against Race*. Foucault, says Gilroy, *"was not haunted, as I believe we should still be,* by the famous image of an orangutan carrying off a Negro girl that provides the frontispiece for Linnaeus' *Genuine and Universal System of Natural History"* (44–45; emphasis mine). I agree with Gilroy that we all need to be haunted: the presence of the ghost challenges the assumption that presence, the present, and re-presentation can be dissociated; both the body and its ghost disrupt the implicit semantic emphasis on which the unspeakable relies.[24]

To be haunted, I will argue, is to eschew the moral high ground that the unspeakable so seductively supplies and to embrace the complicity of our own situation in structures of violence and power. Like Gilroy, who treats the complicity of humanism in racist violence as an opportunity to rethink not only race and violence but humanism itself, I argue that complicity is a potentially productive site, one that needs to be actively sought out rather than avoided. For, as Gilroy puts it in *The Black Atlantic,* "there might be something useful to have gained from setting these histories [modern racism and the Holocaust] closer to each other . . . as precious resources from which we might learn something valuable . . . about the ideologies of humanism with which these brutal histories can be shown to have been complicit" (217). What I find most heartening about Gilroy's example is his movement to literature as a productive arena in which these concerns can be explored. Significantly, it is in literature's imaginative space—a space both public and private, universal and particular, historical and fictional—that this semantic emphasis can be undone. It is here, perhaps, that a new relation to an exceptionally disturbing history has begun to be forged.

Because *Against the Unspeakable* moves across a number of fields and disciplines (including Holocaust studies, African American studies, and comparative ethnic studies) and alternates broad cultural contexts with close readings of specific critical, literary, and cinematic texts, I offer here a few words about the book's structure and some implications of its argument. Taken as a whole, the book moves from a critique of the unspeakable in writings about the Holocaust (the focus of chap. 1) to an ethics of complicity (which I address in the conclusion). I argue that the unspeakable, that evocative space of silence, is an attractive rhetorical strategy for literary and critical writing about events like the Holocaust and slavery. The attraction of the unspeakable lies in the seeming separation it performs between the literary writer or the critic on the one hand and the moral problematics of her subject on the other—a separation that seems to mimetically reflect experiential incommensurability. To abandon the unspeakable is to abandon the lure of the moral high ground and to recognize that all of us, literary authors and critics alike, are the producers and the products of our cultures and hence always already complicit in the ugliest aspects of our histories. Rather than disqualifying our judgment, our attitude, or our being from productive ethical intervention in the moral problematics with which we engage, complicity cements our relation to them. In this way, the affirmation of complicity is also and equally an affirmation of presence: there is something to be gained by relinquishing the unspeakable, and that something is nothing less than our own fragile corporeality and a constructive engagement with the fragile corporeality of others.

The movement from a focus on the unspeakable to an ethics of complicity, then, is paralleled by a movement from a focus on language, representation, and its limits on the one hand to an engagement with the corporeal on the other. This movement begins in chapter 3, which focuses on representations of Holocaust testimonies, an especially fruitful site for exploring the tension between historical fact and cultural artifact, a tension (literally) embodied, I claim, by the figure of the speaking corpse. I continue to trace the emergence of corporeality from the unspeakable in chapters 4 and 5, reading novels about American slavery to address how the body, as well as its speech, is implicated in the mechanisms of persecution—a complicity that, like our own, is the condition of possibility for ethics. Thus this book not only offers a critique of the unspeakable but outlines a reading practice that is, I hope, both ethically and critically productive. To read texts like Steven Spielberg's *Schindler's List* not for what should or should not, can or cannot be represented but for what the work of representation makes possible offers new insight into texts that have received extensive critical attention (like Elie Wiesel's *Night* or Toni Morrison's *Beloved*) and reopens texts that, like William Styron's *Confessions of Nat Turner,* have been subjected to controversy so acrimonious as to practically prohibit productive critical work.

Chapter 1, "Thinking 'After Auschwitz,'" is an introduction to and anatomy of the unspeakable, exploring the range of forms it takes and the modalities of its operations. For the unspeakable, language's exclusions (of alterity, of negativity, of trauma) and inclusions (of silence, of absence, of the work of mourning) become rhetorical structures through which the Holocaust appears as itself unspeakable, and hence incomprehensible or posing a specific challenge to comprehension. Such rhetorical work is not unique to the Holocaust, but its prevalence in writing about the Holocaust, the pervasiveness of the phrase "after Auschwitz" as a presumed designation of the contemporary human condition, and, as further chapters demonstrate, the appropriation of this rhetoric for other atrocities indicate that close scrutiny of the unspeakable merits our attention.

Opening with the question, just what part of "Auschwitz" don't we understand? I argue that "Auschwitz" is posited as what is a priori incomprehensible, and that the tendency to refer to the Holocaust as "Auschwitz" actually performs a metonymic substitution according to which what we can historically know about a vast network of destruction, involving the active and tacit participation of millions and occurring over a significant period of time, is divorced from a particular evil posited—but only heuristically—as its culmination. To think "after Auschwitz" is to rethink the politics of representation, both linguistic (a synecdochic trope, attractively alliterative, works as metonymic performance) and epistemological: Auschwitz, wrenched from its specific historical and political context, comes to signify the challenges to communication, comprehension, and thought associated with the Holocaust—a historical event that has itself garnered a vast body of scholarship.

Holocaust scholars address these politics of representation in a variety of ways, not the least interesting of which is their rigorous dissociation from the term "Holocaust" itself, and this chapter analyzes texts from four main areas of Holocaust scholarship (history, literary criticism, psychoanalysis, and philosophy), identifying the operations of the unspeakable in each. For these scholars, I argue, the unspeakable is imbued with what I call an ethical imperative which presumes that to translate another's experience into language is to perform some sort of violence, and which advocates that the limits of language be delineated in order to make space for cultural, experiential, or epistemological difference. Thus silence, absence, and incomprehensibility replace crucial issues of human volition, responsibility, and complicity, just as "Auschwitz" replaces the broader concerns of the Holocaust. This chapter ends with an emphasis on *speaking* the unspeakable, and urges an explicit confrontation with the inevitable complicity that such speech would perform.

The second chapter, "Speaking *Schindler's List*," provides a working example of the previous chapter's injunction to "speak" the unspeakable and to confront complicity. In her introduction to a collection of critical essays about the film, Yosefa Loshitzky writes: "*Schindler's List* provides fertile ground for general reflections about the limits and problems associated with the representation of the Holocaust precisely because it challenges those limits by making the unimaginable imaginable, the unrepresentable representable" (2). Such a statement—a fair representation of many critics' discomfort with the film—is based on two assumptions: (1) the Holocaust is unimaginable, unrepresentable; (2) this particular film has succeeded in enabling the imagination or representation of what had previously been deemed unimaginable and unrepresentable. In other words, *Schindler's List* enables its viewers, or other filmmakers, or post-Holocaust society, or someone, somehow, to speak what Loshitzky assumes to be unspeakable.

I argue that *Schindler's List* should be examined, not in terms of the relation of representation to its object, but rather in terms of the relation of representation to its audience. The film constructs, controls, and directs our acts of seeing and creates situations in which sight underscores or undercuts comprehension. We need to ask, then, To what extent is the viewer empowered or disempowered by what she sees? What viewer reactions are scripted, and what reactions are scripted as unspeakable? Analyzing some key scenes from the film in light of these questions, I attempt to delineate a more productive approach to images of atrocity: speaking *Schindler's List* involves spelling out the complex articulations of complicity that are expressed or effaced by the act of seeing, by the agency required for comprehending, by the complexities of representation and of the work of memory.

Testimony contributes an additional, crucial dimension to the unspeakable. Given that testimony is a narrative that is accorded truth-value by an institution, negotiating the vicissitudes of testimony requires addressing not only the complexities of representation, its relation to history, the evocation of memory, and the institutional practices and spaces (the courtroom, the camera, the archive) in and through which representation and memory signify, but also the relation of knowledge to a reality that is informed by a range of assumptions about what constitutes experience and who is authorized to speak. In the next two chapters I focus on representations of testimony: chapter 3 ("The Story of My Death") discusses representations of Holocaust testimony, and chapter 4 ("Nat Turner's Key") focuses on representations of Nat Turner's confession (Thomas R. Gray's 1831 pamphlet, William Styron's 1967 novel, and contemporary historical studies and critical readings of both).

Scholars of Holocaust testimony—Lawrence Langer and Shoshana Felman are prominent examples—focus on renegotiating the presence of the unspeakable into testimony so that representation's potential for truth-value can be maintained. But this urgent work fails to distinguish between the survivor's inability or unwillingness to speak and rhetorical evocations of the unspeakable, effectively situating material experience beyond the limits of representation. As an alternative to this approach, I focus on a recurring image, as yet unexplored, that appears both in survivor testimony and in studies and representations of Holocaust testimony: the figure of the speaking corpse. I identify this figure in a wide range of mediums: it appears in the writings of Elie Wiesel, Primo Levi, and Jorge Semprun; in Art Spiegelman's graphic novel *Maus* and Claude Lanzmann's cinematic testimony *Shoah;* and in the critical and philosophical writings of Jacques Derrida, Shoshana Felman, and Giorgio Agamben. When the unspeakable encounters the complexities of testimony, and the stakes become the relation between experience and its (institutional) verification and validation, the speaking corpse— significantly, a *literary* image—emerges, and this image both forces and embodies the confrontation between language and the corporeal. Thus, I argue, the figure of the speaking corpse shatters the unspeakable, forcing us to re-member ourselves as palpable entities as well as discursive constructions. The chapters that follow trace the function of the unspeakable in articulations of identity that are in a more mediated relation to the Holocaust than those discussed heretofore, with an eye to performing an integration of experience—the body and her actions—into an economy of language, community, and ethics.

William Styron's controversial novel *The Confessions of Nat Turner,* like Spielberg's *Schindler's List,* raised critical ire by virtue of its representational gestures toward a presumably unrepresentable reality. Unlike *Schindler's*

List, however, Styron's problematic depiction of the Turner rebellion generated a debate in which the ethics of representation were explicitly linked to ethnic identity. The initial controversy—defined by *William Styron's Nat Turner: Ten Black Writers Respond,* edited by John Henrick Clarke—condemned the novel as an articulation of its author's implicit racism and performed an identity politics in which assertions of historical fact merge with the authority assumed by a history of suffering to produce a reality claimed as a crucial constituent of identity. Contemporary readings of the debate, however, focus on the strategic rhetorics and the historical contexts of the controversy, effectively eschewing the issues of identity politics that the original controversy urges and that remain a crucial constituent of ethnic identity, especially in the United States today.

In chapter 4, "*Nat Turner's* Key," I address how the original "Confessions" by Thomas Gray reflects an uncomfortable negotiation of a problematic body and its murderous actions into a textual performance, and that Styron's novel (loosely based on Gray's pamphlet) reanimates this body and ascribes it a raced and gendered identity perceived by the novel's critics as immensely problematic. Recalling the complexities of language and materiality posed by testimony, I argue that these paradigms offer a reading of the novel that shows us a body—not only Turner's but also Gray's and, significantly, Styron's—both silenced and animated by text. *The Confessions of Nat Turner* and the debate it produced, then, reveal some crucial aspects of how the unspeakable is mobilized in the service of identity politics, effectively masking the appropriation—not of atrocity, but of identity—with the patina of ethical urgency.

The function of the unspeakable in identity politics in the United States encloses my discussion of Toni Morrison's novel *Beloved* in the following chapter, "The One Word That Mattered." I begin with a rereading of the controversy raised by the dedication of the novel to "60 million and more." Critics have expressed concern about the extent to which "60 million" reflects an appropriation of the Holocaust. I demonstrate, however, that this figure is not an appropriation of the Holocaust but an appropriation of the unspeakable, discussing the implications of such appropriation for the purpose of comparative atrocities. Reading the novel as a demonstration of multiple levels of complicity, I note that this complicity is effaced, in critical work on the novel, by evocations of the unspeakable—a tendency implicitly encouraged by Morrison herself in her speeches and interviews. The "one word that mattered" is "Beloved," an inscription on a child's tombstone, and the appropriation of that text by a living breathing body haunts the novel, its characters, and its critics, performing the violation of language's limits by the presence of the corporeal.

If I have heretofore insisted on the necessity of speaking what has been posited as unspeakable and on confronting the inevitable complicity that such speech imposes, "the one word that mattered" identifies the form that such confrontation should take: the speaking corpse and her disturbing corporeality forces materiality back into language—a materiality that the unspeakable deliberately works to exclude—and challenges the assumption that what is excluded from "speech" is excluded from the world in which that speech functions. The speech that speaking the unspeakable produces is the speech of the living breathing body, defined and circumscribed by her physical palpability and by her actions in *Beloved*'s material world. Such actions, unlike rhetoric, cannot gesture toward their own inefficacy under the guise of ethical practice, and force us to re-member ourselves—as palpable entities as well as rhetorical constructions. If we, like the characters in *Beloved*, are haunted by a speaking corpse, what we are haunted by is the fact of our own corporeality, our own vulnerability to suffering, our own inevitable complicity in victimization. Rendering a painful history unspeakable makes these sad facts too easy to forget.

The conclusion articulates the trajectory of the book's argument in terms of the bodies of work—Holocaust studies and African American studies— it brings into dialogue, unpacking the manifestations of "complicity" that have been in play in the course of the preceding chapters. With the help of Primo Levi's meditations on "the gray zone," I begin to disentangle the concept of complicity from the charge of collaboration and the verdict of culpability in order to redefine complicity as a series of actions on which judgment *has yet* to fall. This definition has the virtue of expanding the sphere of complicity to include a range of questionable actions. Focusing on these actions—and on their relation to the evil in which they are implicated—enables a refocus of the critical gaze from the object of speech to the speaking, and acting, self. It is this self—articulated against and complicit in the discourses that form and sustain it—that *Against the Unspeakable* reveals.

Chapter 1

Thinking "After Auschwitz"

I use the name of Auschwitz to point out the irrelevance
of empirical matter, the stuff of recent past history, in terms
of the modern claim to help mankind to emancipate itself.
—Jean-François Lyotard, "Defining the Postmodern"

What it might mean, after Auschwitz, to live a life thoughtfully
"beyond good and evil" is, in short, worth finding out.
—James Miller, The Passion of Michel Foucault

When Adorno situated contemporary culture "after Auschwitz," he coined a
phrase that has been accumulating significance and intensity as this culture
moves on into the future and Auschwitz recedes into the past. In the course
of this movement, "Auschwitz" has come to signify more than the sum of its
particular parts. When we say "Auschwitz" we do not mean the concentration camp in occupied Poland, or we do not mean merely that; we are also
referring to the vast network of bureaucracy, red tape, regional and personal
politics, personal and impersonal betrayals and hatreds, German national-
ist and racist presumptions that found expression in National Socialism
and a leader in Hitler, the scapegoat mentality and delusional ideology produced by a centuries-old anti-Semitism—in short, the immense, cumula-

tive, complex, profound, prosaic, stunning, and disturbingly banal process that produced what is known as the Holocaust.

So when we refer to "Auschwitz" we mean something else; when we say we exist "after Auschwitz" we are making a statement about our own relation to history and to an especially painful past. Just what that relation is and what that past contains rise bleakly to mind: a train station, cattle cars, bewildered naked people, some go to the right, some go to the left, gas, ovens, chimney, smoke. A process stunning in its simplicity—the reduction of living people to smoke and ashes—while overwhelming in its implications: the reduction of living people to smoke and ashes. "Auschwitz" emblematizes this simplicity, giving the process a specific location and a name, while enacting its complexity: specifying, locating, and naming. Like any word or any name, "Auschwitz" both signifies and effaces, refers and defers. To be "after Auschwitz" is to be in the spectral presence of the people who died there as well as in the accusing presence of the people who survived it. It is to be forced to confront these deaths, this presence, and the disquieting effacement that "after Auschwitz" performs on both.

In the second half of the twentieth century, this effacement has come to take central stage as "after Auschwitz" both compels the project of living, as Miller puts it, "thoughtfully" and just as compellingly gestures determinedly toward the perils of thought. Given the extent of suffering that "Holocaust" represents, "thinking the unthinkable," "speaking the unspeakable," and "representing the unrepresentable" are not only legitimate projects but projects of legitimation, articulating indissoluble paradoxicality as an essential constituent of contemporary thought. The more we speak about Auschwitz, it seems, the more prevalent and compelling the gestures toward the limits of speech, thought, knowledge, and world.

When such gestures are enacted by early Holocaust writers like George Steiner, for whom "the world of Auschwitz lies outside speech as it lies outside reason" ("K" 123); or intellectuals like Lionel Trilling, who, when confronted with photographs of the liberation of Buchenwald in 1948 concluded that "before what we now know the mind stops" (qtd. in Rosenfeld, *Thinking* 11); or advocates of Holocaust sacralization like Elie Wiesel, for whom "Auschwitz negates all systems, destroys all doctrines" ("The Holocaust" 7), one may well dismiss them as manifestations of an archaic aesthetic, a specific historical moment, or a particular worldview. But with the emergence of "Holocaust studies" as a distinct field these early writings have garnered a degree of institutional reification that makes such dismissal a tricky proposition. In 1997 Alvin Rosenfeld ascribed to Trilling's statement a "sense of cognitive arrest" which he identified as "characteristic of much of the most thoughtful writing about the Nazi crimes against the Jews" (*Thinking* xi). When "cognitive arrest" is evoked as a criterion of "thoughtfulness," thinking "after Auschwitz" becomes a formidable project indeed.

Within the broader spectrum of debates about discourse, realism, and representation, the Holocaust's traditional role as the paradigmatic challenge to all these categories is affirmed or relinquished but rarely ignored. Critics who do not subscribe to the unspeakability of the Holocaust nonetheless tend to gesture respectfully toward it. Michael Rothberg, for example, discussing conceptual approaches to the Holocaust, identifies "seemingly irresolvable contradictions between the event's 'uniqueness' and its 'typicality,' its 'extremity' and its 'banality,' its 'incomprehensibility' and its susceptibility to 'normal understanding.'" Though in no way a proponent of Holocaust sacralization, Rothberg avoids "choosing a side," preferring to "preserve the tensions between these conflicting understandings" (3). Hilene Flanzbaum, distancing herself from the Holocaust's "incomparability and unspeakability," nonetheless clarifies that "this is not because the Holocaust is not unique or incomparable or indescribable; it may be all three" (15). Resilient even in denial, gestures toward the limits of thought eloquently and compellingly delineate critical work that takes the Holocaust as its subject. As Gary Weissman puts it, "the problem of the unrepresentable Holocaust will not go away" (207).

These eloquent gestures toward the limits of thought reverberate in contemporary critical theory and philosophy's explorations of language, history, community, and ethics, realms in which the Holocaust maintains a formidable presence.[1] Jean-François Lyotard posits Auschwitz as a *differend*—the space that cannot (yet) be filled by discourses of history, politics, or philosophy. As paradigms of disaster, Maurice Blanchot chooses "Holocaust" and "Auschwitz." Giorgio Agamben's project *Homo Sacer* is predicated on the disquieting presence of the Holocaust in history. Amy Hungerford and James Berger both note that Jacques Derrida's work on literature participates in this trend, though Derrida explicitly destabilizes the referent of "holocaust."[2] For Lyotard, Blanchot, Agamben, and Derrida, the Holocaust—along with the implications of its representation—is not itself the object of their study but, rather, a catalyst that activates a sense of moral urgency and heightens the discussion's implicit stakes. Here, the Holocaust's association with the disruption of all limits is mobilized in order to illustrate a moral nadir, aporia, or rupture from which a new concept of text, race, humanism, ethics, or identity must arise. Evoking the Holocaust in this manner, however, retains and thus perpetuates the assumption that, once evoked, the Holocaust's role as an emblem of crisis requires no further scrutiny. As Miller's casual reference in the epigraph to this chapter attests, "ethics after Auschwitz" invites the question, What ethics? not Why Auschwitz?

Further, this fundamental designation of contemporary identity (we are all, somehow, presumably "after Auschwitz") poses crucial problems for the articulation of presence and the present in relation to this particular past. What, precisely, does it means to *be* "after Auschwitz"? What ontological stance is afforded by this mystic merging of space and time? How is being "after Auschwitz" different from being "after" any historical event, or "after" history itself, assuming that the past can be sufficiently dissociated from the present as to enable the present to be, effectively, *after* it? Geoffrey Hartman has suggested that while we may be "after" Auschwitz, we are not yet "beyond" it (*Longest Shadow* 11). But this substitution of a temporal metaphor with a spatial one only reaffirms the unthinkability of "Auschwitz" itself. Rather than asking, what does it mean to be "after Auschwitz," we may well ask: *what does "after Auschwitz" mean?*

Approaching the issue in this manner highlights the assumption that everyone who encounters the phrase "after Auschwitz" knows, as if instinctively, precisely what it means. But as Hungerford points out, "this claim about unspeakability and the unimaginable condenses a number of assumptions" that prove "difficult to sort out" (15). The last couple of decades have revealed the extent to which articulating *any* identity raises crucial issues of silence and exclusion, not to mention the uncomfortable economics of representation forced on such articulation in political contexts for political means, and the implications of defining an identity on the basis of lack and loss. If, as Rothberg puts it, "[a]fter Auschwitz," has become "a two-word sound bite . . . the intellectual equivalent of the political poster slogan, 'Never Again!'" (25), Wendy Brown has noted that the prominence of subjection in articulations of identity can produce an identity "invested in its own subjection . . . even while it seeks to assuage the pain of its powerlessness through its vengeful moralizing, through its wide distribution of suffering, through its reproach of power as such" (70). Such an identity, Brown continues, "is as likely to seek generalized political paralysis, to feast on generalized political impotence, as it is to seek its own or collective liberation through empowerment" (71). Caught between activism and paralysis, the issues of identity and identity politics forced by the assumption of a "we" that is, presumably, "after Auschwitz" raise these questions: What happens when "after Auschwitz" appears on the rhetorical scene? What work is this phrase expected to do? What work does it actually do? And is this work worth doing?

Just What Part of "After Auschwitz" Don't We Understand?

Choosing a concentration camp to stand for the Holocaust seems to imply that it is the killing, and the killing alone, that eludes comprehension. One imagines a well-oiled operation by which victims—generally but not exclusively Jews—are unloaded from trains, undergo a selection process, are herded into gas chambers, and cremated—a strangely sterile, abstract proceeding, perhaps what Heidegger was thinking about when he referred to "the manufacture of corpses." Shocking as this image may be, it is still a relatively reductive account that effaces the more complex and far more disturbing issue of how these people got to Auschwitz in the first place, while the passivity of the victims as they are unloaded, selected, herded, gassed, and cremated elides the complexities of life within, around, and after the camp. Further, by giving the horror a specific location and a name, the horror is localized, abstracted, and isolated, as if the Holocaust is what occurred at the camps. But the fact remains that family members, friends, neighbors, coworkers, students, teachers, employers, employees, religious leaders, municipal and government officials, real and imagined allies, were all potential betrayers or murderers, and it is this dissolution of an entire network of human relations, not just the killing, that constitutes the Holocaust. Calling it "Auschwitz" effaces this fact, makes it too easy to face.[3]

This is not to say that the enunciation of "Auschwitz" is an attempt to deny the broader context in which the camp functioned or to deliberately dissociate oneself from the broader historical context. On the contrary, a thoughtful and rigorous engagement with history propels Saul Friedlander to refer to "'Auschwitz'" (the quotation marks are his) as the referent for "the proper historization of National Socialism" (*Probing the Limits* 2). But in the conflation of what Auschwitz stands for with Auschwitz itself, something gets lost, and it is that "something" that is Friedlander's main concern, the elusive "something" which, as Jürgen Habermas puts it, "happened there that no one could previously have thought even possible," but which nonetheless instantiates Auschwitz as "the signature of an entire epoch" (251).[4]

Lawrence Kritzman performs a similar conflation in his introduction to *Auschwitz and After*, where "Auschwitz" serves as a referent both for the Vichy government's collaboration with the Nazis and for the implications of this collaboration for representations of the Holocaust in France. "The memory of Auschwitz and the question of Jewish identity," Kritzman writes, "have been key critical *topoi* in French political, cultural, and intellectual life since the end of World War II" (1). If the issue is *French* identity and *France's* collaborationist past, why mention Auschwitz (a concentration camp in Poland) at all? Despite his expressed concern with collaboration, Kritzman's gesture toward Auschwitz rather than Vichy enacts a turn toward "humanity" and away from the specificities of "Jewish identity" and "French political, cultural and intellectual life," away from French collaboration and toward an expansion of "Auschwitz" into a general comment on the responsibilities and ethics of memory. "[T]he problem of remembering Auschwitz," concludes Kritzman, "is how to remember it in order not to forget what happened at Auschwitz, or how to talk about Auschwitz without betraying or trivializing it" (8).

We see here what Debarati Sanyal describes as "[t]he extension of the concentration camp . . . from fact to concept" (15), in which culpability becomes generalized and very real differences and distinctions are effaced. Sanyal locates the origin of this generalization and consequent effacement in the assumption that "silence [is] the only adequate mode of apprehending a historical reality that confounds representation" (15).[5] Sanyal is right, but Kritzman's essay extends the problem from silence to language and, specifically, *language's limits*. "Since Auschwitz," Kritzman writes, "*every word* evoking its dark past either dissimulates guilt or simply denies the reality of the extermination" (1; emphasis mine). I would suggest that it is not every word since Auschwitz but "Auschwitz" itself that performs the dissimulation Kritzman finds so troubling and emblematizes the generalization Sanyal finds so problematic. By naming Auschwitz, rather than Vichy, as a referent for his enunciation of a "we," Kritzman provides an illustration of how Auschwitz, wrenched from its specific historical and political context, comes to signify the challenges to communication, comprehension, and thought associated with the Holocaust. The word refers to the limit of words, a realm that is in-accessible to knowledge; to define ourselves as "after Auschwitz" implies, as Kritzman puts it, a compelling ethical imperative: we must not forget, we must not trivialize, we must not betray. But the obscurity and inaccessibility that characterize Auschwitz, this emphasis on our inability to understand it, severely qualify this ethical stance: if we cannot "know" Auschwitz, how can we know what not to betray, how not to trivialize, when to remember, why not to forget?

It is this detachment of Auschwitz from the work of historicization—a detachment that produces an "almost comfortable demonization" of the camp—that Debórah Dwork and Robert Jan van Pelt address in *Auschwitz, 1270 to the Present* (11). Assumptions of the Holocaust's incomprehensibility, they argue, "[distance] us from an all too concrete historical reality, sup-pressing the local, regional, and national context of the greatest catastrophe western civilization both permitted and endured, and obscuring the re-sponsibility of the thousands of individuals who enacted this atrocity step by step" (11). Dwork and van Pelt examine the referent "Auschwitz," re-creating the specific historical and economic context through which it came to exist, with the expectation that displaying the concrete, prosaic networks that en-abled Auschwitz to become a killing center will demythologize the killing, replacing incomprehensibility with knowledge and enabling a more re-sponsible commemoration of the function the camp served and the suffer-ing it inflicted. Such rigorous historicism, Dwork and van Pelt assume, should dispel the mythologization surrounding "planet Auschwitz" and reestablish its uncanny closeness and similarity to the culture that produced it as well as to the culture that remembers it. As a concrete place produced by concrete, prosaic processes, Auschwitz promises to gain significance and relevance—we should no longer be able to dismiss it as an abstract para-digm of evil, "separated from the rest of the world," as Dwork and van Pelt put it, "by 'night' and 'fog'" (10–11).

But the project fails at this strategic point. In the chapter devoted to the process of killing, titled "The Holocaust," a bleak recital of the existing facts (who designed the building, who constructed the furnaces, how the flames were fanned, how the gas chambers were constructed, how and when the system of mass extermination became operational and the extent of its pro-ductivity) leads the authors to foreground the limitations of their study. "We *know* all of that. But we *understand* very little about many issues central to this machinery of death. Research into the history of the region, the intended future of the town, the development of the camp, and the changing design of the crematoria has been useful, but it is not the whole story about the Holocaust at Auschwitz. It is the questions of the victims and the survivors which loom large" (352; emphasis mine).

Dwork and van Pelt close the distance between Auschwitz and the present, then, only to reopen it. Contrasting what we know with what we can understand, they open a space of incomprehensibility by gesturing toward silence, absence, and impossibility: the unheard, unhearable questions of the victims and the unanswered, unanswerable questions of the survivors. These questions, according to Dwork and van Pelt, redirect the issue away from *how* the atrocity could happen to *why*. Quoting a survivor's experience of the selection process, the authors focus on this statement: "They went to the left, and we went to the right. *And I said, 'Why?'*" (352; emphasis in the original).

When the historically specific Auschwitz meets the broader phenomenon of the Holocaust, then, the limits of knowledge must be firmly set. Thus the authors conclude this chapter with a double gesture: they defer to the voice of the survivor ("Sara's question remains") and repeat the survivor's question ("And I said, 'Why?'" [353]). Marking the limits of their ability to understand with repetition and deferral, the authors make themselves absent and silent, relinquishing their voice to that of the survivor. Her question—unanswered, unanswerable—is surrounded by silence, answered with absence. The following, and final, chapter of the study focuses on the construction of Auschwitz as a memorial site, emphasizing the inadequacy of memorials to answer Sara's question or to convey the victims' fate.

Such strategic evocation of and retreat into silence, absence, and impossibility is a gesture toward what I characterize as *the unspeakable*, a concept that will be the focus of this book. More than a vehement emphasis on the Holocaust's incommensurability to existing modes of representation, the unspeakable evokes the limits of comprehension, the limits of language, the limits of acceptable social discourse, and what Saul Friedlander calls "the intangible but nonetheless perceived boundaries" that "should not be but can easily be transgressed" (*Probing* 3). The unspeakable, I will argue here, collapses the space beyond these limits with the work of their evocation. To say that something is unspeakable is not only to conjure "something" and describe it; it is, moreover, an act of speech, a discursive move that produces knowledge even as it gestures toward knowledge's limits. As a discursive move the unspeakable is informed by an articulable context that the concern with "transgression" too often makes mute. It is well worth considering what might emerge were this gesture to be undone.

The Unspeakable

"Unspeakable" evokes a range of concepts that will be in play in this study. Significant for this term is the conjunction of physical articulation, language, and community in the term "to speak." "To speak" implies the presence of a speaker, an audience for her speech (one that shares enough of the speaker's culture to be able to recognize the speaker as such, apprehend her speech, and assess its rhetorical significance), a public arena in which her speech takes place (hence my choice of "to speak" over the more informal connotations of "to say"), and the assumption that such speech—by virtue of its presence, its audience, its public context—*does something* (or, just as significantly, valiantly attempts to do something and fails). Thus the fact of speech conjoins the act of physical articulation, the performative quality of language, the space (however virtual) of a public arena, and the presence of community.

This conjunction, and each of its elements, are both evoked and erased by the determined negation of "*un*speakable." What is "unspeakable" welds an inability to articulate to the impossibility of communication; it presents a crucial challenge both to language and to community. This challenge has its own seductive eloquence and has generated a formidable body of writing in literature, philosophy, history, psychoanalysis, critical theory, postcolonial studies, and cultural studies. By drawing attention to the semantic (language's limits), the unspeakable directs the critical gaze away from physical presence, effecting a certain dissociation from the body of the speaker and from her act of speech. By virtue of its prevalence in discourse on the Holocaust, the unspeakable proffers and perpetuates the framework by which the Holocaust is imagined, again and again, as posing a challenge to the categories of comprehension that are mobilized to apprehend it. This proffering and perpetuation deserve a closer look. Put differently: the question is not, is the Holocaust unspeakable? but rather, when we say that the Holocaust is unspeakable, *what do we do?*

Given deconstruction's focus on language's evocation of its limits and poststructuralism's account of discourse's formation of knowledge, few will disagree with the assumption that since silence is a part of language, the unspeakable will delineate speech.[6] Further, since language is a human enterprise, the inhuman—alterity, in the form of radical evil, infinite good, absolute beauty, or the idea of God—poses a specific challenge to the potential of human conceptualization and hence to language.[7] When we say that what the Nazis did to the Jews is unspeakable, then, we are not only saying that language fails at the articulation of the Final Solution (as it failed Himmler in Poznan).[8] We are doing that and more: we are identifying this action as "inhuman" and hence as inaccessible to human understanding, external to the speech community that forms human culture. This work of exclusion, and the dichotomies it implies, will come into play in the vehement assertions that Nazis cannot or should not (the distinction is deliberately elided) be perceived as traumatized by the implications of their actions, as well as in strategic designations of the ideological enemy of the moment as "Nazi"— a designation that facilitates vilification and, ultimately, violence.

Such vilification is aligned with a dichotomous thinking in which the opposition of inhuman/human is mapped onto Nazi/Jew, perpetrator/victim, guilty/innocent, wrong/wronged. We need not profess skepticism toward dichotomous thinking per se in order to see how quickly such thinking transforms complex categories into absolutes, and how one dichotomy quickly evokes another, most notably when in its final form it precipitates the translation from inaccuracy or incompetence to morally suspect, from wrong as an adjective to wrong as a noun. It is this translation that informs the denunciation of Holocaust revisionists as anti-Semitic demagogues rather than incompetent historians.[9] More subtly, it facilitates the denigration of thoughtful critical work like Hannah Arendt's *Eichmann in Jerusalem* and Peter Novick's *The Holocaust in American Life* as lacking such "ethical" attributes as empathy or care.[10] When sympathy is aligned with knowledge, and the lack of one is wielded to demonstrate the absence of the other, evoking the unspeakable takes the form not of knowledge's abnegation but of its legislation: an unacceptable truth that, sympathy dictates, cannot be uttered.

I assume, then, that it is not merely an ironic paradox that the most thoroughly documented atrocity in human history is figured as the emblem of the incomprehensibility of this history. While we might like to think that the sheer magnitude of the destruction (in Poland alone: 500,000 by mobile operations, 550,000 in the ghettos, 1.95 million in the camps, 3 million all together)[11] would require a physical challenge to articulation, these figures slip easily off the tongue, forcing us to address the distinction between what is physically unspeakable, what is socially unspeakable, how these realms are determined, and the extent to which they interact. As Judith Butler eloquently reminds us in *Precarious Life,* the explanatory frameworks that emerge in the context of violence render some positions utterable while silencing others (4–5). The Holocaust's unspeakability, I am going to argue here, is such an explanatory framework, especially if under "explanatory" we include, as we ought to, "impossible to explain."

Avoiding "Holocaust"

It is traditional for discussions of the Holocaust to comment on the choice of terminology, to express some discomfort with the term "holocaust" (because of its Greek origins denoting a fiery sacrifice), and to point toward alternate designations like "Shoah" or "the event."[12] Rather than rehearse here the reasons for this discomfort (which I assume are familiar), I want to examine some representative expressions of this discomfort with an eye to uncovering what is articulated when "Holocaust" is not. What does avoiding "Holocaust" make possible?

Bruno Bettelheim, who takes exception to the term "Holocaust," calls it a heuristic that permits us to "manage . . . intellectually" what would "overwhelm us emotionally," hinting that this "linguistic circumlocution" is somehow similar to the Nazi's term "Final Solution" and the technical term "genocide" (*Surviving* 91).[13] In an oft-repeated critique of the term, Bettelheim refers to the Greek origin of the word—a burnt offering, entirely consumed by fire—and vehemently eschews the sacralization implied. "To call these most wretched victims of a murderous delusion, of destructive drives run rampant, martyrs or a burnt offering is a distortion invented for our comfort, small as it may be," he writes (93). By focusing on the motivations of naming, Bettelheim is alerting us to the cultural, social, and psychological assumptions that determine the assignation of language to any event. His concern is that with "Holocaust," language is employed for the benefit of the post-Holocaust world alone. Rather than responsibly mourning the victims of the Holocaust itself, the term "robs them of the last recognition which could be theirs, denies them the last dignity we could accord them: to face and accept what their death was all about" (93).

Just what was their death all about? That issue, like Dwork and van Pelt's question, "Why?" is left unexplored. By refocusing the role of naming from "us"—inhabitants of the post-Holocaust world—to the victims, Bettelheim is making a gesture similar to Dwork and van Pelt's: evoking the unspeakable. This is why he employs terminology of the sacred while critiquing the implicit sacralization in "Holocaust": the term is "a sacrilege, a profanation" (92). While ostensibly dismissing the implicit sacralization in "Holocaust," then, Bettelheim affirms the Holocaust's heterogeneity to the secular, contingent, "profaning" operations of language; while critiquing one term by which the Holocaust is spoken, he retains the notion of the Holocaust as unspeakable. It is this circumlocution—not unlike that of the Nazis with which Bettelheim opened his discussion—that characterizes the eschewal of the term "Holocaust" in contemporary discussions of the Nazi persecution of Jews in Europe.[14]

Sacralizing the Holocaust—referring to it as a "burnt offering" and to its victims and survivors as "martyrs," or otherwise situating it in a tradition of ineffability that stems from a centuries-old discussion of the limitations posed to language by the presence or the idea of the divine—generates a series of associations with religious (specifically Judaic and Christian) narratives. These associations, as Peter Haidu points out, "functionalize" the Holocaust, situating it firmly within the narratives that grant significance to a widespread series of cultural acts. The Holocaust becomes "a burnt offering, a sacrifice willingly offered divinity, a divinity apparently hungry and thirsty for the blood of innocents, a sacrifice which, properly enacted, might allow the victims the possibility of an eventual redemption" (279).[15] Paradoxically, the unspeakable—the notion, as Agamben puts it, that "Auschwitz is 'unsayable' or 'incomprehensible'"—reiterates this sacralization: it is, Agamben continues, "equivalent to *euphemein*, to adoring in silence, as one does with a god. Regardless of one's intentions, this contributes to its glory" (*Remnants* 32–33).[16]

Such reservations toward the term express discomfort with the meaning "Holocaust" makes, especially in the context of identity most broadly conceived: what it means, "after Auschwitz," to be human. Not only does "Holocaust" evoke, as Haidu puts it, "a divinity apparently hungry and thirsty for the blood of innocents," it constructs humanity as participants in the

sacrifice demanded by such a divinity, and offers the possibility of "an eventual redemption" for the victims, indicating that their deaths could, somehow, make sense in this narrative (279). Because "Holocaust" weds an image
of humanity's participation in the "sacrifice" (it is "willingly offered") with
the victims' possible "eventual redemption," it should, the logic goes, be
avoided. By shunning the functionalization posed by the term "Holocaust,"
then, articulations of discomfort about the term do something else: they
shun the potential of complicity—both God's and man's—with this act
which, when renamed "sacrifice," might give meaning to the victims' suffering. It is this potential complicity—not only with the act but with the generation of meaning—which may cause the "profanation of God and man"
that Bettelheim thinks is sacrilegious in the term "Holocaust." By avoiding
"Holocaust," then, we avoid stating our own complicity with evil and maintain the incommensurability of the victims' suffering with the sense-
making mechanisms of redemption.

This silencing of complicity will emerge, in the course of this chapter, as
a crucial element of the unspeakable and as its central motive. But first we
should ask: For whom, precisely, is the Holocaust functionalized? For Jews?
For humanity? For the victims? For God? And can this functionalizaton, or
its impossibility, be limited to a specific recipient? If "Holocaust," as a paradigm of absolute evil, poses a challenge to mankind's relation to God, what
is assumed to be the specifically Jewish character of the Holocaust becomes
secondary to what are perceived as the broader implications of this historical event. Such functionalization informs much discussion of Holocaust
memorials and memorialization and the role that the Nazi Judeocide plays
,in this activity—an "ideology of remembrance," for example, that produces
an "Auschwitz without Jews."[17] To concern with the past, a theological narrative adds the project of imagining the future. Robert McAfee Brown, asking
"how can one speak about the unspeakable?" (47), concludes that the Holocaust must remain as a warning, an illumination of our moral landscape,
to forestall other, similar evils: "[T]here is hope that the Holocaust, unre-
deemably evil in itself, could be a grotesque beacon, in the light of which we
could gird ourselves against its repetition toward any people in any time, in
any place. *And I believe that unless we can use it as such a beacon, the Nazis have
finally won*" ("The Holocaust" 62).

Brown, then, functionalizes the Holocaust as a narrative of potential redemption, if not for the victims of the Holocaust itself (their deaths are, pre-

sumably, unredeemable), then perhaps for future victims of future atrocities (but what would be redeemable about *their* deaths?). The stakes of this functionalization are no less than humanity per se: the Nazis might yet "win" (win what?) if we fail to use the Holocaust as a "beacon."[18] Brown's discussion is a central example of how speaking about what has been initially posited as unspeakable facilitates a certain mistranslation: a historically, temporally, geographically specific atrocity is turned into a test of his faith, and the fact that the Holocaust poses, for Brown, a test of Christian faith is an extremely unsettling concept for those who think of the Holocaust as something a Christian culture did to Jews.[19]

The point is that once the unspeakable is constructed as a theological narrative of destruction, sacrifice, and potential redemption by the term "Holocaust," it becomes appropriable—not merely by Brown as a test of his Christian faith but as a generic, almost comfortable, appellation for a broad spectrum of disasters: hence the use of "Holocaust" to refer to African American and American Indian histories, the AIDS crisis, and abortion—to limit this appropriation to public discourse in the United States alone.[20] Concern with appropriation motivates replacing "Holocaust" with the Hebrew term *Shoah.*[21] Such a replacement generates an illusion of controlling the referent: a Hebrew (and therefore, one assumes, Jewish) word can only refer to a Jewish catastrophe, safeguarding such a catastrophe from possible appropriation, retaining its specificity (the Judeocide perpetrated by Nazi Germany in Europe during the 1930s and '40s) as well as positing it as a cumulative moment in a Jewish history of persecution, perhaps signifying the end of that history and the beginning of a new one with the establishment of the state of Israel. While Shoah, too, has religious connotations (as Haidu notes, the term implies that "the disaster is sent from God" [279]) the term is usually used as a paradigm of disaster, specific to the Jewish people, that is located in history rather than in divine will. Berel Lang submits that Shoah and Churban "are more accurately descriptive than 'Holocaust,' because they imply a breach or turning point in history" (*Act* xxi).

What reservations about "Holocaust" point to, then, are not merely the problematic consequences of its induction into narratives of contemporary identity but also the specific questions of identity politics—Holocaust as Judeocide—that this induction invites. Referring to the Holocaust in Hebrew raises issues of translatability between languages and between cultures, and the use of the Hebrew term *Shoah* to safeguard the specific Jewish identity of the Holocaust poses such translatability as impossible: a disconcerting dilemma for those who emphasize "never again!"—for the Jews, perhaps, but not necessarily for the rest of us. Attempts to ensure the specificity of the Holocaust construct the Holocaust as incommensurable and—as scholars like Haidu and Yehuda Bauer fear—as potentially irrelevant to contemporary history.[22] Finally, emphasizing such untranslatability posits the Holocaust as the property only of those who have a claim on Hebrew—although the idea that Hebrew-speaking Israeli Arabs or non-Jewish Israeli residents might refer to their own histories as containing a Shoah demonstrates that a claim on Hebrew does not ensure the specifically Jewish character of the Holocaust.[23]

I have chosen "Holocaust" for this project in light of these issues, not despite them. Reservations about "Holocaust" reveal an unwillingness to face the salvationist implications of the narrative evoked by "sacrifice," discomfort over potential complicity with the God who demanded this sacrifice or with the human beings who performed it, and a reluctance to enable or facilitate the appropriation of this narrative by other histories or other cultures. I maintain that complicity and appropriation need to be confronted, not avoided; it is the reluctance, the eschewals, and the flights from language that need to be examined.

The Lure of Totality

Despite prevailing concerns about their propriety, "Holocaust" and *Shoah* persist as referents to the Nazi genocide of Jews. The reason for this is the powerful connotation, in both "Holocaust" and in *Shoah*, of immensity, of totality: both terms evoke a *total* destruction, a *complete* annihilation, an *absolute* devastation. This sense of total destruction would seem to indicate that (a) all the Jews were destroyed, or (b) the destruction itself was total. Both assumptions are inaccurate: Jewish communities out of the Nazis' reach—in North and South America, Africa, the Middle and Far East, as well as in countries where Nazi policies were actively resisted, like Denmark and, to a lesser extent, Bulgaria—were not destroyed. And yet, assuming that the destruction of Central and Eastern European Jewish communities is tantamount to the destruction of the Jewish people or at least a (potentially fatal) blow to the "heart" of the Jewish people remains a prominent element of Holocaust scholarship, reflecting a dismaying cultural centrism. David

Vital, for example, identifies European Jewry as the "veritable core" of all Jewry and adds that

> it cannot be stressed too often, or too strongly, that in Poland and the Baltic countries, in Russia and Romania, in Czechoslovakia and Hungary, were to be found those communities that, taken together (as they should be), constituted the most homogeneous, the most coherent, the least assimilated, least self-conscious, most compact, and, of course, far and away the most numerous and lively—and in so many ways, the most remarkable—of all Jewish conglomerations in modern times. It is not too much to say that to all intents and purposes they were the Jewish nation—all other communities, no matter how distinguished or ancient or prosperous, being peripheral to them. (123)[24]

The exclusion of African and Middle Eastern communities (communities that are, as a rule, nonwhite and primarily Arabic- or Amharic-speaking) lends weight to Vital's rhetoric of total destruction. Identifying the European Jews as the essence of the Jewish nation constructs this nation as essentially European. Constructing the Jewish people as a European nation facilitates imagining the Holocaust as the loss of that nation. Even if we were to grant Vital's assumption that the Holocaust destroyed "the most remarkable . . . of all Jewish conglomerations in modern times," the presence of Jewish thought and life in Europe after the Holocaust qualifies any assertion that the Holocaust completely destroyed the European Jews. Here it is useful to recall Jonathan Boyarin's definition of genocide as "the destruction of an imagined national collective, the loss of a 'people'" (7). Since, Boyarin notes, such a collective, such a "people," is itself a construction, its loss is equally a construction.[25] It is also important to recall the distinction Hungerford draws between culture and people; forgetting this distinction, she warns, privileges arguments that are emotionally powerful over those that are coherent (156). "Hate-crimes or genocidal acts need to be punished more severely," she writes, "not because what they destroy is somehow different from what is destroyed by other kinds of large-scale violences and oppression but because the ideology motivating that destruction reduces an entire group of persons to the status of nonpersons" (157).

Despite its inaccuracy, though, a rhetoric of total destruction persists, enacted by the connotations of totality implicit in "Holocaust" and *Shoah* and reiterated by a corresponding emphasis on the challenge that such totality poses to attempts to comprehend it. While it is not surprising that the Holocaust is perceived in terms of totality or that the sheer magnitude of the destruction is considered to pose a specific problem to comprehension (the Holocaust is, indeed, a vast and violent event), what is surprising is that in the case of the Holocaust, this vastness and violence are assumed to be unique, offering a specific and apparently irresolvable problem to experience, imagination, conceptualization, and, finally, representation. Christopher Browning, for example, writes,

> The Holocaust is not an abstraction. It was a real event in which more than five million Jews were murdered, most in a manner so violent and on a scale so vast that historians and others trying to write about these events have experienced nothing in their personal lives that remotely compares. Historians of the Holocaust, in short, know nothing—in an experiential sense—about their subject. This experiential shortcoming is quite different from their not having experienced, for example, the Constitutional Convention in Philadelphia or Caesar's conquest of Gaul. (25)

That Browning doesn't feel the necessity to qualify or explain just *why* or *how* the experiential shortcoming posed by the Holocaust is different from the experiential shortcoming posed by any other moment in history should alert us to how, in the case of the Holocaust, this difference is assumed, not concluded. The question to be asked, then, is what purpose does this assumption of "experiential shortcoming," conveyed and enacted by the rhetoric of totality in the terms "Holocaust" and *Shoah,* serve? What does this rhetoric enable those who evoke it to *do?*

To assume—and by assumption I mean both the act of taking on oneself and the act of postulating—the Holocaust's *totality,* the *absolute* quality of its evil, is to take up the burden of its challenge to all limits. In the context of this assumption, the Holocaust is not just any event; it is, in Bettelheim's words, the "*most* callous, *most* brutal, *most* horrid, *most* heinous mass murder" (92). It is this hyperbole that may force a rhetoric of the sacred back into Bettelheim's argument; totality, like the divine, challenges language with its limits. Infinity will only be mistranslated if forced into sense, giving rise to Saul Friedlander's impression that "this event, perceived in its totality, may signify more than the sum of its components" (*Probing* 3). In the course of representing totality, then, the limits of representation must be evoked, established, and addressed.

This assumption of totality, and its corresponding emphasis on limits, is the conceptual force behind much of Friedlander's work. In *Memory, History, and the Extermination of the Jews in Europe,* he describes the implementation of the Final Solution in terms of an apocalypse and casts the dilemma of Holocaust representation in terms of the impossibility of contemporary life to contain totality.[26] "The total dissonance between the apocalypse that was and the normality that is makes adequate representation elusive, because the human imagination stumbles when faced with the fundamental contradiction of apocalypse within normality" (51). But when he concludes from this that "the representation of the Shoah does not seem to have played any significant role" in Western ideology and culture (51), and that "the catastrophe of European Jewry has not been incorporated into any compelling framework of meaning in public consciousness, either within the Jewish world or on the Western cultural scene in general" (43), one wonders just what "framework" or "role" would be deemed sufficiently "compelling" or "significant" a repository for such a catastrophe? How do you represent an apocalypse? Once the Holocaust is perceived in terms of total destruction, statements such as "the representation of the Shoah does not seem to have played any significant role" are always already qualified by the impossibility of any such role. By positing the Holocaust as total destruction, then, Friedlander constructs it as unspeakable.

From this context of totality and subsequent unspeakability emerges the urgent evocation of interpretation's limits. As Friedlander puts it, "[T]his very perception of limits—about the nature of which one can have any number of arguments, but the sense of which is compelling, may indicate that we are possibly facing an exceptional situation which calls for a fusion of moral and cognitive categories in the course of the historical analysis as such" (*Memory* 56). Returning to this argument in his introduction to *Probing the Limits of Representation,* Friedlander will add "representation" to "interpretation," emphasizing the perceived limits of both: "The problem is neither scientific nor blatantly ideological: one cannot define exactly what is wrong with a certain representation of the events, but . . . one senses when some interpretation or representation is wrong" (3–4). "Sense" and "feeling" establish limits without determining or defining the nature of these limits.

Indeed, these limits *must* remain within the amorphous realm of (unutterable) sensibilities, since to define the limits of interpretation would be to establish what is and is not interpretable, work that would situate the Holocaust within a specific interpretive framework.

Friedlander's emphasis on sense and feeling in the face of representation's limits also recalls a tradition of negativity according to which language's inevitable exclusions are recuperated by a sense of the ineffable. Negativity, like totality, foregrounds the limits of representation and delineates a realm of the unspeakable; like totality, negativity is unapproachable by language (hence the rhetorical devices of apostrophe, elision, irony, or silence). Such negativity, in the form of absence, may, as Sanford Budick and Wolfgang Iser point out, work as "a kind of ordained enabling structure" (xiii), facilitating and qualifying its own presence. Berel Lang ends his introduction to *Writing and the Holocaust* with a gesture toward such absence:

> We do not know, of course, what writings there might now be before us—written from Vilna or Prague, from Warsaw or Vienna—if the Holocaust had not occurred. But we know enough, as we imagine reading those unwritten texts, to speculate about them—and to understand that they would also have been significant and life-giving. To be sure, if they existed, the work included in this volume would not—and that fact itself remains an aspect of the volume's content. It is no substitute, however, for those writings which are not present now, but should be, and which in this sense are also to be counted among the writings of the Holocaust—a larger instance of what Isaac Babel had earlier founded as the "genre of silence." Their absence remains in fact the most closely literal representation of the Holocaust. (15)

The "unwritten texts" that Lang imagines us reading reflect what Budick and Iser call "reified negativity" (xiii)—a negativity that, like Hegel's, operates as an antithesis that, within the enabling structure of the dialectic, enables synthesis and thus generates meaning. Against this reified negativity, which is fundamentally enabling, Budick and Iser proffer a concept of negativity "which is traceable only through its impact" (xii), a project that echoes Blanchot's explorations of negativity in *The Writing of the Disaster*. Assuming that "the disaster . . . cannot be measured in terms of failure or as pure and simple loss" (2), Blanchot focuses not on the disaster per se but on the *writ-*

ing of the disaster and the extent to which such writing can convey the inexpressible.[27] Rather than a simple dichotomy in which presence and absence establish, qualify, and reflect each other, as Lang poses in his evocation of "unwritten texts," Blanchot posits the concept of passivity, with its connotations of subjection and negation (the French *pas*), which enables Blanchot to speak of the disaster without incorporating it into such sense-making mechanisms as desire (which necessitates a distinction between a desiring subject and an object of desire), temporality (which necessitates a distinction between past, present, and future), and language (which necessitates a distinction between a writing subject and a written text). In other words: Blanchot's passivity in the face of the disaster that is Auschwitz makes possible a thinking about negativity that does not run the risk, detailed by Budick and Iser, of applying an enabling or productive framework to the Holocaust.

I have lingered on Friedlander's assumptions of totality and Lang's and Blanchot's concepts of negativity in order to stress how, in the work of these scholars, the Holocaust (for Blanchot, in the form of the disaster) is repeatedly figured as heterogeneous to conceptualizing systems. It is totality, for Friedlander; for Lang, an absence that qualifies, informs, and pervades any evocation of presence. In Blanchot's more sophisticated analysis it appears as a name "alien [*hors*] to naming" (47). In each case, the Holocaust is relegated to the realm of the unspeakable: external to, but inseparable from, the discourses that it forces, enables, or interrupts.

Trauma and the Unspeakable

In the course of this discussion I have been treating the unspeakable as a deliberate rhetorical move, evoked to further specific, if implicit or unacknowledged, agendas. But the unspeakable is also what cannot be physically spoken or pronounced, like an infinite word or an infinite scream. Its dimensions are located in the challenge posed to the psyche by a traumatic experience, and it is manifested in the repetitions and deferrals that constitute the work of mourning. These psychic dimensions of the unspeakable are echoed in the taboos or injunctions against certain speech acts by a community: our reluctance to shout "Auschwitz" on a crowded street corner or to force Holocaust survivors to address what they prefer not to confront. In such cases the unspeakable takes the form of trauma, not merely for the individual survivors but for a collective post-Holocaust culture that is perceived to be "traumatized" by the presence of the Holocaust in its history. In this manner, what is psychically impossible (for the individual survivor) becomes a rhetorical expression of psychic impossibility (contemporary culture's trauma in the wake of the Holocaust).

Thinking of the Holocaust as a manifestation of trauma draws our attention to the different orders of experience that such a statement puts in play. The survivor's trauma is, of course, of a different order than that of the witness, the scholar, the historian, or the student, and to refer to all as "traumatic" is to precipitate their overlap. This overlapping is both enabling and problematic. It is enabling because the survivor's inability to psychically process her traumatic experience offers, for the trauma theorist, a productive and imaginative epistemological model, one that is simultaneously predicated on silence and that articulates silence as such. If the survivor is silenced by trauma, trauma theory gives this silence a voice, affirming the survivor's experience and articulating, as Shoshana Felman and Dori Laub put it, "the ways in which our cultural frames of reference and our preexisting categories which delimit and determine our perception of reality have failed, essentially, both to contain, and to account for, the scale of what has happened in contemporary history" (xv). Here, the unspeakable works as a responsible space of "witnessing" an otherwise unwitnessable past; the survivor and the one to whom she speaks are linked in this ethical gesture.

But this overlapping of two orders of traumatic reality can also be problematic, in that the ethical gesture linking the traumatic experience with the experience of trauma facilitates the conflation of the two, proposing, as Sanyal puts it, "an infinitely elastic notion of victimhood" (9) and producing, as Hungerford puts it, "trauma without experience" (110) that enables too easy a slippage between lived suffering and its production through the act of reading.[28] Here the unspeakable that Felman and Laub evoke generates a space of silence into which too many can step, and the very ethical gesture that informed the work of witnessing can facilitate the appropriation of suffering, raising questions about who can, or cannot, be "traumatized." Hence, for example, Felman's reading of Paul de Man's writings for the collaborationist publication *Le Soir* has been critiqued—most significantly by Dominick LaCapra ("The Personal, the Political")—as exonerating de Man from the charge of collaboration and positioning him as a witness to "the radical loss—or death—of truth, and therefore . . . a radical loss—or death—of self" (Felman, "After the Apocalypse" 135) that the presence of the

Holocaust in history performs. Hungerford identifies Felman's reading of de Man "as the logical limit case of the trauma theory *Testimony* as a whole puts forward" (109).

These possibilities and limitations of trauma theory will structure my exploration of the question, what happens when a rhetoric of trauma is applied to the Holocaust? Merely asking this question is, of course, a difficult undertaking, since it does not presume that the Holocaust is, in itself, inherently traumatic. Indeed, the widespread identification of Holocaust suffering as unspeakable and personal suffering as incommensurable almost prohibits the question itself, denigrating such assumption of empirical inquiry as the product of hegemony or of hubris that may, by forcing suffering into "meaning" or "coherence," further victimize the victim and put her story in the service of our own agendas, as Freud, hauntingly, did with Dora and Anna O. "The unrepresentable, unspeakable nature of the Holocaust is at once an epistemological proposition (we can't fathom it) and an ethical injunction: we wouldn't want to try for fear of betraying it," writes Sanyal of this dilemma (20). Like "the Holocaust is unspeakable," "the Holocaust is trauma" reflects a basic intentional fallacy by which a cultural production is posited as an irrefutable fact or at least a painful reality. It is on the level of this assumption of the Holocaust as *the* paradigmatic traumatic event that the implicit cultural and political agendas of trauma theory need to be approached.

Felman and Laub's *Testimony: Crises of Witnessing in Literature, Psychoanalysis, and History* plays a crucial role in introducing a discourse of trauma through which to address the presence of the Holocaust in history, its implications for narrative and culture, and responses to this presence and its implications (which they term "testimony"). But the traumatic nature of this history, and the nature of its impact (the traumatization of contemporary culture by the Holocaust), are, like Browning's "experiential shortcoming," assumed and not concluded. Felman and Laub situate their discussion after "the historic trauma of the Second World War,"

> a trauma we consider as the watershed of our times and which the book will come to view not as an event encapsulated in the past, but as a history which is essentially *not over*, a history whose repercussions are not simply omnipresent (whether consciously or not) in all our cultural activities, but whose traumatic consequences are still actively *evolving*

(Eastern Europe and the Gulf War are two obvious examples) in today's political, historical, cultural and artistic scene, the scene in which we read and psychoanalyze, and from within whose tumult and whose fluctuations we strive both to educate and write. (xiv; emphasis in the original)

Despite their gestures toward World War II in the introduction, the Holocaust dominates Felman and Laub's study (no other World War II atrocities are addressed in any detail in *Testimony*). This conflation of World War II with the Holocaust elides the ideological underpinnings of identifying the Holocaust (which happened in Europe, to people who are, today, perceived as technically "white")[29] as a trauma that reverberates through "contemporary culture," while the rhetorical evocation of "we" facilitates an unquestioned (because "obvious") collapse of contemporary political scenarios ("Eastern Europe and the Gulf War") into a history (pre)determined by the Holocaust, but without addressing the crucial questions that such collapsing raises (What do the Gulf War and the Holocaust have in common? Just what does "Eastern Europe" metonymically represent?) or the ideological implications of any of these questions' many answers. Felman and Laub's move here is an example of how, as Hungerford points out, the emphasis on trauma as an essentially linguistic and textual, rather than experiential, event facilitates the "transmission" of cultural identity, specifically, a cultural identity that is structured around the (imagined) experience of trauma (116–19). I would add that this inclusive "transmission" can mask an exclusive identification: when trauma is aligned, unproblematically, with "Holocaust," such alignment reiterates the cultural assumption according to which what happened in Europe reverberates globally.

Implicit in the concept of the Holocaust as trauma is the assumption that group identities and individual identities can be approached similarly (Felman and Laub's "we" can refer equally to the authors or to the imagined community of contemporary culture). Further, identifying the Holocaust as a traumatic event generates a discourse that is predicated on the assumption that the Holocaust cannot be approached directly but only perceived indirectly, though its effects and repercussions: the "traumatic consequences" that Felman and Laub mention.[30] In other words, "the Holocaust is trauma" posits the Holocaust as engendering the very discourse that renders it unspeakable, while "the Holocaust is traumatic" posits a subjectivity for whom the unspeakable offers the terms of its articulation. Given the traumatic event's inherent unspeakability (Hungerford describes trauma as "that experience which cannot be fully understood or known" [113]; Sanyal as "something that resists immediate knowing and representation" [10]), positing the Holocaust as a "traumatic" event reiterates its presupposed heterogeneity to conceptual structures, a heterogeneity that facilitates the conflation of the limits of psychic experience with the limits of conceptual work. It is at the point of this conflation that trauma theory merges with the work of literary criticism, aligning psychoanalysis with philosophy; as Hartman puts it, "every time we are tempted to say 'I see' when 'I understand' is meant, we do not see, or else we do not understand" ("On Traumatic Knowledge" 540).

My concern here is less with the possibility that this unspeakability can be occupied by an "inauthentically traumatized" identity like Bruno Dössekker's or Paul de Man's than with how *history as holocaust* (Felman's term, "Camus' *Plague*" 95) constructs history as unspeakable.[31] In the articulation of such a history and of the subjectivity that is traumatized by it, gestures toward the unspeakable take on a certain ethical urgency. When, as Felman puts it, "[n]arrative has . . . become the very writing of the impossibility of writing history" ("Camus' *Fall*" 200–201), the narratives by which, as Hayden White puts it, we "emplot" history must retain unspeakability in order to be "responsible" to "a new form of historical reality," one defined by "a profound sense of the incapacity of our sciences to *explain*, let alone control or contain these [supposedly unspeakable events]; and a growing awareness of the incapacity of our traditional modes of representation even to *describe* them adequately" (White 52; emphasis in the original).

White's identification of the unspeakable as a "responsible" relation to "a new form of historical reality" echoes in the assumption that trauma theory is a vehicle for an active engagement with history, an engagement codified as an ethical wrestling with the past via the very vocabulary of silence that trauma theory engenders. Both the notion of history as trauma and of trauma as a space for ethical engagement are, Sanyal suggests, sites for "an ethical investment in the unrepresentability of both history and subjectivity" (11). Very different approaches to trauma come together in their alignment of this specific discourse with ethical work. "There is an opening," Hartman says, "that leads from trauma studies to public . . . issues, an opening with ethical, cultural, and religious implications" ("On Traumatic Knowledge" 544). Cathy Caruth and Dominick LaCapra respond to this "opening" in a variety of ways. In *Unclaimed Experience,* Caruth offers a "new mode of reading and listening" to our own wounds and, crucially, to others' (9) and describes a history in which "we are implicated in each other's traumas" (24). LaCapra's concept of "muted trauma" not only offers a rethinking of the relation between history and theory but also posits trauma studies as a form of sociocultural and political critique (*Representing* 4). Hartman (a literary scholar), Caruth (whose psychoanalytical approach is informed by deconstruction), and LaCapra (an intellectual historian) speak from very different points of the diverse field of trauma theory, but all suggest that the gestures toward the limits of knowledge that characterize the unspeakable need not separate or exclude but, rather, enable an emphatic, responsible engagement with cultural and political otherness. Unlike the unspeakability of the sacred or the sublime, from which we can only recoil in awe, trauma theory promises an active mode of engagement with the limits of understanding that "Holocaust" presents.

Approaching trauma as a linguistic and textual, rather than solely experiential, event raises these questions: In the translation from history to text, what gets lost? In the translation of culture to psyche, who gets excluded? We can begin to answer these questions by remembering what Caruth points out in *Unclaimed Experience:* that the original meaning of trauma is that of a wound, an "injury inflicted on a body" (3), a phrase that strongly distinguishes the act of inflicting an injury from the body that receives it. This distinction—which effectively separates the wounded from the wounding— remains intact when the wounding is imagined to take place not on a body but on a mind. I will turn to the implications of this dissociation from the physical in chapter 3; at present, I want to point out that the movement of trauma from a psychic to a cultural phenomenon has been accompanied by surprisingly little attention to the political contexts that facilitate this movement or to the implications of such a movement for cultural identity.[32] Further, in the context of this movement, the issue of agency becomes a source for critical concern: separating the wounded from the wounding (whether physical or psychic) ascribes passivity to the former, activity to the latter, identifies one as victim, the other as perpetrator, and encourages a rigorous distinction between the two. While learning to hear the silent stories of trauma is indeed important work, equally important work needs to be done in answering these questions: Who is offered access to the traumatized psyche? Which historical events can be granted the imprimatur of "traumatic" and which can—or should—not?

In the context of these questions, what is enabling about trauma theory takes on a somewhat prohibitive cast. Since trauma theory facilitates an active engagement with the past, the distinctions between an event and its perception, the survivor and the nonsurvivor, the (legitimately) traumatized and those who are not offer opportunities for urgent critical intervention. Ruth Leys's scathing critique of Caruth's *Unclaimed Experience* provides an idea of how high the stakes of such an intervention can be.[33] Caruth addresses the presence of trauma in history and the necessity to rethink history in the wake of trauma's radical challenge to reference. This broader definition of trauma enables her to detach trauma from its historical manifestations and to translate the psychic experience of trauma into a linguistic phenomenon: trauma, for Caruth, is a metaphor for a specific manifestation of the limits of reference. In this translation, a broad range of experiences— imagined, mythical, historical, psychological—are collapsed into the unifying text of trauma, producing "trauma" as a universal concept, a common denominator of various histories.[34]

Leys argues that this universalizing of trauma exposes Caruth's "primary commitment to making victimhood unlocatable in any particular person or place, thereby permitting it to migrate or spread contagiously to others" (296).[35] As an example of the dangers inherent in this dissociation of specificity, Leys evokes the Holocaust, in relation to which, she writes, "it is as if she [Caruth] proposes that whether we experienced the trauma of the Holocaust directly or not, each of us, in the post-Holocaust period, is always already a split or dissociated subject, simultaneously victim and witness, and hence always marked by the difference and division that characterizes the traumatized subject" (297). What Leys finds most disturbing about Caruth's logic is that it can efface the distinction between trauma's perpetrators and its victims: Caruth's theory of trauma "would turn the executioners of the Jews into victims and the 'cries' of the Jews into testimony to the trauma suffered by the Nazis" (297).

When considering Leys's critique of Caruth, it is useful to remember that her analysis of the discourse of trauma, like Caruth's, does not address the Holocaust directly. Leys's *Trauma: A Genealogy* offers a history of the concept of trauma in the fields of neuroscience, psychology, and literary criticism;

she "approach[es] the literature on the Holocaust indirectly, as a contribution to the modern definition of PTSD" (16). Nor does Leys treat Caruth as a Holocaust scholar; she describes Caruth as a literary theorist who utilizes neurobiological claims in her postmodernist and deconstructivist approach, "epitomiz[ing] the contemporary literary-critical fascination with the allegedly unrepresentable and unspeakable nature of trauma" (16), a fascination in which the Holocaust "in effect stands in for trauma generally" (16). But in Leys's critique, the specific historical event of the Holocaust is imported into Caruth's argument in order to demonstrate a moral limit case: the potential elision, via the traumatic space, of crucial distinctions between victim and executioner, Nazi (to borrow Leys's formulation) and Jew.

Given Caruth's deconstructivist methodology, her neglect of distinctions, binaries, and dichotomous oppositions should not be surprising. But as LaCapra notes in *Representing the Holocaust,* deconstruction's "critique of pure binary oppositions or sheer dichotomies . . . eventuates in problematic distinctions—not in utter confusion, free play, or homogenization of all differences" (9). "More hangs on certain distinctions than on others," he adds, and refers to attempts to problematize the distinction between victim and perpetrator of Holocaust horror (attempts that he describes as "of dubious nature" [10]) as an example of this context's ethical and political stakes.[36] "Victim," writes LaCapra elsewhere, is a "social, political and ethical category," not a psychological one (*Writing History* 79)—an important definition, since it allows for the alignment of "victim" with "innocent," a definition that the psychological category of victim does not.[37] As a social, political, and ethical category, "victim" prohibits the assumption that Nazis may be traumatized by the atrocities *they* committed, and it is this prohibition that motivates Leys to import the Holocaust into Caruth's argument in order to reassert the distinctions between victim and perpetrator that she, with LaCapra, deems so crucial. Ironically, her ultimate critique of Caruth's argument is that it "contributes to that collapse of distinctions," a collapse that she views as "a general problem in current approaches to trauma" (17). But in the context of this critique, Leys collapses another important distinction: the distinction between traumatized and victimized, reasserting (to return to LaCapra's definition) the social, the political, and the ethical in *Trauma: A Genealogy*'s psychoanalytical context. In other words, when the Holocaust becomes the test case for Caruth's theory, ethics manifests itself at the point where the distinction between victim and perpetrator of Holocaust horror is threatened with collapse.

I am not arguing here that we must consider Nazis as victims of their persecution of the Jews.[38] The point I am trying to make is that the Holocaust, informed by the moral dichotomy of Nazis–persecutors/Jews–victims, does important work as an assumed context for trauma theory: it generates a sense of ethical urgency informed by this moral dichotomy, itself posited as unquestionable and absolute.[39] Evoked as a vehicle to distinguish between Nazis and Jews, the assignation of "traumatized" works as a kind of moral arbiter, aligning trauma theory the role generally accorded to juridical institutions for which the assignation of certain actions, not reactions, distinguish perpetrator from victim. To collapse "victimized" with "traumatized," and to refuse Nazis the position of either, is to do more than presume that perpetrators do not inhabit a fragile and vulnerable subjectivity: it reinstates unassailable dichotomies, reiterating that as the victim is human, the perpetrator is inhuman; as the victim is innocent, the perpetrator is guilty. Such an assumption (that Nazis cannot or, more precisely, should not be traumatized) constructs Holocaust victims as victims of inhuman, impersonal, abstract evil; at the same time, it evokes an ethical alignment with this victim. Further, if we follow Leys's model of trauma as a "purely external event coming to a sovereign if passive victim" (10), we can see that the assumption of contemporary culture as "traumatized" by the Holocaust posits contemporary culture as the essentially passive victim of the Holocaust's impact on its constructed collective psyche, evading crucial questions about volition, agency, and responsibility that "after Auschwitz," that evocative phrase, invites. The Holocaust becomes (merely) the product of unexplained, incomprehensible, random evil, like an asteroid hitting the earth; as Terrence Des Pres puts it, "Survivors do not bear witness to guilt, neither theirs nor ours, but to *objective conditions of evil*" (*Survivor* 49; emphasis mine).

Leys's critique of Caruth, like LaCapra's and Hungerford's critiques of Felman's reading of de Man, demonstrates how the alignment of trauma with ethics renders criticism subject to a certain policing activity: the limits of the argument are made manifest when moral distinctions have been breached. In these cases, the critical gaze is directed toward the argument (Felman's or Caruth's), not toward the assumption of these limits and the implications of their evocation. If trauma theory offers a language with which to "speak" the silenced stories of the traumatized, the limits of this language lie at the moment where collaborators' (de Man's) or perpetrators' (Nazis') "speech" can be heard. The alignment of trauma with ethical engagement reestablishes inclusive and exclusive communities, here identified not geopolitically but juridically: to be traumatized is to be innocent; to be outside the limits of trauma's discourse is to be guilty. When susceptibility to trauma becomes legislated in this way, access to the ability to be traumatized becomes an index of ethical commitment, whether directly, for the victim (for whom, LaCapra writes, "*not* being traumatized [by certain events] would itself call for explanation" [*Writing* 79]), or indirectly, for the critic: "[W]hat is necessary," he writes elsewhere, "is a discourse of trauma that itself undergoes—*and indicates that one undergoes*—a process of at least muted trauma insofar as one has tried to understand events and empathize with victims" (*Representing* 220–21; emphasis mine).[40]

Access to trauma is also access to the attractive position of responsibility and empathy. When trauma is identified with European history, and access to the position of "traumatized" by this history is thus monitored, trauma theory becomes both the subject and the object of cultural and ethical surveillance. Not merely the product of empathy and an attempt to understand the victims' experience, trauma is mobilized as a referent of the psychic toil such work demands. It becomes, as Weissman puts it, "the sign of one's authentic relationship to the Holocaust: if one has really faced the Holocaust, felt its horror and remembered its victims, one must be 'traumatized' by the experience" (21). As an index of ethical commitment, trauma functions as currency in what Weissman calls a "hierarchy of suffering," an index to "one's intellect and moral fiber" (21). The role of the unspeakable in this hierarchy is indicated in Sanyal's description of trauma theory as "a critical discourse that, paradoxically, claims historical validity and ethical weight by virtue of its appeal to what cannot be coaxed into discourse" (16).

For the theorists discussed here, this identification of trauma with ethics is further complicated by how trauma figures less as a psychoanalytical diagnosis than as a discursive space for encounters with the real—encounters characterized by the eloquence of their gestures toward the real's inaccessibility. Again, to pair very different approaches to trauma, Caruth describes trauma as "the story of a wound that cries out" and suggests that "a new mode of listening" is demanded by "the silence of its mute repetition of suffering" (9), while for Rothberg, trauma "entails not only the exile of the real but also its insistence" (140). "The absence of the real," he continues, "a real absence, makes itself felt in the familiar plenitude of reality" (140). The elegance of these articulations both performs and reflects the multilayered complexity of their subject, one aspect of which is the laudable project of making room for affect in critical studies. But when eloquence and affect are compounded with the aesthetic and psychic challenge to representation that mass suffering (metonymically represented by the Holocaust) is assumed to pose, the critic who ventures to critique this discursive space finds herself at odds with the very qualities of compassion, ethics, and political engagement that trauma theory claims to provide.

The Ethical Imperative of the Unspeakable

The previous sections traced the movement from thinking the unthinkable fact of the Holocaust to analyzing the operations of its unspeakability in contemporary discourses of subjectivity, identity, and perception. In this movement, we can discern a certain shift in perspective: our focus has moved from the relation between the object of representation (the Holocaust) and the representation of that object (in philosophy and history) to the role played by critical work that analyzes these representations and, more importantly, the implications of this critical work for its practitioners. "The representation of the Holocaust," writes Flanzbaum, "has entered the realm of common discourse. And accordingly it has become the *responsible* critic's job to evaluate, to analyze, to contextualize, and to make choices among the many renderings of the Holocaust we have in our national culture" (15; emphasis mine). Lang also focuses on the moral implications of evaluating representations of the Holocaust. For Lang, who, like Flanzbaum, distances himself from the assumption that the Holocaust is "unspeakable" or "unsayable" (*Holocaust Representation* 5), a Holocaust representation is "good" if it answers to ethical criteria in which representation's *limits* are expected to play a prominent role. Such a collapse of aesthetics into ethics in the evaluation of representation raises important questions about the ethics of criticism—Flanzbaum's "responsibility." But as I hope to demonstrate in chapters 2 and 3, these ethics are too often informed by what Sara Horowitz calls the "essential contradiction" between "an impossibility to express the experience, coupled with a psychological and moral obligation to do so" (*Voicing* 16). My point is that attention to the ethics of Holocaust representation and to the critic's "responsibility" and "obligation" maintains the assumption that the Holocaust does pose some challenge that ethics and responsibility are mobilized to address. In other words, regardless of whether the Holocaust can or cannot, should or should not be represented, the challenge the Holocaust is assumed to pose to representation remains implicit but intact.

As we have seen, the flight of scholars from the term "Holocaust" reflects their eschewal of the sense-making mechanisms of religion, of totality, and of history that the term implies. This abstention reflects a moral decision according to which refraining from comprehension facilitates the operation of a kind of identity politics that determines "Holocaust," like trauma, to be accessible to some, denied to others. Further, it highlights the role of human volition in language and representation and in wielding the limits of language and representation for political purposes. I have tried to demonstrate, in the discussion of trauma theory, how in the attempt to ethically engage with a traumatic event, the unilateral alignment of the Holocaust with trauma precipitates urgent gestures toward the limits of this engagement and, hence, toward the limits of ethics. When we consider how trauma, as the limit case of perception, participates in the unspeakable, we can see how the unspeakable problematizes this issue of volition in its emphasis on psychic or cultural violation. This concern with volition is, then, equally a concern with violation, and the widespread emphasis on the Holocaust as "unspeakable" facilitates the eschewal of both. This is the unspeakable at its most seductive: the rhetorical performance of foregrounding the limits of knowledge and gesturing toward the incomprehensible is, through an alchemy of trauma theory's problematization of agency, transmuted into ethical practice.

The origin of this alchemy is not in trauma theory itself but rather in the role accorded to language and representation in the generation of what, by the beginning of the twenty-first century, is accorded the status of reality. If we agree with Lang's observation, in *Act and Idea in the Nazi Genocide*, that "genocide" requires the rigorous definition of its object, we must, with Lang, ascribe a (however heuristic) degree of agency to this term, and hence accord a significant degree of responsibility to language.[41] Significantly but not atypically, Lang does not effectively distinguish between responsibility and agency in his discussion of the term: genocide requires "deliberation, first in conceptualizing and generalizing its object—and then by intending and realizing a process of annihilation as a matter of principle" (*Act* 23).

This assignation of agency enables him to argue against the mystification and sacralization of the Holocaust: since genocide requires a specific level of awareness and rationalization, it cannot be assigned to an unconscious, ignorant, or unwilled realm; evil, for Lang, is "a conscious and deliberate—intended—choice," and the awareness and rationalization implicit in "genocide" require us to "establish a relation between human intentions and the status of evil" (29).[42] For him, this inseparability of moral culpability, language, and evil reveals the extent to which *language* can be, or can be perceived as being, a participant in this evil: "[T]here is evidence of the same general purpose at once to rationalize language and to subordinate it to authority, that is, to make it into a political instrument which in its own structure would incorporate the features of moral violation" (96).

But by focusing on the relation of language to the human evil it is forced to enact, the issue of *human* culpability, with which Lang opened his discussion, is relocated to *language*. Discussing the term "Final Solution," Lang concludes that this term cannot be described by existing figurative language: it is not irony, or metaphor, or synecdoche, or metonymy, nor is it a euphemism. It is, Lang concludes, a lie forced upon language: "A person who denies having done something he knowingly did is lying—but it is not the language that then does the lying, it is the speaker. By contrast, calling genocide a Final Solution turns the phrase itself into a lie" (*Act* 92). In other words: unlike a person who lies and who must face the consequences, the phrase "Final Solution" forces language to lie.[43]

Once language is perceived as culpable for the evil into which it has been forced, "the process of representation becomes morally accountable" (Lang, *Act* 150), and the limits of language and of representation—what I have been calling here the unspeakable—are invested with ethical weight.[44] The Holocaust, for Lang, foregrounds the moral implications of the *act of writing*, especially in the context of what are perceived as the far more compelling and valuable possibilities of silence: "Once writing is viewed as an act, to be judged for what it 'does' to its subject and to its readers, then the enormity of the Nazi genocide in its historical or nonliterary character necessarily affects—enlarges—the risks incurred in its literary representation. . . . The most radical alternative to any particular representation of the Nazi genocide is not a different or contradictory one—but the possibility of not having written at all; that is, the writer's decision for silence" (*Act* 160).

Lang's logic demonstrates what makes the unspeakable especially compelling: when agency, responsibility, and culpability are ascribed to language, what language "does" to its subject, what it "does" to its readers, is aligned with what Nazis did to their victims. The fallacy of this logic is obvious enough, but in its inverted form this logic is most seductive: when language is perceived as culpable, silence avoids language and evades culpability. Thus, the "decision for silence" serves as an exculpatory mechanism through which rhetorical gestures toward the limits of comprehension effectively masquerade as ethical practice. The power of the unspeakable lies in what I call this ethical imperative, as evocations of the unspeakable are read as assumptions of responsibility to the dead, to history, even to the problem of evil in the world. Such eschewal of conceptual categories occurs even in the context of engaging with culpability or collaboration: remember Kritzman's flight to the unspeakable in the context of his gestures toward the collaborationist Vichy regime in France with which this chapter began. Indeed, an urgent dissociation from culpability is intricately linked to evocations of the unspeakable, and it is this relation between the unspeakable and the culpability it is evoked to avoid that I turn to here.

In *The Drowned and the Saved,* Primo Levi writes compellingly about the "gray zone" of the concentration camp. Addressing the painful issue of the victims' forced collaboration with their aggressors, a collaboration that, he argues, only enhances their victimization, Levi rigorously distances this issue from comprehension, which he identifies as simplification, associating it with a childlike Manichaean tendency to clearly demarcate good from evil. For Levi, comprehension, which is inevitably simplistic, equally inevitably judges and accuses. While he does distinguish the category of "innocent" from that of "victim" ("the condition of the offended," he writes, "does not exclude culpability" [44]), Levi is also careful to add, "I know of no human tribunal to which one could delegate the judgment." Again, then, the unspeakable—in the form of comprehension's limits (the "human tribunal" of which Levi *does not know*)—is evoked both to distinguish the offended from culpability in the offense and to avoid the violence that comprehension would of necessity perform, this even in the context of Levi's courageous engagement with complicity in evil.[45]

Levi's "gray zone" is a tricky and misunderstood concept, and I will return to it in the conclusion. At present, my concern is with the role that the unspeakable plays in the context of the "gray zone." Levi's reference to the limits of comprehension works, as I noted above, as an admonition against a simplistic Manichaean tendency to judge. In an expansive and far-ranging reading of Levi, Giorgio Agamben posits the "gray zone" as the emblem of contemporary culture's inextricability from the horrors of its past. The "gray zone," writes Agamben, "knows no time and is in every place. Hence the anguish and shame of the survivors . . . but also hence our shame, the shame of those who did not know the camps" (*Remnants* 26). This extension of culpability from the historical specificity that Levi describes to a more generalized sense of contemporary "shame" reflects what Sanyal calls "a general sense of contamination . . . a sense of second-hand culpability, or implication" (3), and Sanyal takes Agamben to task for conflating "several incommensurate and undefined forms of violence" (6). "To suggest," writes Sanyal,

> that primary and secondary witnesses have a comparable experience of the traumatic inner dislocation Agamben describes is an untenable conflation of literal and metaphorical victimization, complicity, and survival. *For how can the "we" interpellated by Agamben, as secondary witnesses, fully grasp* the shame Levi describes as, in silent defeat, he watches a Sonderkommando defiantly shout out "Comrades, I am the last one!" before being executed for his participation in the revolt that blew up a Birkenau crematorium? Or the wave of nausea gripping the narrator of Borowski's short story, "This Way for the Gas, Ladies and Gentlemen" as he participates in divesting the truckloads of prisoners entering the camps of their possessions? (8; emphasis mine)

We cannot, as Sanyal puts it, "fully grasp" what Levi describes. Like the unanswered, unanswerable question, "And I said, 'Why?'" with which Dwork and van Pelt marked the limits of knowledge in *Auschwitz, 1270 to the Present*, Sanyal evokes and establishes a crucial incommensurability between the victim's experience and the apprehension of this experience. If Dwork and van Pelt's move is, as I discussed at the beginning of this chapter, a classic example of evoking the unspeakable, Sanyal seems to be doing something very similar. What distinguishes Sanyal's evocation from Dwork and van Pelt's is that for Sanyal the unspeakable is evoked not to delineate the limits of knowledge but to safeguard historical specificity: in Agamben's hands, writes Sanyal, "the infernal conditions of the gray zone's emergence undergo a sort of spatiotemporal erasure" (7), an erasure that "robs this past of its singularity and particularity" (11). Here, the unspeakable, in the form of what we cannot "fully grasp," is posited as a way to forestall violence—not to the survivor (who, Sanyal says, Agamben "disregards" [8]) but to history, and Sanyal's response to this violence is to emphasize an inviolable incommensurability that replicates the unspeakable's form (evoking the limits of comprehension) and function (its ethical imperative).

It is here that I part ways with Sanyal, from whom the "intractable violence" (21) perpetrated on "the historical specificity of the Holocaust" (3) elicits an urgent demarcation of incommensurable orders of experience, essentially (if not explicitly) evoking the unspeakable. I am not suggesting that such incommensurability does not exist. What I am suggesting is that more can be accomplished by assuming that violation has always already occurred and by working with it to produce more meaning, not less. In the course of this book I will refer to such work as "being complicit," though in the context of doing so, some important distinctions will need to be drawn in distinguishing complicity from culpability or collaboration (distinctions that Sanyal, otherwise so careful, neglects to draw). I posit here—a point that I will return to in the conclusion—that complicity differs from collaboration (a charge) or culpability (a verdict) by being *the condition of possibility* for the articulation of both. We may be—and, I will argue, we should be—complicit in the violence of representation, of comprehension, of speaking the unspeakable. Such complicity does not mean that we are culpable for Nazi crimes (as Agamben suggests). Distinguishing complicity from collaboration and culpability enables us to engage a history of atrocity while maintaining the incommensurability of two orders of experience. Further, and even more importantly, it frees us from the unspeakable's siren song that lures us ever closer to that elusive, and fictitious, "moral high ground."

"After Auschwitz" Revisited

"After Auschwitz," says Wiesel, "everything brings us back to Auschwitz" (*Confronting* 205). I conclude this chapter by following Wiesel's logic and by reexamining the chapter's beginning: Adorno's situating of contemporary culture "after Auschwitz," and the readings and misreadings of his statement through a rhetoric of unspeakability by which complicity is expressly avoided, deflected, and obscured.

"To write poetry after Auschwitz is barbaric," says Adorno in "Cultural Criticism and Society" (34)—a statement that appears in various forms in virtually every piece of Holocaust scholarship. Occasionally, it is accompanied by a footnote or a parenthetical comment mentioning Adorno's retraction of the statement in the final chapter of *Negative Dialectics* ("it may have been wrong to say that after Auschwitz you could no longer write poems" [362]). Whether writings about the Holocaust cite Adorno's statement or its retraction, "to write poetry after Auschwitz is barbaric" stands firm as a marker of the challenge the Holocaust poses to meaning, to writing, to comprehension, and to aesthetics.

Situating the Holocaust in this manner, though, misses how, in the context of Adorno's broader concerns about the position of cultural criticism in the wake of the Holocaust, this challenge emerges as the result of a radical *complicity*. Adorno's concern in "Cultural Criticism and Society" is, after all, the extent to which the critic is *implicated* in the culture he or she examines. Since culture has produced the critic, the critic's position of objectivity, superiority, or detachment from culture is a false idea, one produced and perpetuated by culture and by the critic's position in it. "The cultural critic is not happy with civilization, to which alone he owes his discontent," writes Adorno. "He speaks as if he represented either unadulterated nature or a higher historical stage. Yet he is necessarily of the same essence as that to which he fancies himself superior" ("Cultural Criticism" 19). Critiquing culture, for Adorno, is an implicit reification of culture itself and of the critic's position in it. In his important analysis of the role "Auschwitz" plays in Adorno's writing of the period, Rothberg points out that Adorno's concern is not Auschwitz per se but this reification. Reading the passage in context, writes Rothberg, reveals that "the agent of the impossibility is 'absolute reification,' the process that 'absorb[s] the mind entirely'" (35).

My reading of this phrase in Adorno departs from Rothberg's in its focus on Adorno's concern not with history or with modernity but with complicity. To critique culture is to establish it, to perpetuate it, and hence to establish and perpetuate one's own position in relation to it: "[C]ulture and criticism," writes Adorno, "for better or for worse, are intertwined" ("Cultural Criticism" 22). For Adorno, the situation is definitely "for worse," as he situates his discussion of "cultural criticism and society" in the wake of "the threatening annihilation of uncounted human beings" (20). And in this context, cultural criticism cannot be innocent: its "guilt" lies in that, by the act of putting culture to scrutiny, the cultural critic helps to efface culture's disturbing operations. "Even in the accusing gesture, the critic clings to the notion of culture," writes Adorno, "where there is despair and measureless misery, he sees only spiritual phenomena, the state of man's consciousness, the decline of norms" (19). The critic's work "detracts from the true horrors" (28), as cultural critics "help to weave the veil" (20).

Adorno's proposition in face of this seemingly inevitable complicity is to posit an "immanent criticism": an "unideological thought" that "does not permit itself to be reduced to 'operational terms' and instead strives solely to help the things themselves to that articulation from which they are otherwise cut off by the prevailing language" (29). In helping to the articulation of that which was silenced, immanent criticism literally speaks the unspeakable, and while Adorno says that immanent criticism should avoid transcendence and harmony, focusing on and highlighting—rather than resolving—the contradictions between reality and ideology, he also recognizes that this "immanent method," too, will inevitably succumb to complicity: it is likely to be "dragged into the abyss by its object," to be incorporated into the "causal dependence of culture" (34).

Adorno's "immanent criticism," complete with its heuristic designation "Auschwitz," has migrated almost intact into ethically invested and politically engaged scholarship that emphasizes the work of highlighting contradictions, tensions, discrepancies, and aporias. A crucial example of the effects of this migration is Lyotard's study of Adorno in *Le Différend*. "Born from a wrong and signaled by a silence" (57), a *différend* is the product of the conflict of incommensurate discourses, an incommensurability that reinforces the practitioner of one discourse while silencing, and hence victimizing, the other; Lyotard's book has, as David Carroll notes, an explicitly "critical-political" goal: "to formulate a political strategy and to practice a justice in terms of the nonresolution of *différends*" ("Rephrasing" 78).

If *Le Différend* is engaging in the same kind of "immanent criticism" that Adorno highlighted in "Cultural Criticism and Society," Lyotard misses this crucial point: in offering the idea of "immanent criticism," Adorno is not proffering a solution, he is describing a crisis. The crisis is that of culture in the wake of the Holocaust and in light of totalitarian regimes (specifically in Russia). Adorno ends his essay by expressing the paradoxical nature of the mind's attempt to escape the reification imposed on it by dialectical thought:

"The more total society becomes, the greater the reification of the mind and the more paradoxical its effort to escape reification on its own. Even the most extreme consciousness of doom threatens to degenerate into idle chatter" (34). From the context of this collapse of consciousness of doom into doom, of the mind's reification into its attempt to escape this reification, Adorno concludes that "[t]o write poetry after Auschwitz is barbaric," adding that "this corrodes even the knowledge of why it has become impossible to write poetry today" (34).

Poetry after Auschwitz, then, is directly complicit with the culture that produced Auschwitz: the "barbarism" of writing poetry after Auschwitz shares in culture's barbarity. And this complicity in culture, and in the barbarism that culture has proved itself to be, cannot be articulated or even known: the essential barbarism inherent in poetry after Auschwitz "corrodes"—or contaminates—"even *the knowledge of why* it has become impossible to write poetry today." Adorno ends his discussion of cultural criticism and society, then, with a delineation of the widespread complicity of culture with the barbarism it produced, a complicity that subsumes even the knowledge of its manifestations.

This concern with complicity, not with the propriety of poetry after Auschwitz, is what informs the oft-cited "retraction" in *Negative Dialectics*. "Perennial suffering has as much right to expression as a tortured man has to scream; hence it may have been wrong to say that after Auschwitz you could no longer write poems," Adorno writes (362), adding to this renunciation of the unspeakable an emphasis on an existence after Auschwitz that is defined by "drastic guilt." "[I]t is not wrong," he says, "to raise the less cultural question whether after Auschwitz you can go on living—especially whether one who escaped by accident, one who by rights should have been killed, may go on living. His mere survival calls for the coldness, the basic principle of bourgeois subjectivity, without which there could have been no Auschwitz; this is the drastic guilt of him who was spared" (*Negative Dialectics*, 362–63).

Rothberg reads this passage as "anticipat[ing] psychological insights about what has come to be known as 'survivor's guilt,' but, more importantly, recogniz[ing] the implications of those insights for culture at large and point[ing] us toward the social framework in which this condition's symptoms should be read" (47). This reading of "the drastic guilt of him who was spared" testifies to the resilience of the alignment of the Holocaust with trauma. Rothberg's approach to trauma does not partake in the psychoanalytical model of, say, Leys; rather, he reads trauma as a "sign" under which modern history is thought (49), a discursive space for encounters with the real. But even if this "guilt" is read philosophically, as consciousness's encounter with its other (that "other of consciousness" is, for Rothberg, the Holocaust), such a reading maintains the inherent challenge the Holocaust poses to consciousness. "If consciousness and 'the other of consciousness,' that is, genocide and its aftermath, grounds philosophy after Auschwitz," writes Rothberg, "it also strips away its ground, since it produces the traumatic 'shock' that these nonintegratable moments of guilt cannot be reconciled with any existing philosophy of history" (48). "Adorno's late work," Rothberg concludes, "attempts to bring theory into line with the cultural confrontation with trauma and the attempts at the work of mourning happening all around him" (48). My approach differs from Rothberg's, again, in my attempt to avoid the manifestations of unspeakability, however implicit, in articulations of "after Auschwitz" while focusing on the complicity that Adorno identified as this phrase's referent. When Adorno posited contemporary culture "after Auschwitz," he was assigning that culture a quality of complicity with the horrors of the Holocaust; when "Auschwitz" is rendered unspeakable, that complicity is effaced.

The central role that Auschwitz plays in Le Différend indicates the degree to which Lyotard's project, for all its philosophical sophistication, participates in the unspeakable and in this rhetoric's ethical imperative. Discussing Adorno's use of "Auschwitz" in Negative Dialectics, Lyotard describes Auschwitz as "the name of something (of a paraexperience, of a paraempiricity) wherein dialectics encounters a non-negatable negative [un négatif non niable] and abides in the impossibility of redoubling that negative into a 'result'" ("Discussions" 152). Further, for Lyotard, Auschwitz is an "anonym": "'[W]ithin Auschwitz' . . . would be found a name 'within' which we cannot think, or not completely . . . it would be a name for the nameless . . . it would be a name which designates what has no name in speculation, a name for the anonymous" ("Discussions" 152–53). In choosing Auschwitz to exemplify the différend, Lyotard is explicitly responding to Adorno's concerns with the state of culture "after Auschwitz." However, the complicity that Adorno identified as the situation of culture "after Auschwitz" is silenced when Auschwitz is read as a différend: rather than a "corroded" knowledge, Auschwitz becomes the paradigm of "what is not presentable

under the rules of knowledge" (*Le Différend* 57). Lyotard translates Auschwitz into the unspeakable, and this translation effaces the complicity that
was Adorno's concern. If we agree with Adorno that the rules of knowledge
are corrupt and corroded, the notion of Auschwitz as "that which is not presentable under the rules of knowledge" enables us to avoid the inevitable
complicity that this knowledge forces upon us.

Earlier in this chapter I suggested that the unspeakable collapses the
space beyond language's limits with the work of these limits' evocation: to
say that something is unspeakable is not merely to conjure "something" and
describe it; it is, moreover, an act of speech, a discursive move that produces
knowledge even as it gestures toward knowledge's limits. Absence, silence,
and the limits of comprehension, all manifestations of the unspeakable,
have, after Auschwitz, played too central a role. I conclude here by urging a
shift of the critical gaze away from the unspeakable's manifestations and toward the context in which it operates and that defines its evocations. This
context, and the complicity that informs it, come to the fore when the unspeakable is eschewed. To be "after Auschwitz" is to be irrevocably complicit in the culture that produced it; to think "after Auschwitz" is to actively
integrate complicity into our ongoing projects of self-articulation, projects
that must take into account no less momentous an issue than the relation
between language, experience, and ethics. For when the unspeakable pro-
claims, "We can never know what she [the survivor] experienced, so we have
no right to speak it," it distinguishes language and community (implicit in
speaking and its production of knowledge) from experience (which is constituted as unknowable) and imbues this distinction with an ethical injunction: "we have no right." The rhetorical performance of refraining from
speech, when confronted with experience, is, then, perceived as an ethical
practice.

In this context, a number of questions arise: If we could "know" the survivor's experience, would we then have the right to "speak" it? If we have no
right to speak, does that mean, conversely, that we have the right *not* to
speak? Rather than attempting to answer these unanswerable questions
(with their evocation of an undefined sovereignty that grants such "rights"
or withholds them), I turn to what they make possible or prohibit. For regardless of whether we can or cannot "know," or whether we do or do not
possess the right to "speak," the issue of "experience" is consistently maintained, in this context, as external to the rhetorical performance of speech

and to the implication of speech with knowledge. The unspeakable, then, by seeming to privilege experience (specifically, the unbearable experience of suffering) as the locus, origin, or performance of the limits of speech, keeps experience under erasure. Further, while claiming to preserve the uniqueness, sanctity, and inviolability of atrocity, this rhetoric silences suffering's crucial corporeality and facilitates a forgetting of our own corporeality, our own vulnerability to suffering. Our flight from knowledge is, then, equally a flight from experience: by rendering the atrocity unspeakable, we silence ourselves. Speaking the unspeakable, thinking "after Auschwitz," should force the recognition of a pervasive complicity that we, heirs to the horrors of the twentieth century, cannot afford to ignore.

After the residents of the Kraków ghetto have been rounded up like cattle and sent to labor camps or extermination, the German soldiers search the houses for Jews still in hiding. A stethoscope is pressed to a wall. Children scramble out of drawers and peep from cupboards. An empty bed is overturned to reveal a figure strapped to the frame. A chance flashlight beam, like the burst of a camera flash, illuminates a family posed tensely in a corner. Caught in the light, they silently raise their hands. On the floor above, a young man climbs out of a piano. The sound of his foot hitting the keys galvanizes the soldiers into action and they rush up the stairs. Shooting begins, accompanied by hurried piano music. The young man is revealed sitting at the keyboard and playing the opening movement of Bach's English Suite no. 2 in A Minor.

Two German soldiers halt in the doorway, arrested by the unexpected concert. Automatically, they remove their caps. "What is that?" one of them calls to the musician, "Bach? Is it Bach?"

"No, no," says the other soldier, nudging his friend. "It's Mozart."

"Mozart?" inquires the first soldier incredulously, turning away from the musician to his comrade.

"Sure," replies the soldier, with a distinctly European shrug. The music remains as the camera lifts to a panoramic view of the ghetto street, the night dark pierced with machine-gun-fire light.

Steven Spielberg has always been adept at imagining the commonplace—a child's toys, a Christmas gift, a plate of mashed potatoes—as a space for fantasy and wonder. In the liquidation of the ghetto, he compellingly renders the familiar and homely (the cupboard, the family photo, the childish trick of hiding under the bed) as spaces of unbearable tension and fear. Like the boy whose face lights up with wonder as he sees his toys come alive, the childlike Jews, with their large eyes, stunned faces, and helpless passivity as they are painfully, inevitably tagged in this deadly game of hide-and-seek, appeal to the child in all of us. In this powerful sequence, Spielberg gives his viewers a glimpse of one of the most devastating aspects of Nazi horror: its capacity to transform the familiar and safe into a space of vulnerability, terror, and violent death.[1]

The paradox of culture and genocide is a familiar one: how could a people who produced artists like Goethe and Beethoven act in so barbarous a manner? Like the machine-gun fire that illuminates the darkness of the ghetto at night, the "light" of German culture is explicitly sinister, and the questions posed by this paradox (did the Germans act in such a barbaric manner because of their culture or in spite of it?) are gestured toward but never answered. In this scene the paradox is rendered even more complex, since the soldiers are cultured enough to be arrested by the music, yet not cultured enough to know what they are hearing: they misidentify the composer (the pianist is playing Bach, not Mozart) and their inaccurate choice of Mozart over Bach is significant since Mozart, unlike Bach, was not German.

How can the viewer respond to this scene? What can *I* say? Like the German soldiers, my own cultural status is in question: I understand the "Bach?" "No, Mozart" conversation even though it takes place in a foreign language with no subtitles. Do I believe the soldiers and assume that the music is Mozart's ("Wow, these guys sure know their classical music"), ceding them the respect and authority accorded in the United States to European culture and education? To do so would be to accept the soldiers' authority and status as a cultured nation, an acceptance that would make it difficult to dissociate myself from their murderous actions. Do I correct the soldiers ("No, you idiots, it's Bach"), mentally participating in their conversation? To do so would be to assume, like the soldiers, the disturbing position of allowing the music to divert my own attention from the killing. Any response to this scene renders me complicit in the alignment of culture with genocide. I cannot say anything that would not incriminate me, therefore I say nothing. This scene silences me. Hence it is unspeakable.

When critics express concern about the unselfconscious gestures toward realism performed by *Schindler's List,* they are ultimately saying that the film does not sufficiently acknowledge the limitations that its subject matter is supposed to pose to representation. Representations of the Holocaust that posit themselves as "realistic" are generally regarded with suspicion by those who assume that Holocaust reality is unspeakable, or inaccessible to contemporary imagination. Claude Lanzmann, for example, says that the Holocaust is "unique in the sense that it erects around itself, in a circle of flames, a borderline that cannot be crossed because there is a certain ultimate degree of horror that cannot be transmitted. To claim it is possible to do so is to be guilty of the most serious transgression" ("Why Spielberg").[2] But Lanzmann is ignoring the fact that "transmission" is aimed at an audience, and in the case of a comprehensible transmission, like Spielberg's, the audience participates in the transgression of comprehension. In the scene I have discussed, it is the *viewer's* position that is rendered unspeakable. Anything I could say about this scene would implicate me in its comprehensibility and hence in its transgression. And since there is no ethically comfortable position from which I can articulate a response to this alignment of culture with genocide without being myself somehow complicit in this alignment, the audience, not the Holocaust, is silenced by this film: "The reactions at the end were tears, stunned silence, and a smattering of applause that was cut short as if somehow out of place" (Craig R. Whitney, qtd. in Hoberman 28).

Describing the audience as "silenced" may sound odd in light of the immense amount of public response that *Schindler's List* generated when it was released in 1993. Oprah Winfrey's declaration that the mere act of seeing *Schindler's List* made her "a better person" (qtd. in Horowitz, "But Is It" 119) may give rise to a sense that any "silencing" performed by this film has been insufficient at best. But just as the Holocaust, posited as unspeakable, has generated a tremendous body of literature, the amount of discussion generated by *Schindler's List* is no reliable index of the limits it imposes on speech. What is significant is the fact that Oprah Winfrey is talking about the Holocaust on national television in the first place, and the discomfort with this fact is a discomfort with the perceived induction of the Holocaust into the (always slightly suspect) realm of popular culture, aptly confirmed by Spielberg's juxtaposition of "the six million who cannot watch it tonight with the one billion who are watching us now" at the Academy Awards ceremony as he received the Oscar for best director (qtd. in Loshitzky, intro. 1).

Images for the Unimaginable?

In her introduction to a collection of critical essays about the film, Yosefa Loshitzky writes: "*Schindler's List* provides fertile ground for general reflections about the limits and problems associated with the representation of the Holocaust precisely because it challenges those limits by making the unimaginable imaginable, the unrepresentable representable" (2). Loshitzky's statement, offered as a matter of fact, merits an exploration of the assumptions that underlie it: (1) the Holocaust is unimaginable, unrepresentable; (2) this particular film has succeeded in enabling the imagination or representation of what had previously been deemed unimaginable and unrepresentable. In other words, *Schindler's List* enables its viewers, or other filmmakers, or post-Holocaust society, to speak what Loshitzky assumes to be unspeakable. But what makes Loshitzky think that Spielberg's film challenges the limits of representation, and what form does such a challenge take? What is it about *Schindler's List* that makes Loshitzky assume that Spielberg's particular version of the Holocaust has succeeded in representing the unrepresentable so successfully that previously intact limits now require reflection?

Critical responses to the film have offered a variety of answers to these questions. Some critics are concerned with the feel-good quality of the story of a German who dared save Jews, feeling that while the film tells a story that is technically "true," this "truth" is not indicative of the reality that the film claims to represent. Thus the film, while posing as a realistic depiction of a true story, is not sufficiently realistic to be "really" "true." Omer Bartov describes how "within the context of the Holocaust, [Schindler's story] was so unique as to be untrue in the sense of not reflecting (or even negating) the fate of the vast majority of victims who were in turn swallowed up in a unique and unprecedented, and therefore (at least as far as Hollywood conventions are concerned) unrepresentable murder machine" (46–47). In addition, critics are concerned that the Hollywood conventions that dictate the parameters of the plot and the film's unquestioning assumption of the epic genre work to emphasize individual action, initiative, and redemption—an emphasis that obscures the collective concerns, vulnerability, and destruction that was the fate of one-third of the Jews in Europe.[3]

Other critics are concerned with the degree of realism that the film undertakes. While *Schindler's List* tells a fantastic story of good in the face of evil, this story is presented with all the trappings of a realistic depiction. Disturbed by the deliberate utilization of a documentary style, the black-and-white film's connotations of authentic newsreel footage, the CNN-style reportage evoked by handheld cameras, and Spielberg's own comment during the film's premiere in Kraków that he had made "a document, not an entertainment" (qtd. in Zelizer 28), critics see in such gestures Hollywood's ultimate usurpation of reality and history. This becomes especially problematic in light of the specific reality and precise moment in history that the film portrays. As Miriam Hansen puts it, critics are concerned with the extent to which "the film enhances the fallacy of an immediate and unmediated access to the past . . . by posing as 'the real thing' the film usurps the place of the actual event" (300). She adds: "What is worse, it does so with an event that defies depiction, whose horror renders any attempt at direct representation obscene" (300–301).[4]

What underlines Loshitzky's statement, then, is not that this particular film has represented the Holocaust in an unprecedented manner that would require us to rethink the "limits of representation," but that it has represented the Holocaust at all. The argument that Spielberg's film—either by excessive or insufficient authenticity—violates some representative taboo is based on the assumption that any Holocaust representation, merely by virtue of being a representation, is somewhat reprehensible. Like Lanzmann, Loshitzky locates this violation in the nature of the subject matter, which she imagines as imbued with an inherent quality of sacred unspeakability. "Spielberg was the first mainstream Hollywood Jewish filmmaker to break the taboo of explicitly imagining the Holocaust and the gas chamber as its ultimate sacred center and horrifying metaphor. In essence, Spielberg violated the ancient Jewish biblical prohibition against creating images as it had been unconsciously resurrected in the moral taboo on representing the Holocaust" ("Holocaust Others" 110–11).

A responsible representation of the Holocaust, the assumption goes, must situate itself somehow in relation to representation's limits, acknowledge its own inadequacy, and, in the form of ellipses, gaps, or other deferential gestures, retain a space for what exceeds these limits, for the unspeakable. The failure of *Schindler's List* to do so is perceived by its critics as an ethical and aesthetic drawback. "Spielberg does not display any of the restraints, hesitations, or stammers that have become characteristic of *authentic* artistic responses to the Holocaust," writes Ilan Avisar. "[T]he film conveys no sense that the events were much worse, indeed unrepresentable, unimaginable, incomprehensible" (50–51; emphasis mine). "Although Spielberg's *Schindler's List* is about morality," writes Sara Horowitz, "it is not a moral film. The filmmaker's unexamined use of the epic genre limits the moral complexity of the film" ("But Is It" 136). She adds a plea for reticence in the face of the inevitable limits the Holocaust is assumed to impose on generic categories: "Perhaps, too, a Holocaust film needs to stand in humility in the face of unspeakable horror, rather than accommodate itself to the hubris of the epic" (138).

How is such unspeakable horror to be retained in the specifically *visual* medium of film? What happens when the unspeakable is *seen*? In "The Cinema Animal," Geoffrey Hartman notes that visual technology poses ethical challenges to representation and expresses concern about the specific capability of the visual medium to elide a recognition of its own limits. "There are things that should not be represented," he writes. "Yet because our modern technical expertise is such that simulacra can be provided for almost any experience however extreme, it is more today a question of *should not* rather than *cannot*. What should not be represented remains a moral decision" (130). Unlike literature or an oral tradition, which requires the reader to exert her imagination and confront its limits, the visual medium casts "a magnetic spell that alone seems able to convey the magnitude of the evil. . . . The 'ineluctable modality of the visual,' with its evacuation of inwardness, fixates imagination more than the formulas of oral tradition" (131).

Hartman's concern is with the complex moral situation this medium forces on the viewer, since the imagination, thus "fixated," will be unable to confront its own limits or take responsibility toward what it confronts. "Spielberg has created a fact on the screen," he writes, "and the moral challenge passes to the viewers. Can we, either during the movie, or as those images recall themselves in the mind, become like the Perceval of legend, who must decide what to ask or what not to ask of an extraordinary sight?" ("Cinema Animal" 131). He returns to this question and rephrases it: "How do we respond to such sights? In our very impotence, do we protest and turn away, or find some other defense? Have we no choice but to demand that these representations be labeled unpresentable?" (134). Ultimately, Hartman is more comfortable with Haim Gouri's *The Eighty-First Blow* and Claude Lanzmann's *Shoah,* both of which privilege an oral, rather than visual, tradition through the techniques of voice-over and oral testimony. This privileging of the oral indicates that for Hartman, as well as for critics like Horowitz and Avisar who are uncomfortable with the film's lack of ellipses and gaps, Holocaust depictions that do *not* confront the reader with the moral challenge of unselfconscious visual realism are preferable to *Schindler's List.*

But as I have demonstrated, it is precisely this challenge that renders the viewer reluctant, or even unable, to speak, and the film itself unspeakable. The fact that we have no refuge in ellipses or gaps forces us to confront what we may have assumed to be safely beyond the limits of representation. Significantly, what we are confronting is not the historical fact of Nazi genocide (Holocaust revisionists are unlikely to be convinced by *Schindler's List*) but, rather, the extent to which our own self-interests, not the mere spectacle of atrocity, dictate the limits of our seeing. Therefore, while we may not learn much about the details of Nazi genocide from this film, we are in a position to learn a great deal about the interaction of image and viewer and, specifically, the ethical negotiations and responsibilities that the work of seeing entails. To speak *Schindler's List* is to confront the complexity of our position as active participants in a comprehensible representation of the Holocaust. Such a position is inescapably complicit, not merely with the alignment of culture with genocide, but with the moral challenge posed by genocide itself, its uncanny familiarity as an inherent constituent of our collective identity at the dawn of the twenty-first century.

The infamous shower scene, in which the women on Schindler's list, mistakenly routed to Auschwitz, are forced to strip and are crowded into a room that has all the familiar trappings of a gas chamber, is a crucial example of this challenge. The explicit representation of (what appears to be) the inside of a gas chamber disturbs many critics who, like Loshitzky, feel that, in following the women into the chamber, Spielberg is essentially entering the "Holy of Holies" and violating some sort of sacred taboo. Significantly, critical readings of this scene focus on its implications for the viewer's integrity, which, critics assume, is problematized by the scene's eroticism and melo-drama. Horowitz says that "the shower scene provides another occasion for the camera to eroticize the Jewish female body" ("But Is It" 129). Hartman calls the scene "an unnecessary touch . . . [it is] melodramatic, and leaves the audience confused (like the terrified prisoners, in that crucial moment of uncertainty, when the lights go out) about the issue of disinfecting showers and gas showers" ("Cinema Animal" 129). Bartov, specifically concerned with the extent to which this scene catapults the viewer into complicity with the women's victimization, says that the scene is "more appropriate to a soft-porn sadomasochistic film than to its context," adding that "the fact that this 'actually' happened is, of course, wholly beside the point, since in most cases it did not, and even when it did, the only eyes which might have derived any sexual pleasure from watching such scenes belonged to the SS. Hence, by including this scene, Spielberg makes the viewers complicit with the SS, both in sharing their voyeurism and in blocking out the reality of the gas chambers" (49).

What's significant about these reservations is that Horowitz, Hartman, and Bartov are disturbed precisely by what this scene does to the *viewer:* forc-ing her into an erotic or voyeuristic gaze, aligning her with the prisoners' confusion, and leaving her ignorant. Their dislike of the scene is predicated on the extent to which it forces the viewer into a potentially complicit posi-tion. Vehemently critiquing this scene, then, is a way for critics to safeguard the viewer from the problematic implications of participating in *Schindler's List*'s transgressive, because comprehensible, transmission. For these crit-ics, viewer complicity is something to be avoided, and a scene that makes the viewer complicit is to be derided.

My understanding of this scene, on the other hand, is aligned around this question: now that I have readily and easily identified the visual signs that make me think "gas chamber," what is my response to Spielberg's manipu-lating my expectations and deflating the tension with the water from the shower? Without attempting to safeguard the viewer from potential com-plicity in the scene's "transgressive" quality, I would offer the following an-swer: having followed Schindler's Jews into the showers, and waited, with them, for the gas, and gasped (with relief?) at the water, I cannot ignore the fact that this scene worked, not because I *didn't* know what was going to hap-pen, but because I *did* know what happened, and did or didn't want to see it take place. The camera is not leading me into unfamiliar territory, but reminding me of what is disturbingly familiar and recognizable. By virtue of this recognition, this scene ceases to be about the Jewish victims and, instead, directly addresses the issue of what *I* know, what *I* recognize, and what *I* am willing and able to watch. If I gasp with disappointment, it is because I recognize my complicity with the camera's voyeuristic gaze. It is a gasp for myself, a gasp that says, "I wanted to watch them die." If I gasp with relief, my relief is not for the Jewish women who emerge intact from the jaws of the Nazi death machine, it is for myself, it is a gasp that says, "I didn't want to watch them die."

The Work of Seeing

Schindler's List should be examined, then, not in terms of what we do or don't see and the extent to which what we see is "authentic" or "realistic," but rather with an emphasis on how the film constructs, controls, and directs our acts of seeing and the extent to which such seeing underscores or undercuts comprehension. To what extent is the viewer empowered or disempowered by what she sees? What viewer reactions are scripted, and what reactions are scripted as unspeakable? Focusing on the expository introduction sequence, I will demonstrate that a close examination of empowering and disempowering the viewer—irrespective of how realistic or explicit the image being viewed—offers a new way of seeing, evaluating, and analyzing Holocaust films.

The opening sequences of any film direct the viewer how to see, offering types of information to look for and to choose among, and inviting her to begin to construct meaning and significance that will be either reinforced or undercut in the course of the film. In the opening sequence of *Schindler's List*, we move from an image of a family lighting the Sabbath candles (in color) to Jews registering at the Kraków train station (black-and-white) and the enigmatic figure of Schindler preparing to make his way into the higher echelons of Nazi society, ending with a close-up on Schindler's Nazi pin. This sequence of scenes, structured by the juxtaposition of parallel and contrasting images and sutured by nondiegetic music and sound,[5] introduces the viewer to a number of crucial elements that will prove essential to comprehending the film: the relation of the black-and-white film "proper" to the moments in color that open and end it; the locus and operation of historical information (specifically, explanatory paragraphs providing names and functions of places and individuals) in this "documentary" depiction; the crucial dichotomies and juxtapositions of power and powerlessness that will characterize the relations of Schindler and "his" Jews.)

The film opens in color, in late afternoon, with the lighting of the Sabbath candles before sunset. As the candles burn down, the daylight fades, and the switch from color to black-and-white is subtly aligned with the fading of daylight to night. The Holocaust, then, by virtue of the switch from color to black-and-white, is identified as the realm of Night, and Day will not return until the final scene, in color, as the *Schindlerjuden,* literally awoken by a Russian soldier who informs them they have been liberated, walk out of the nightmare and back into life, across a green pasture to the present and to the Promised Land.[6]

The realm of Night is alien, mythic, inaccessible, and informed, like dreams, by visual symbols. The transition from color (day, life, here-and-now) to black-and-white (night, death, the Holocaust) is therefore enacted through prominent Holocaust images: the extinguished candles, the infamous deportation trains, and the smoke that connects the two. As the candle burns out and smoke rises from the extinguished flame, the sound of a train is heard, and the rising smoke from the extinguished candle is replaced with the stark black-and-white image of rising smoke from the engine of a train bringing displaced Jews to Kraków. "Hmm, fire and trains," muttered a fellow moviegoer, "this must be a film about the Holocaust."

In the course of distancing the Holocaust from the viewer by rendering it in the realm of Night and in the somewhat alienating, because archaic, black-and-white of authentic footage, the film puts the viewer in the powerful position of identifying the construction of this distance—we are aware that a movement from color to black-and-white has been effected—and of comprehending the symbolic gestures that inform it: the recognition of fire and trains and the identification of the candle's rising smoke with that of the smokestack and its inevitable crematoria connotations. These visual images work to establish a dreamlike symbolic, visual, and associative continuum appropriate to the realm of Night: "The candles burn down, literalizing the term Holocaust as an offering to God wholly consumed by flames. Thus the candles symbolize the extinguishing of European Jewish life and the burning of Jews in the crematoria" (Horowitz, "But Is It" 124).

But these Holocaust symbols and the identifications they evoke are undercut by the matter-of-fact tone of the explanatory paragraphs which note that after the defeat of the Polish army, Jews are forced to relocate from the countryside to the city. The train smoke, we realize, is not crematoria smoke at all. It is not even the smoke of the cattle cars that carted the Jews to extermination. It is the smoke of a train bringing Jews to Kraków, not taking them away. It heralds the Jews' presence in Kraków, not their absence from it. Thus, while the film puts the viewer in a powerful position of identifying and deciphering the symbolic visual images that inform this nightmare world, it also, through the documentary-style explanatory paragraph, undercuts that position. On the one hand, we are in the world of Night, confidently identifying and reading familiar symbols. On the other hand, a different kind of reading—of the explanatory paragraph—informs us that the initial symbolic meaning we had been invited to construct is inaccurate.

The documentary style, however, does not maintain this alignment with historical accuracy which would consistently contradict the symbolic level of these opening moments. In fact, the cabaret sequence that immediately follows the opening sequence will undercut the documentary style as well. In the cabaret, we observe Schindler as he ingeniously inserts himself into Nazi society, and the crucial instrument that enables him to do so is the photographer's camera. Photographs, which convey the sense of direct reference to the photographed reality (Barthes describes the photograph as "literally an emanation of the referent" [80]), offer an aura of authenticity that is presented, in this scene, as explicitly staged. This scene, then, renders us witnesses to the construction and manipulation of historical documents, somewhat undercutting the film's own claim to "document" status. The photograph of a Nazi officer moving in front of and obscuring a woman in order to document his friendship with Schindler is an especially good example of this—so good an example, in fact, that it merits a reappearance later in the film, when Schindler uses these cabaret photos to bribe Nazi officials for army contracts.

Were the film consistently to set up and then to debunk the associations surrounding Holocaust symbols and its own documentary style, it would have been a very different film. The viewer would have been able to assume an ironic distance from the operations of the visual medium, and the film would have lost most of its affective power. As a result, it would be far less successful in rendering itself unspeakable. Therefore, this initial debunking of the viewer's reading is presented concurrently with a reliable, stable power relation that informs the entire film: the clear contrast between Jews registering at the train station, speaking loudly and clearly over the sound of the train as the camera focuses on their faces and their names are entered on the lists, and the silent, enigmatic, faceless figure preparing for an evening out. Nondiegetic waltz music sutures the two scenes, underscoring the conceptual connection that the viewer is invited to create. In stark contrast to the exposed names and faces of the previous scene, Schindler's face is hidden, his name as yet unspoken, and we see only his hands and objects that connote power (watch, whiskey, cash, etc.).

The function of these contrasting scenes is to establish the relation of power and powerlessness that will inform the film's plot: those who have to give their names and whose faces are visible, like the Jews on the platform, are vulnerable (a hypothesis borne out as Schindler gets Stern off the train deporting Jews to extermination by demanding the names of the soldiers in charge of the transport); those who can hide their names and faces (like Schindler) have power. This structure of power is enhanced by virtue of the viewer's preexisting knowledge of Hollywood filmic traditions that the scene draws on: the accoutrements of power surrounding Schindler's appearance clearly establish him as our enigmatic hero. Thus, in addition to setting up a reliable series of power relations that inform this film (to which Rothberg, in a reading of the film's publicity posters, adds "the strong hand and forearm lifting up a smaller, more childlike hand" [228]), these scenes correct the initial evocation and undercutting of Holocaust symbols, reinstating the viewer in a position of authority: her gaze draws clear connections and constructs hierarchies of power, hierarchies that will be reaffirmed in the course of the film and that essentially inform its plot and illustrate its theme.

What to do, then, with Schindler's Nazi pin in the construction of these hierarchies? In the predictable privileging of individual vs. collective, enigmatic vs. vulnerable, powerful vs. powerless, the pin adds Nazi vs. Jew. Unlike the other dichotomies, however, which remain intact throughout the plot, the Nazi vs. Jew dichotomy will dissolve in the course of the film as Schindler (technically a Nazi) uses his position as a member of the Nazi Party to save Jews from destruction. In Schindler's final scene—the "I could have done more" speech to which I will return at the end of this chapter—this same pin will function as the emblem of potentially saved lives, not destroyed ones: "this pin . . . two more lives." As if to underscore the instability of this final dichotomy, the waltz, which has connected this scene with the preceding train station scene, comes to a leisurely end as the camera

Against the Unspeakable

zooms in to focus on the pin. Both the visual and aural levels of the film work to exclude this pin, and the Nazi vs. Jew paradigm it evokes, from the system of coherence constructed by the viewer's gaze. In this manner, Schindler's membership in the Nazi Party, his collaboration with the instrument of destruction, is rendered incomprehensible (outside the coherent hierarchies set up in this sequence) and hence unspeakable.[7]

Schindler's List's Viewer

An approach to Holocaust films that evaluates the operation and manipulation of the viewer's gaze and emphasizes her agency in constructing coherence from the images on the screen requires that the role and identity of the viewer be central to the operation of the visual medium. Such an attitude toward the viewer is at the heart of the complex and diverse entertainment industry that we refer to as "Hollywood," with its explicitly "American" identity and orientation and its perceived emphasis on focus groups, prerelease hype, and the politics and strategies of domestic, international, and home video release. And yet, situating the viewer at center stage is disturbing to many critics of *Schindler's List,* as doing so reiterates the film's role in an industry that is often reviled for its appeal to the lowest common denominator, reinstating the uncomfortable pun of "Shoah-business" and, most significantly, locating the Holocaust as subject matter within the minds and hearts of moviegoers, rather than safely behind the cultural and aesthetic boundaries of foreign language, temporal distance, and the relatively inaccessible medium of the "art film."

But, as Omer Bartov puts it, "any representation of the Holocaust comes with a heavy price" (51). In this particular representation of the Holocaust, a complex and disturbing economy is evoked: on the one hand, the director of *E.T.* emplots the Holocaust as a narrative of individualistic redemption, complete with happy end; *Schindler's List* is Hollywood at its most simplistic, sentimental, and disturbing. On the other hand, the film's box-office success has exposed many people to a representation of the Holocaust that they might otherwise have managed to avoid. As a result, Spielberg's relatively upbeat version of history, precisely by virtue of its Hollywood credentials and box-office success, is touted as a powerful tool for Holocaust education in particular and the fight against contemporary racism in the United States in general.[8] "Is it worth it?" critics ask, a question that obscures the players in this complex economy of representation. Just as Amon Goeth, asked by Schindler, "How much is a person worth?" turns the question around and responds, "How much is a person worth, *to you?*" the economy of Holocaust representation galvanized by *Schindler's List* is not, is it worth it? but *what* is it worth, and *to whom?*

Horowitz, wondering whether *Schindler's List* is an "important" film, answers immediately: "Yes, by virtue of its popularity. Spielberg's film may well be the one vehicle by which many Americans come to learn of the Holocaust" ("But Is It" 138). In her emphasis on Americans for whom the Holocaust occurred in a far country, a long time ago, to other people, and in a foreign language, Horowitz is pointing to the crucial role played by the *medium* in Holocaust representations in the United States. While Europeans and Americans may be equally ignorant about the Holocaust (in Israel, where the Holocaust plays a prominent role in the curriculum, the media, and public discourse, ignorance is assumed to be less of a concern), the means of alleviating this ignorance in the United States is more media dependent than in Europe, where linguistic and geographical barriers do not pose the same obstruction, and where there is easier access to the sites of atrocity that actively construct or obscure memory.[9] As a result, Americans are more readily imagined as "learning about the Holocaust" through the media than Europeans are. In her emphasis on the medium's responsibility toward educating Americans in particular, Horowitz is voicing a widespread, though reluctant, consensus: while *Schindler's List* is a profoundly flawed representation of the Holocaust, a profoundly flawed representation is better than profound ignorance, and Spielberg's film at least serves the purpose of introducing the Holocaust to a far larger audience than, say, Claude Lanzmann's far more sophisticated film, *Shoah*.[10] The film could be better, but *Schindler's List*'s popularity ultimately outweighs its faults.

In order to reach this conclusion, however, one must make this calculation in the context of an imagined audience for whom the film, despite its heavy reliance on fictional elements, serves as a "document," informing— or, more precisely, misinforming—otherwise ignorant Americans about history. In addition, one must assume that this representation exists alone, rather than in a broader spectrum where it could be challenged by other, conflicting, revisionist representations; and that it is, necessarily, inadequate to the reality that it purports to represent.[11] For if we were to imagine an American audience confronted with a wide variety of Holocaust films, like they are confronted with a wide variety of Vietnam War films, such an audience would be far more likely to see *Schindler's List* as "just one more film about the Holocaust" instead of mistaking it for "*the* Holocaust film" or even for "the Holocaust" itself. Thus, expressing discomfort with the extent to which the film's representation of the Holocaust replaces or obscures the "real" Holocaust functions as an expression of discomfort with Holocaust representation per se.

But just what kind of audience is being posited in this argument? Who are these Americans for whom, Horowitz assumes, "the film's version of Holocaust suffering will stand unrefuted by other sources" ("But Is It" 138) and for whom, writes Bartov, "a relatively minor, and quite extraordinary case, has been transformed into a representative segment of the 'story' as a whole" (46)? If, as Lanzmann puts it, Spielberg "could not tell Schindler's story without also saying what the Holocaust was" (14), does telling Schindler's story neglect the facts that "in the 'real' Holocaust, most of the Jews died, most of the Germans collaborated with the perpetrators or remained passive bystanders, most of the victims sent to the showers were gassed, and most of the survivors did not walk across green meadows to Palestine" (Bartov 46)? Is neglecting these facts tantamount to, as Bartov suggests, obliterating the truth?

Schindler's List's viewer must be ignorant, since a viewer who does know "what the Holocaust was," as Lanzmann puts it, is in no danger of believing that Schindler's actions are indicative of German behavior in Nazi Germany, that Jews were not gassed in the showers, and that the more glaring inaccuracies and the general "feel-good" quality of the story do not function as crucial deterrents in the film's gestures toward realism and authenticity. Assuming an ignorant viewer of this film also requires that the viewer be gullible, willing to "buy" Spielberg's version as an accurate representation of an otherwise inaccessible reality (rendered even more so by the archaic black-and-white format, the European settings, and the foreign accents). It is difficult to imagine a viewer who is ignorant but not gullible; one who, without additional factual background than that communicated by the film, could walk out of *Schindler's List* and declare, "No, actually, it was worse." Such a declaration would indicate that the Holocaust is readily accessible by basic Western principles of logic and common sense, principles that would then be necessarily implicated in the Holocaust itself. In such a case, the Holocaust's "speakability" would reside in the overt realm of our own volition: it would be something we could, conceivably, speak about. Such an assumption, as I will demonstrate, is not only undercut by the film itself but also directly contradicts prevailing concepts of the Holocaust as beyond the realm of human comprehension.

What purpose is served by positing such a viewer? An ignorant and gullible viewer, who assumes that *Schindler's List* is a faithful and accurate depiction of history, might come to the conclusion that the Holocaust, after all, wasn't so bad: "Sure, a lot of people must have died, but hey, fortunately there were good folks around like this Schindler guy."[12] Such a viewer might also assume that after watching *Schindler's List,* he or she has filled some sort of "Holocaust quota" and therefore does not "need" to see any more (possibly more accurate) Holocaust films, implicitly reinforcing the position of *Schindler's List* as "*the* Holocaust film."[13] This ignorant, gullible viewer works to reinforce assumptions of the Holocaust's unspeakability: such a viewer's erroneous attitude merely highlights the perceived need to emphasize that the Holocaust was, in fact, worse than anything imaginable and that no representation can do it justice, facilitating the argument that Spielberg's imagination of the Holocaust is transgressive in its representation of an ultimately "feel-good" reality.[14] In this manner, the ignorant and gullible viewer works as a construct according to which critics of the film can reiterate their assumption that the Holocaust is unspeakable.

The construction of an American viewer who will know "nothing" or "very little" about the Holocaust other than what she has seen in the theater while watching *Schindler's List* is, I argue, too easy. It effaces the viewer's presence, experience, judgment, and agency. It posits that the viewer is absent from the meaning-making operations of the film. But the viewer of a film is anything but passive, and *Schindler's List* is no exception. *Schindler's List's* viewer is consistently recognizing images, responding and dissociating herself affectively, making judgments and evaluations that are reinforced or undercut by the available visual information, and finding herself propelled in and out of a disturbing emotional or intellectual complicity with what she sees, hears, and understands.

As Goeth and his soldiers exhume and burn bodies of Jews murdered in Plazsów and the Kraków ghetto massacre, a Nazi soldier, emerging from the smoke of burning bodies, screams directly into the camera, momentarily obliterating the distance between the viewer and the horrendous scene by the immediacy of his gaze and the intensity of his response. I recognize his emotion, he articulates my horror, he screams for me, he *is* me. But immediately after screaming he looks away from the camera and chuckles, I see him laughing and shooting randomly into a pile of bodies; I realize with relief that he is mad. The moment's affective quality does not make such scenes easier to watch; what I have recognized as an expression of my affective response is in fact a type of murderous insanity that I would have liked to assume is unrecognizable.

Avoiding a Complicit Gaze

I am not exonerating *Schindler's List* from sentimentality, or saying that the film, by rendering itself at moments unspeakable, is more complex and therefore a "better" or more "responsible" Holocaust film. An approach to Holocaust films that evaluates the effect of a scene or a sequence on the viewer, rather than the "responsibility" assumed by its director toward the subject matter, does not ensure that the systems of coherence the viewer constructs will inevitably propel her into an ethical engagement with the act of seeing. Such an approach could equally identify moments in which the viewer is safeguarded from, rather than propelled into, a morally challenging gaze.

During the liquidation of the ghetto, the artificial color of a little girl's red coat serves to safeguard the viewer in precisely this fashion. In this controversial scene, often deplored for its sentimentality,[15] the presence of a child is signaled by background music of children singing, the first nondiegetic sound in this painfully realistic sequence; the viewer, alerted by the soundtrack, searches for and finds an enigmatic red dot which takes on form and becomes recognizable as a child's coat. Both the red coat and nondiegetic music are welcome artificialities in this sequence, the relentless realism of which is emotionally and even physically exhausting. By searching for and identifying a child, we are momentarily relieved from "the chaos of terror made physically painful to the viewer's eyes by hand-held, unsteady cameras, as if the eyes had to be punished for what they could not feel" (Hartman, "Cinema Animal" 127).

The wide camera angle of this scene conjures a panorama of destruction that forces the viewer to decide which atrocities to look at and which to ignore. Such a gaze, implicitly selecting some deaths to be witnessed and relegating others to oblivion, would be complicit in the massacre. The little girl's red coat saves the viewer from such a choice and such a gaze. In addition, by actively directing our gaze toward the little girl in the red coat, the camera keeps us from emotionally withdrawing from a view that, like Bosch's rendition of Hell, is literally stunning in its sheer plentitude of horrifying detail. Such a withdrawal would align us with the role of passive bystanders during the Nazi regime and would also reiterate the emotional withdrawal from spectacle enabled by the relatively passive visual medium of film, where we have grown accustomed to viewing far more horrific scenes than this.

The cuts to Schindler's intent face indicate that he sees this coat and that it is his gaze that follows it. In addition, the frequent cuts to Schindler's face hint that it may be his gaze that colors the coat. The association of the coat's redness with Schindler's gaze frees the viewer from the disturbing sense that she is being emotionally manipulated by Spielberg; rather, the viewer (merely) shares Schindler's individualizing, humanizing, and compassionate viewpoint. Finally, Schindler's attempts to keep the child in view (by wheeling his horse about and straining in the saddle) give the impression that his gaze not only colors the child's coat but also keeps her safe. When the child does disappear from Schindler's view, the redness of her coat remains a little longer, as if the viewer, having taken on Schindler's gaze, continues to hold the coat's color and, in the absence of his compassionate looking, keeps the child safe in his place. The red color fades only as the child appears to be, for the moment at least, out of danger, ensconced in a hiding place under the bed.

The red coat makes a final appearance as Goeth is incinerating the bodies of the Jews killed in the ghetto liquidation, accompanied with similar cuts to Schindler's face. Perhaps, at this moment, Schindler realizes that his gaze did not keep the child safe. To some extent, this is the turning point in the film, since only after the incineration scene does Schindler begin to actively work to save "his" Jews. In this manner, the red coat works as an instrument of salvation: in generating an individualizing, humanizing gaze, it enables Schindler to extend this gaze to the 1,100 people he does succeed in saving. By extension, the red coat's function of engaging our emotions and keeping us from a passive, complicit gaze emplots us in this narrative of salvation, as if the fact, or quality, of our affective response is somehow connected to saving human lives.

The artificial color of the child's red coat, then, keeps us from the complicity inherent in emotional withdrawal from the scene of atrocity and constructs us as active participants in a humanizing gaze. Had there been no red coat, we would have most likely missed the child and not participated in the gaze that individualizes her; we would have looked on the scene merely as a spectacle, incapable of singling out any individual and following their fate. In fact, had there been no red coat, the viewer would of necessity have participated in a passive, uncaring, dehumanizing gaze that dispassionately observes tiny dark figures scurrying, like the vermin Jews were often likened to, from extermination.

Avoiding a Complicit Comprehension

The red coat aligns us affectively with the fate of a child, employing our emotions to keep us from the complicity inherent in a passive, uncaring gaze. In a similar manner, the presentation and representation of Amon Goeth's murderous rampages works to disqualify our intellect from the complicity of active comprehension. As Goeth shoots at Jewish prisoners in Plaszów from the balcony of his villa, the camera angle aligns the viewer's gaze with that of the Nazi commander: we are looking through his rifle sights at his potential victims. This point of view is an especially uncomfortable one, since it makes the viewer participate with Goeth's murderous gaze on what Hansen calls "the unconscious level of cinematic discourse" (300).

But on the conscious level, Goeth's murders are, in this scene, chillingly logical: the people he shoots are the only figures within his view who are not actively employed in some kind of labor. The camera, following Goeth's gaze through his rifle sights, cuts back repeatedly to a woman kneeling by her wheelbarrow before we see him shoot her, and we guess, correctly, that she is to be his target. Our hypothesis about his reasoning is confirmed as he shoots the man idling on the barracks steps. Thus not only does the viewer share Goeth's murderous gaze, she quite consciously *comprehends* his actions, *anticipates* his decisions, and *participates* in his logic. Goeth's murderousness, which we would like to assume is illogical and insane, the irrational realm of absolute evil, is in fact rendered painfully logical, systematic, and comprehensible from the viewer's point of view.

This complicit gaze, however, is contradicted on the verbal level of the film by Helen Hirsch's oral testimony in the cellar. Describing Goeth's killing sprees, Hirsch represents his murderousness as illogical, random, and inexplicable: she relates seeing Goeth kill a woman "no fatter or thinner or faster or slower than any other woman and I couldn't *think* . . . what she had done." Hirsch's position, sitting tensely in a chair under a single lamp as Schindler paces in the background, is reminiscent of a prison interrogation. There is some sense of Hirsch confessing to a crime, and her emphasis on "I couldn't *think*" implies that her crime is precisely her inability to comprehend. As he assures her that the slain woman was, for Goeth, "part of a series, neither pleasing nor displeasing him," Schindler seems to exculpate Hirsch from the crime of incomprehension, indicating that it's okay not to think, locating her (and with her, the viewer, as we identify with Hirsch throughout) safely in an amorphous realm of incomprehensible evil for which no responsibility need be assumed.

The oral testimony that we hear in the cellar, then, directly contradicts the visual reality we have witnessed, (re)constructing that reality as random and illogical, and safeguarding the viewer from the uncomfortable recognition of the method in Goeth's madness. More significantly, Hirsch's oral testimony and Schindler's assent to it also work to undercut the value of our gaze and hence of our ability to draw on our own logic and common sense in relation to the Holocaust. The film is ultimately telling us, "look, but don't think you can understand what you see." Finally, this scene establishes the limits of responsibility and comprehension as our uncomfortable intimacy with Goeth's mode of reasoning is neutralized by Schindler, who disarms intimacy's destructive potential. This scene ends with Schindler kissing Hirsch chastely on the forehead, another potentially invasive and illicit intimacy which Schindler effectively neutralizes: "It's not that kind of kiss."[16]

The Work of Memory

The possibility that cinematic images created by Spielberg in particular and Hollywood in general may, by virtue of the film's popularity and critical acclaim, enter as "memory" into its viewers' minds is the source of much of the urgency that underlies critical writing about the film. "Will this film not only preserve the Holocaust in the world's historical memory but also define the shape and dominant imagery of this memory?" asks Loshitzky, who appears disturbed that "myths and symbols constructed and perpetuated by Hollywood have become permanent features of America and the world's historical consciousness" (intro. 1–2). For with *Schindler's List*, not only has the representative taboo been broken ("images for the unimaginable"), it has been broken by Steven Spielberg, whose choice of a main character named "Oskar" can hardly have been an innocent one, and by Hollywood, whose representation of the Holocaust was perceived in Europe (where it happened) and Israel (which claims to represent those to whom it happened) as a disturbing manifestation of U.S. cultural hegemony.[17]

The issue is, ultimately, that of the construction, fictionalization, and propagation of memory. Once the representative taboo is perceived as being broken, the relation between memory and representation becomes especially crucial. What is the relation of images to memory? Who has the right to remember (i.e., to represent, to create images or efface them), and how (if at all) can such representations be controlled? At stake is the definition of memory in light of Spielberg's supposed desecration of the second commandment. According to such assumptions, *Schindler's List*'s unapologetic realism has contaminated memory with representation, rendered the unspeakable speakable, endowed it with volition, responsibility, and the potential of complicity.

Rothberg notes that the release of *Schindler's List* coincided with the inauguration of the U.S. Holocaust Memorial Museum to produce what ABC's *Nightline*, on December 28, 1993, called "The Year of the Holocaust" (221–22). The film, suggests Rothberg, shares with the museum a memorial function, producing a situation in which "praise for, and citation of, the film . . . stand in for memorialization of the genocide itself" (223), a situation that propels Rothberg to consider the place of the Holocaust in the contemporary United States. Hansen's discussion of *Schindler's List* in the context of "the second commandment, popular modernism, and public memory" concludes with an emphasis on the film's significance in the politics of contemporary mass-mediated memory culture. While being careful not to defend the film "on aesthetic grounds" (305), she urges critics to take seriously the film's function in the culture that produced it: "To dismiss the film because of the *a priori* established unrepresentability of what it purports to represent may be justified on ethical and epistemological grounds, but it means missing a chance to understand the significance of the Shoah in the present, in the ongoing and undecided struggles over which past gets remembered and how" (311–12).

Without dismissing such struggles and the constituencies that inform them, it's worth examining the gestures the film itself makes toward remembering the past and the extent to which such gestures propel the viewer in and out of the active responsibility and agency required to participate in the work of memory. My concern here is not, *what* memories of the Holocaust are instilled in our minds by *Schindler's List*? but rather *how* does the film represent memory, what attitude toward memory is the viewer invited to assume, and what work of memory does the film itself undertake?

The film ends with two significant gestures toward memory. The first occurs as the *Schindlerjuden* bid farewell to their protector after the surrender of the Third Reich to the Allied forces. Schindler, giving Stern last-minute instructions, starts toward his car, and Stern stops him and hands him a paper. "We've written a letter," says Stern, "trying to explain. Every worker signed it." Stern's words (*"trying"* but inevitably failing "to explain") indicate that as this fantastic event recedes into (however recent) history, explanations and words fall short. It is the gold ring that Stern presents to Schindler that is a much more significant and active repository for the story the film has told, and Stern holds the ring for a moment and turns it so it will flash, alerting us as well as Schindler to the importance of this next gift:

Stern: [*Presents Schindler with the ring*] It's Hebrew from the Talmud.
It says whoever saves one life saves the world entire.
[*Schindler looks at his wife, looks at Stern, drops the ring, picks it up, raises his hand in full view of the surrounding congregation, and slides the ring on to his wedding ring finger*]

Schindler's gestures here are especially telling. In accepting the ring, he is now "married" to the Jewish people. His glance toward his wife and then back at Stern indicates that he is aware of the potential friction such acceptance entails: marriage is an exclusive relationship, as his wife, with her emphasis on not being mistaken for anyone but "Mrs. Schindler," has stipulated throughout the film. While Schindler's "marriage" to the Jewish people is not sexual and hence does not detract from Schindler's new-found sexual virtue,[18] his glance toward his wife before accepting the ring does indicate that an exclusive relationship is being reimagined as inclusive, a potential site of tension is being disarmed. This moment indicates that since inscription, history, and other attempts at "explanation" must be inadequate, the proper commemoration of Schindler's actions during the Holocaust can only be performed in the relatively safe space of ritual: in this case, the marriage ceremony.[19] This ritual and the reimagination of it inform the film's gestures toward responsibility and ultimately toward memory, as the protagonist's and the film's omissions and failures are transmuted to an inclusive, ritualistic realm that functions as a safe repository for the necessarily excluded:

> Schindler: [*Bending toward Stern, as if telling a secret*] I could have got more out. [*Stern inclines his head toward Schindler to hear*] I could have got more.
> Stern: [*Shakes his head*] I don't know.
> Schindler: If I'd just . . . I could have got more . . .
> Stern: Oskar, there are eleven hundred people are alive because of you look at them.
> Schindler: If I'd made more money . . . [*Laughs*] I threw away so much money . . . you have no idea . . . if I'd just . . .
> Stern: There will be generations because of what you did.
> Schindler: I didn't do enough.
> Stern: You did so much.

Schindler's sense of loss is juxtaposed with his gain: "If I'd made more money," he says. "I threw away so much money." At the same time, loss is positioned as external to the system of exchange: money, we gather, is not the issue; the presence of "generations" is. And Schindler's confession "I didn't do enough" is, without being contradicted, simply counterpoised and equated with Stern's "You did so much." This exclusion of value from the system of representation that informs it serves to qualify the radical revaluation of representation that follows, as physical objects come to stand for lives lost and saved:

> Schindler: [*Moves away from Stern*] This car . . . Goeth would have bought this car. Why did I keep the car? Ten people right there. Ten people . . . [*Camera pans to watching Jews—about ten people*] . . . ten more people . . . This pin [*Takes it off his coat*] two people . . . [*Looks at the pin*] This is gold. Two more people. He would have given me two for it. At least one. He would have given me one more. One

more person. A person, Stern. For this . . . [*Stumbles, Stern embraces him*] I could have gotten one more person and I didn't . . . [*Weeps*] . . . I didn't . . .

[*Jews move to embrace him, obscuring him from view. Jewish woman picks up empty coat and turns away, unbuttoning it*]

While appearing to gesture toward responsibility, guilt, and grief, Schindler's speech and the camera work that accompanies it divert our attention from what it means to retain any object in a world where objects are used to purchase human life. In the course of this film we have seen objects change hands from Schindler (the hero) to Stern (his sidekick) to Goldberg (the collaborator) and Goeth (the villain), and these images of objects are accompanied by corresponding images of the faces or names of the people purchased by them. In this speech, as Schindler moves away from and back to Stern, the perpetrator's crucial function in this system of exchange ("Goeth would have bought this car") is gradually effaced and replaced with an address to the survivor: "A person, Stern." The representative value of objects is also effaced, to be replaced with the image, and finally the idea, of the victim: we move from the visual equation of car = ten people to the realm of the absent and the paradigmatic, the one person Schindler could have saved and didn't.

As Schindler breaks down under an overwhelming sense of a responsibility unfilled, his figure is hidden from view by the surviving Jews who move to embrace him. In this manner, Schindler himself, and his very real guilt at not having done enough, are literally effaced, replaced with the figures of the survivors and, we gather, their collective assumption of the responsibility to remember. Indeed, Schindler's inclusion of Stern in the work of imagining the absent person he could have saved indicates the assignation of the work of memory to the survivor, an assignation reiterated as another survivor, holding the empty coat, turns away from the Jews comforting Schindler. It is she, we gather, who will remember the person Schindler did not save.

What makes this scene especially compelling is the extent to which it, albeit momentarily, catapults an entire system of representation into complicity. When objects stand for human lives, the work of buying and selling requires a disturbing intimacy with the perpetrator ("Goeth would have bought this car"), and merely retaining objects is tantamount to participating in the work of killing. Hence Schindler's very real guilt that he could have saved one more person and didn't. In this scene, the guilt, like Schindler's figure, is immediately effaced, replaced with the survivor's work of memory (the woman with the coat that represents the person Schindler didn't save). In this process, the viewer is able to assume the relatively comfortable position of forgiving Schindler for not having saved more people and overlooking the inevitable insufficiency of any act of resistance while, at the same time, affectively registering the immense sense of loss without the disturbing sense of her own responsibility to engage in the work of memory. Such a position is infinitely more comfortable than to agree that yes, in fact, Schindler could and should have saved more people with his car and his pin. The people he didn't save are not comfortably ensconced in the memory of the survivors. Their loss cries out from each and every object that could have been employed to save them. And no cinematic scene, no matter how gut-wrenching, can ever change that fact.

The concept that representation replaces or effaces that which it represents is the motive behind many critics' invocation of *Bilderverbot* in reference to the Holocaust in general and *Schindler's List* in particular. Such evocations express concern that Spielberg's "feel-good" version of the Holocaust will replace and (for an ignorant, gullible American audience) obscure what J. Hoberman calls "the ultimate feel-bad experience of the 20th century" (qtd. in Hansen 297). In this scene, representation itself, by virtue of such effacement and replacement, becomes a site of complicity. Just as monetary value is rendered pointless in the light of "generations," numerical value and, ultimately, any system in which objects stand for human beings (bribery, the black market, printed names on a list) are rendered disturbingly transparent. Thus, despite the presence of the 1,100 people that, as Stern puts it, "are alive because of you look at them," Schindler (and, by virtue of the camera point of view which aligns our gaze with his, the audience) see the potential human beings represented (and replaced) by the car and the pin. The redirection of our gaze toward the living does not outweigh the spectral presence of the one person Schindler could have saved. The idea of the potential human value that is effaced by monetary, numerical, or object value, however briefly it is gestured toward, is a potentially devastating concept, since it makes representation itself complicit in the Holocaust—at least, in the specific version of the Holocaust that is represented by *Schindler's List*.[20]

It is significant, then, that the film's second and more powerful gesture toward memory redeems representation from complicity. By virtue of color film and the return to the present ("the Schindler Jews today," reads the caption), this scene is granted a certain priority over the preceding narrative, which was, after all, only a story and—by virtue of its initial relegation to the realm of Night and the mysterious sleep that the Jews seem to fall into after Schindler's departure (a sleep that overtakes them immediately and collectively and causes them to drop off where they stand and from which they, like members of Sleeping Beauty's court, are awoken by a lone soldier on horseback who informs them of their liberation)—only a dream. We are back in the here and now, and the here and now is established as the realm, not of representation, but of ritual and of memory: the *Schindlerjuden,* accompanied by the actors who portrayed them, file past Schindler's grave in Jerusalem, and in a Jewish memorial ritual, each leaves a stone on the tomb. In this manner the survivors' effacement of Schindler's grieving figure in the previous scene is reenacted. This time, however, the survivors do not obscure the living figure but commemorate the dead one, obscured already by the tombstone. This reenaction, then, translates the issue at hand from the complicity of representation to the ritual of memory.

Since the actors participate in this ritual together with the survivors, accompanied by the film's signature theme music, representation is portrayed as being strongly in the service of memory, rather than threatening to efface or replace it.[21] The stones on the grave do not obscure Schindler's name or the dates and places of his birth and death. In fact, this information is bordered by the stones, which have been cleared to form the shape of a crucifix, illustrating that in this memorial gesture Christian images and Jewish rituals exist side by side in harmony, much like Schindler's Christian and Jewish "marriage partners" were imagined in the previous scene. Finally, Spielberg's figure, as he lays a rose on the grave, is also exonerated from any complicity inherent in "representing the unrepresentable" and safely aligned with the ritual of commemoration, strengthening the impression that with *Schindler's List,* Spielberg has not only represented the Holocaust *to* us but also remembered the Holocaust *for* us.[22] In this manner, the film's final scene safeguards the viewer from the necessity to engage in, and take responsibility for, the problematic implications that the complex work of memory entails.[23]

Much of the critical concern with *Schindler's List* has, significantly, avoided dealing with the film directly and focused instead on the film's function in the cultural conversation which it enters into and which, by virtue of its blockbuster status, extensive critical acclaim, and general prominence in the media, it is assumed to reflect. In this context, the film has been perceived as a powerful and undeniable statement about the complexities of representation, of the relation of image to memory, of the appropriation and politicization of memory and image, and the implications of such appropriations for the interrelation of film, memory, and history. Critical responses to the film tend to gesture toward these broader issues and the implications the profound impact of the film on U.S. society holds for them: "In an age when even children understand that the image of an event transcends the event itself," writes J. Hoberman, "*Schindler's List* is more than just a movie" (24).

Critics who do engage with the complex aesthetics of the film itself—and such engagements are relatively few—are careful to distance themselves from the object of their discussion by foregrounding their dislike or distrust of it. Miriam Hansen, for example, while arguing that "*Schindler's List* is a more sophisticated, elliptical, and self-conscious film than its critics acknowledge" (303), is careful to clarify that the close attention she pays to the film's textual work "can only provide a weak answer to the fundamental objections raised by the film's intellectual opponents" and to distance herself from any potential justification of the film "on aesthetic grounds" (305). Horowitz, who recognizes that "criticizing the deep fabric and texture of the film in front of people moved to tears and beyond seems an act of profound insensitivity," justifies her own critique in terms of what she perceives as the broader context in which the film exists and functions. If "Spielberg's film may well be the one vehicle by which many Americans come to learn of the Holocaust," she reasons, then "allowing *Schindler's List* to stand as a master-narrative of the Holocaust seems ethically irresponsible" ("But Is It" 138). Such overt dislike of the film and stated reluctance to justify the film's aesthetics represent a broader tendency: critics, unwilling to engage with the film itself, utilize the film to gesture toward broader parameters, according to which *Schindler's List* and the public discussion it engendered function as powerful indications of the state of American society in particular and the problematics of representing the Holocaust in general.[24] In this manner critics of the film perform a certain silencing of it. *Schindler's List,* like the Holocaust, is posited as an unspeakable event which engenders a discourse but which, itself, carries a certain taboo against its own interrogation.

Speaking *Schindler's List* involves spelling out the complex articulations of complicity that are expressed or effaced by the act of seeing, by the agency required for comprehending, by the complexities of representation, and by the work of memory. A certain degree of responsibility is implied by viewing a film, especially a film generated for mass consumption, since our participation in the economy that such a film enters into inscribes us as members of the "lowest common denominator" implied by popular culture in general and Hollywood in particular. Rigorously critiquing *Schindler's List* for the audacity of its realistic gestures toward a supposedly unrepresentable reality evades, rather than assumes, this responsibility. Such critiques, under the aegis of keeping the Holocaust safe from films like *Schindler's List,* merely work to safeguard the object of representation from representation itself and, by extension, to keep the viewers of this representation from the potential complicity that participating in a comprehensible transmission implies. "Maybe it's naïve to ask film critics or Hollywood moviemakers to be morally sensitive," says Art Spiegelman. "After all, Spielberg's value system was formed by a world that originally brought us Auschwitz" (Hoberman 25). In such a world, gestures away from the complicity of representation with its object and its audience are as misguided as they are futile.

Night, Maus, Shoah, and the Image of the Speaking Corpse

Despite Spielberg's claim that he had made a "document, not an entertainment" (qtd. in Zelizer 28), despite the film's occasional aesthetic of reportage (the hand-held cameras, the black-and-white), and despite the fact that a factory owner named Oskar Schindler did, indeed, save Jews, *Schindler's List* is not a historical document. I mean by this that the film's value as an artifact does not lie in the accuracy with which it makes historical fact available to the contemporary eye. If such a statement appears to be self-evident, its self-evidence is obscured in the context of atrocity commonly imagined to be unspeakable. In this context the limits of representation assume a dual role. To say that "the Holocaust is unspeakable" makes a statement both about the Holocaust and about speech; it describes the Holocaust and evaluates the agency mobilized in that description, simultaneously mirroring and evoking the limits of speech and precipitating a conflation of cultural artifact and historical fact. For the critics of *Schindler's List* discussed in the previous chapter, this conflation works as a technology of critique: *Schindler's List* represents (what they claim is) the unrepresentable, provides images for (what they assume to be) the unimaginable, and otherwise "speaks" (what has been determined to be) the unspeakable. As Andreas Huyssen puts it, critical responses to *Schindler's List* expressed a sense that "Spielberg's film, playing to mass audiences, fails to remember properly because it represents, thus fostering forgetting: Hollywood as fictional substitute for 'real history'" (69).

By casting the matter in these terms—distinguishing historical fact ("real history") from cultural artifact (its fictional substitute)—I do not mean to imply that one cannot participate in the other's work. This chapter explores the relation between the two, the translation of one into the other, and the role that the unspeakable plays in this translation. I explore these issues by focusing on *representations* of survivor testimony by survivors and by non-survivors.[1] In representations of survivor testimony, historical fact becomes cultural artifact, and the limits of speech—the extent to which experience literally evades, eludes, or exceeds its physical articulation by a corporeal being—reside uneasily within, but remain distinct from, these limits' strategic evocation when that corporeal being is absent.

Testimony and the Unspeakable

Because this chapter deals not with survivor testimony per se but with *representations* of survivor testimony, the unspeakable takes on a different form and plays a different role. There is, after all, a distinction between the survivor's inability or unwillingness to speak, on the one hand, and the rhetorical work of the unspeakable, on the other.[2] For if the Holocaust survivor's experience is, by her, unspeakable (which is different from claiming that the Holocaust itself is unspeakable), survivor testimony to that experience speaks the unspeakable, a speech informed by acute silences and epistemological gaps that reflect the impact of a traumatic experience on the speaker's psyche. *Representations* of survivor testimony are representations of such speech, not of the (presumably unrepresentable) Holocaust, nor of the (too often sacralized) survivor. They stand, therefore, in a different relation to representation's limits than the evocations of the unspeakable I have examined thus far, in which the limits of language, representation, and thought were assumed to be objective qualities of the subject matter, not the products of its apprehension.

Such a focus on the reader, viewer, or critic, rather than on the subject, characterizes approaches to representations of testimony. In *Writing and Rewriting the Holocaust,* James Young proceeds from the basic assumption that "we cannot know this—or any—era outside the ways it is transmitted to us in its representations" (149) and stresses that representations of the Holocaust need to be approached with an eye toward "the possible *consequences* of interpretation" (4); the critic's role is to "sustain an awareness of both the need for unmediated facts in this literature and the simultaneous incapacity in narrative to document these facts" (11). In other words, Young posits historical fact as unspeakable by literary representation, and assigns the crucial role of maintaining this unspeakability to the critic. Similarly, in their introduction to *Witnessing the Disaster: Essays on Representation and the Holocaust,* Michael Bernard-Donals and Richard Glejzer propose that both artistic and scholarly representations of the Holocaust provide "*something other than knowledge* [of the Holocaust], something akin to a flash of horror that precedes and disturbs our ability to know" (3; emphasis mine), which they identify as the object of their study. Like Young, Bernard-Donals and Glejzer locate this "something" in the context of representation's reception and apprehension.

Theories of testimony that take the Holocaust as their subject have characterized this apprehension as traumatic, delineating the implications for memory and history when the event remembered is a traumatic experience, and tracing how testimony to trauma reflects a rupture of memory and of history.[3] Hungerford has argued that contemporary trauma theory's privileging of language—and of language's limits, wherein the traumatic event resides—enables the production of "trauma without experience" (97–103). When the experience in question is the Holocaust, the implications of "trauma without experience" are considered to be especially grave. Consider the *Fragments* controversy: although Swiss-born Bruno Dösseker's "memoir" of his childhood in Nazi concentration camps was proved to be a fabrication, the perceived authenticity of the trauma narrated in the memoir persists despite the demonstrated inauthenticity of the experience claimed by its author.[4] And yet, Bernard-Donals expresses a common sensibility about the importance of the traumatic experience's historical verifiability when he writes that to conflate Wilkomirski's trauma with (authentic) trauma "would seem to fly in the face not only of good taste but of human decency as well" (211). Trauma may disrupt the relationship between history and memory, but when history is the Holocaust, empirical, verifiable historical fact assumes paramount importance. "[O]ur jobs, as teachers and as righteous people," continues Bernard-Donals, "should be to honor the memories of the dead" (211).

In the context of the Holocaust, this job is a difficult one. Here, historical fact is considered to be as inviolable as the traumatic quality of the survivor's experience is considered to be sacrosanct. Scholars of Holocaust testimony—Dori Laub and Lawrence Langer are prominent examples—respond to the inaccuracies and inconsistencies to which survivor testimony is inevitably prone by privileging the survivor, and the validity of her memory or her trauma, over historical fact. They do so by aligning the survivor's experience with an order of truth established as much by her physical, living presence *during* the events narrated as by her testimony *to* them. Thus, in his account of a witness's testimony to the uprising at Auschwitz, in which the witness remembered seeing four crematoria in flames (historical documents confirm that only one crematorium was destroyed), Laub passionately critiques historians' dismissal of the witness and evokes another "truth" of which the witness's testimony is an accurate account: "The woman was testifying . . . not to the number of the chimneys blown up, but to something else, more radical, more crucial: the reality of an unimaginable occurrence. . . . That was historical truth" (60). Similarly, in *Holocaust Testimonies: The Ruins of Memory*, Langer dismisses the term "credibility" when applied to testimonies: "[S]ince testimonies are human documents rather than merely historical ones," he continues, "the troubled interaction between past and present achieves a gravity that surpasses the concern with accuracy" (xv). Echoing Young's and Bernard-Donals and Glejzer's approach to the interrelation of historical fact with cultural artifact, Laub and Langer assume that if the witness's testimony is inconsistent with historical fact, it must be consistent with another level of knowledge that is privileged over the "merely" historical and that is in fact *unspeakable by it.*

My point is that in the context of Holocaust survivor testimony a complex alchemy is in effect: the mutual reverence accorded historical fact on the one hand, and this fact's subjective apprehension (the witness's "truth") on the other, produce an approach to testimony that is predicated on *an identification of the body with its speech,* an identification in which the stakes are no less than the relation between ethics and truth. For if to affirm trauma without the body's experience is "to fly in the face . . . of human decency" (Bernard-

Donals 211), to affirm the body's experience without taking trauma into account is to miss "historical truth" (Laub 60). Thus, when Laub's survivor speaks what is (for the historians) unspeakable, her body's experience lends crucial authority to her speech, grounding it in fact rather than fiction: what distinguishes her testimony from Wilkomirski's fabrication is the fact that her body was historically present at the scene.[5]

Representations of survivor testimony, therefore, are not merely representations of the survivor's speech independent of her body; they are representations of the interrelation of the two and the interdependence of both. Approaches to representations of survivor testimony, informed by what I have been calling the unspeakable's ethical imperative, tend to align testimony with speech—and the concurrent evocation of speech's limits, the unspeakable—assuming but neglecting the body's role. Here we should recall the controversy around D. M. Thomas's postmodern novel _The White Hotel_, where Thomas's direct borrowing of eyewitness testimony for his account of the massacre at Babi Yar was considered, by some critics, to be an unacceptable blending of fact and fiction.[6] Both critiques and defenses of Thomas's novel focus on the extent to which it does, or does not, represent the Holocaust, evoking the issue of representation and its limits to acquit or convict the author on moral grounds.[7] Such readings align speech (the transcription of a survivor's testimony which Thomas imported into the novel to depict his protagonist's death at Babi Yar) with the historical event, positing the relationship between fact and fiction in terms of a relationship between texts: one is evoked to lend authority to the other. But couching the relationship between fact and fiction as a relationship between texts elides the body's role as guarantor of speech's authenticity while, paradoxically, couching this authenticity in terms of the body's pain. Hana Wirth-Nesher, for example, in her thoughtful and seminal defense of Thomas, refers to "the pain of the victim" as a "truth" that must not be violated (17), but goes on to address the controversy in terms of the relation between narrative constructs and silence.[8]

If "unspeakable" both evokes and erases the conjunction of physical articulation, language, and community, representations of survivor testimony are representations of a body and of this body's speech.[9] To identify and engage the complex interrelation of body and speech that representations of survivor testimony force readers, auditors, and viewers to confront, I focus on the image of the speaking corpse, an image that is prominent both in these representations and in their critical reception. In the following sections, I will define this image through critical and philosophical writings by Julia Kristeva, Jacques Derrida, Giorgio Agamben, and Diana Fuss. Turning to Jorge Semprun's evocation of this image in *Literature or Life,* I argue that the speaking corpse is produced by the representation of a testimonial encounter. Finally, I employ this image to revisit three different representations of Holocaust testimony in which it figures: Elie Wiesel's *Night,* Art Spiegelman's *Maus,* and textual and cinematic versions of Claude Lanzmann's *Shoah.*

The Speaking Corpse: Kristeva, Derrida, Agamben, Fuss

Why the speaking corpse? This image enables us to focus on the crucial role played by the body in representations of Holocaust testimony (a role that, as I argued above, is too often elided) without mistaking this body for the historical truth it is evoked to guarantee. As a literary image of a literal impossibility, multiply removed from the historical event, the image of the speaking corpse fuses historical reality (the body) with its inevitable mediation (its speech). Further, I view this image as a site in which the presence of the body merges with its re-presentation, a site that projects us into what Derrida calls the spectral realm of the "noncontemporaneous," a realm that invites an active engagement with the presence of the past (I will discuss this point further in the concluding section of this chapter). Finally, this image of the speaking corpse precipitates an engagement with atrocity that is informed both by ethics and by aesthetics.

Corpses, which figure so prominently in images of atrocity, pose particular problems for the *representation* of such atrocities. In *Powers of Horror,* Julia Kristeva identifies the corpse as the image of abjection which erases the distinction between subject and object, imaginary and real. The corpse, says Kristeva, is "a border that has encroached upon everything. It is no longer I who expel, 'I' is expelled. The border has become an object. How can I be without border? That elsewhere that I imagine beyond the present, or that I hallucinate so that I might, in a present time, speak to you, conceive of you—it is now here, jetted, abjected, into 'my' world" (3–4). Challenging the subject and subjectivity (note Kristeva's quotation marks around "I" and "me"), the corpse, radically alien to all systems of coherence, directly threatens such systems, collapsing the space of otherness ("that elsewhere that I

Against the Unspeakable

imagine beyond the present") into the self. The corpse erases borders; it dissolves the distinction between the literal and the literary, imaginary and real, presence and absence, subject and object, other and self (the corpse "beckons to us and ends up engulfing us" [4]). Perhaps it is the peril implied by these formidable dissolutions that traditionally requires the corpse to be *expelled* by, and from, the community: the disruption it embodies poses a radical challenge to communities that are constructed through and identified by systems of coherence—of which language is often the most crucial and distinctive. A *speaking* corpse, the literary embodiment of a literal impossibility, forces the very distinctions that it precludes, posing a formidable threat to the very concept of the testimonial encounter where the listener must, as Laub notes, "feel the victim's victories, defeats and silences, know them from within, so that they can assume the form of testimony," while "preserv[ing] his own separate place, position and perspective" (58).

Despite the threat it poses to testimony, the speaking corpse is a recurrent image in Holocaust testimony and in critical treatments of that testimony. In *Demeure,* an extended reading of Maurice Blanchot's short story "The Instant of My Death"—the title itself posits a speaking corpse—Derrida echoes this interrelation of the literal and the literary as he emphasizes testimony's inseparability from fiction. "As a promise to *make truth,*" writes Derrida, ". . . testimony always goes hand in hand with at least the *possibility* of fiction, perjury, and lie. Were this possibility to be eliminated, no testimony would be possible any longer; it could no longer have the meaning of testimony" (27). "[W]ithout the *possibility* of . . . fiction, without the spectral virtuality of this simulacrum and as a result of this lie or this fragmentation of the true, no truthful testimony would be possible. Consequently, the possibility of literary fiction haunts so-called truthful, responsible, serious, real testimony as its only proper possibility" (72). Echoing, perhaps, the importance of the body as a guarantor of testimony's truth, Derrida describes this "haunting" (to which I will return) in corporeal terms: the speaking corpse—its literal and literary body—may well constitute what Derrida calls "the testimonial message that passes into the blood of reality through the epidermis of fiction" (60).

The image of the speaking corpse also shares Giorgio Agamben's focus, in *Remnants of Auschwitz,* on the figure of the *Muselmann*—the "living dead" (A. Carpi, qtd. in *Remnants* 41) or "staggering corpse, a bundle of physical functions in its last convulsions" (Jean Améry, qtd. in *Remnants*

41).[10] Agamben describes the *Muselmann* as "the untestifiable, that to which no-one has borne witness" (41). But for him, it is the *Muselmann's silence* that makes testimony possible, maintaining, as it does, the presence of the unspeakable in such testimony.[11] For Agamben, the possibility of testimony is predicated on a distinction between "the living being and the speaking being" (157); the image of the *speaking* corpse embodies a challenge to these crucial distinctions and enacts them, adding an aesthetic dimension (the speaking corpse is, after all, a literary image) to the realm of Agamben's ethical investigations.

Diana Fuss's work on corpse poems further contributes to the aesthetic implications of the speaking corpse. Fuss defines a corpse poem as "a first-person poetic utterance, written in the present or past tense and spoken in the voice of the deceased. At the center of every corpse poem is a speaking cadaver, an insensate figure endowed with the power of speech. . . . The speaking corpse belongs to that improbable body of literature one might more properly identify as *ars essendi morti,* the art of being dead. *Ars essendi morti* names a powerful oxymoron, since 'being dead' annihilates the very possibility of 'being' as such" (1–2). But the Holocaust, Fuss continues, "appears to mark this historical limit beyond which the corpse poem hesitates to venture . . . after the unthinkable event of genocide, no fiction of the living dead can possibly be sustained" (19).

The speaking corpse, then, combines Kristeva's emphasis on the dissolution of boundaries and the challenge to subjectivity that the corpse poses, Derrida's interrelation of testimony and fiction and the subsequent haunting of the one by the other, Agamben's investment in the *Muselmann* as the embodiment of silence, and Fuss's evocation of the Holocaust as the limit case of speech. Further: if Derrida's reading of Blanchot's "The Instant of My Death" posits testimony as constructing the relation between fiction and truth in explicitly corporeal terms ("the blood of reality," "the epidermis of fiction"), this interrelation of truth and fiction that Derrida identifies as a condition of possibility for testimony identifies the speaking corpse as a space where Agamben's ethical investigations engage productively with Fuss's aesthetic genealogy.

The corpse addresses us in the present, from the past, and like the ghost of Hamlet's father tells us a story that propels its listener into a crucial responsibility to both. And as a literary image, the speaking corpse produces this disquieting dilemma: like a decomposing corpse that, by the nature of its presence, poses a physical threat to the community, a speakable, comprehensible, reproducible Holocaust testimony would devastate those structures of coherence on which so much relies. Thus the ethical implications of this (aesthetically unappealing) image are rendered literal by this literary device, a point made manifestly evident in Hartman's reading of Adorno's *Negative Dialectics*. "The integration of physical death into culture should be rescinded in theory," writes Adorno, "not . . . for the sake of an ontologically pure being named Death, but for the sake of that which the stench of cadavers expresses" (*Fateful Question* 366).[12] "That stench," Hartman adds, "still comes from the camps: the cadaver is impossible to lay to rest, whatever memorializing or intellectualizing activities we attempt" (119).

Aesthetics as Ethics in Jorge Semprun's *Literature or Life*

To demonstrate the interrelation of ethics and aesthetics, reality and fiction, that the image of the speaking corpse embodies, I turn to Jorge Semprun's reflections in *Literature or Life*. Semprun opens *Literature or Life* with a meditation on testimony, as a newly released inmate of Buchenwald confronts three horrified Allied officers:

> Here I am, the survivor on duty, appearing opportunely before these three Allied officers to tell them of the crematory smoke, the smell of burned flesh hanging over the Ettersberg, the roll calls out in the falling snow, the murderous work details, the exhaustion of life, the inexhaustibility of hope, the savagery of the human animal, the nobility of man, the fraternity and devastation in the naked gaze of our comrades.
> But can the story be told? Can anyone tell it? (12–13)

Considering the challenge posed by "telling the story," Semprun dismisses the notion that his subject is unspeakable. "The 'ineffable' you hear so much about is only an alibi" (13). What makes him question whether "the story [can] be told" is not the relation of the subject to speech but rather the relation of the subject to art: he distinguishes between "articulation," on the one hand, and artistic creation, on the other. Thus, while Semprun asserts that "you can always say everything: language contains everything," by language he means something very specific. It is not just "language" that contains everything but, more precisely, aesthetic language, the "artifice of a masterly narrative" (13). The challenge posed by this aesthetic language is not, Semprun stresses, its subject matter but rather the ethical burden it lays on its addressee.[13]

> But will people hear everything, imagine everything? Will they be able to understand? Will they have the necessary patience, passion, compassion and fortitude? I begin to doubt it, in that first moment, that first meeting with men from before, from the outside, emissaries from life—when I see the stunned, almost hostile, and certainly suspicious look in the eyes of the three officers.
>
> They're speechless, unable to face me. (14)

The silence of this testimonial encounter is, then, not the silence of the witness unable to recount an unspeakable experience but that of the listeners, who are rendered "speechless," reflecting what Langer calls the survivor's "barren belief that the very story you try to tell drives off the audience you seek to capture" (*Holocaust Testimonies* 61).[14] In other words, the unspeakable is relocated from the survivor's testimony to experience to the listeners' experience of testimony. For Semprun, this relocation produces the image of the speaking corpse. His narrator continues:

> I've seen myself for the first time in two years in their horrified gaze. These three jokers have spoiled this first morning for me. I thought I'd made it out alive. Made it back to life, in any case. Guess not. Imagining what my eyes must look like from what I see in theirs, I would say that I haven't left death all that far behind . . .
>
> I have abruptly understood that these soldiers are right to be afraid, to avoid looking into my eyes. Because I have not really survived death. I have not avoided it. I have not escaped it. (14–15)

Langer reads this moment in Semprun's essay as an example of the sense of being simultaneously dead and alive that he identifies as a consistent theme in Holocaust survivor testimony, in which "the positive idea of staying alive is usurped by the negative one of fending off death" ("Pursuit of Death" 379).[15] But he misses the extent to which the speaking corpse does not precede the testimonial encounter but is, rather, *produced by it*. Put differently, the death to which Semprun's narrator is subjected is *not* the result of his sojourn in Buchenwald; his death is, rather, the product of the testimonial encounter in which the aesthetic (Semprun's faith in "the artifice of a masterly narrative") invests speech with an ethics of presence (note the Levinasian implications of the Allied officers' inability to "face" the survivor) to generate a literary image that embodies the essence of an ethical address.

By imbuing aesthetics with ethics, and predicating these ethics on presence, not absence, the speaking corpse is a potentially productive image through which to read representations of Holocaust testimony without recourse to the unspeakable. This image is productive because it enables us to focus on the implications of ethics and aesthetics—specifically, the ethics of the aesthetics of representing atrocity—and the interrelation of the body with its speech. More importantly, it facilitates a crucial refocusing of the critical gaze from the figure of the survivor to the representation of her testimony and, specifically, to the ethical challenge such representation poses. *Literature or Life* follows the narrator from the gates of Buchenwald out of Holocaust hell and into postwar Europe and a series of meditations on atrocity and art. But I want to remain with this image of the speaking corpse and, more precisely, with those Allied officers and their silence. If representations of Holocaust testimonies confront us with a speaking corpse, are we to remain silent, configuring the Holocaust as unspeakable? And if silence is not an option when faced with such a figure, how are we to respond?

"The Story of My Death": Elie Wiesel's *Night*

Night opens with the story of Moshe the Beadle, the narrator's friend and instructor in the small town of Sighet in Transylvania. Because he is a foreigner, Moshe is deported from Sighet in 1942. Several months later he returns, describing the massacre of his fellow deportees. The people of Sighet dismiss Moshe's account as the speech of "madness" or "imagination," the sort of speech that cannot be approached by rational understanding. But their rejection of Moshe's story is posited in terms of a refusal, not just to give credence to, but even to *hear* his story. Moshe does not expect to be understood (as he says to Eliezer, the narrator, "you can't understand"); rather, he pleads for the people of Sighet to *listen:* "Jews, listen to me. It's all I ask of you. I don't want money or pity. Only listen to me" (5). The people's refusal to listen causes Moshe to withdraw from the community and from speech:

"He was weary of speaking. He wandered in the synagogue or in the streets, with his eyes down, his back bent, avoiding people's eyes" (18).

Moshe the Beadle, pleading in vain for his story to be heard, is generally read as the paradigmatic survivor, and *Night*, which opens with this account, as the paradigm of testimony. "[T]he scene of narration of the opening episode . . . prefigures the scene of reading of *Night*" (204), writes Ora Avni, who argues that the text should be read "literally: Moshe came back 'to tell you the story'" (211). But the story Moshe came back to tell is not, as Avni supposes, that of "the absurd, incomprehensible, and unassimilable killings he had witnessed" (212); it is a very specific and particular story: the *story of his death*.

> "You don't understand," [Moshe] said in despair. "You can't understand. I have been saved miraculously. I managed to get back here. Where did I get the strength from? *I wanted to come back to Sighet to tell you the story of my death.* So that you could prepare yourselves while there was still time. To live? I don't attach my importance to my life anymore. I'm alone. No, I wanted to come back, and to warn you. And see how it is, no one will listen to me . . ." (*Night* 16–17; emphasis mine)

Theorists of testimony agree that in the case of a traumatic experience, a radical disjunction can be effected between the victim, or the individual who underwent a particular experience, and the survivor, or the speaker testifying to the experience, rupturing, as Sara Horowitz puts it, "the continuum not only of history but of personal memory, so that the self who remembers cannot emotionally recognize its identity in the self remembered" ("Review Essay" 53). In *Night*'s representation of Moshe's testimony this rupture is figured by Moshe's claim that he, too, died in the forests of Galicia. But this psychic rupture, which transforms Moshe's testimony into "his story and that of his companions" (4), has a physical dimension: his *body* participates in their appalling fate. Like Semprun's narrator, Moshe casts himself as a speaking corpse, and taking the subject of Moshe's story into account requires us to recast his testimony from a factual account of something that literally happened (the massacre near Kolomaye) to the process of generating a literary image: testimony delivered by the dead.

Moshe's return to Sighet "to tell you the story of my death" emphasizes his story's (impossible) content and the extent to which the literal impossibility of this content assumes the form of a literary image. If Moshe's story is unspeakable, what makes it so is not the limits of speech in the face of calamity or even, as Avni puts it, the daunting proposition of "having a community integrate his dehumanizing experience into [its] narratives of self-representation" (212), but rather the unwillingness, or inability, of the community to integrate his impossible corporeality. The figure of the speaking corpse thus poses compelling issues of ownership and appropriation: if we read Moshe's story not as an account of experience but as producing the figure of the speaking corpse, it is not his experience but this corpse that the community is enjoined to claim.[16]

It is in the context of this vexed relationship between claiming or refusing to claim the speaking corpse that I want to read the return of this image—the return of testimony spoken by a dead man—in *Night*'s final scene. This time, Eliezer identifies himself as a dead man and emphasizes that his story, like Moshe's, is a testimony spoken by the dead:

> One day I was able to get up, after gathering all my strength. I wanted to see myself in the mirror hanging on the opposite wall. I had not seen myself since the ghetto.
>
> From the depths of the mirror, a corpse gazed back at me.
>
> The look in his eyes, as they stared into mine, has never left me. (119)

Night ends, then, on this double note: the narrator and the corpse eternally mirror each other, so that wherever Eliezer goes, whatever Eliezer sees, he will be confronted by the corpse's gaze. At the same time, the narrator and the corpse merge—the French text could be more accurately translated as "his look, in my eyes, has never left me" (*son regard dans mes yeux ne me quitte pas*). Whether Eliezer sees a corpse as he searches for his image in the mirror or whether he, like Moshe, is telling the story of his own death, the witness merges with the atrocities he relates. Both readings of this passage, then, exclude the possibility of addressing testimony to an other.

But testimony cannot merely be articulated to oneself—it must be understood by someone else. "[T]o testify," stresses Felman, "is more than simply to report a fact or an event or to relate what has been lived, recorded and remembered. Memory is conjured here essentially in order to *address* another, to *impress* upon a listener, to *appeal* to a community" ("Return" 204). If *Night* opens with a testimony that fails—Moshe's vain attempt, in

Felman's words, to address, impress, and appeal to the people of Sighet—it concludes by asserting testimony's impossibility, an important move toward establishing the Holocaust as posing a unique challenge to testimony per se (a challenge that Felman and Laub will enshrine in their *Testimony: Crises of Witnessing in Literature, Psychoanalysis, and History;* that history is, of course, the Holocaust).[17]

Traditional readings of *Night* echo this move, identifying the challenge to testimony that the novella represents with the challenge to representation that the Holocaust is assumed to pose, emphasizing, like Avni, language and its limits.[18] By doing so, they miss the crucial role that the body plays in both the novella's opening gesture and in its final scene. Focusing not on the speaker but on his speech—whether the story can or cannot be heard, understood, or communicated—enables critics to treat the text's ellipses and gaps as a quality of the novella's subject matter, which they distinguish, naively, from the aesthetic of its representation.[19] But if we keep in mind that *Night,* like Moshe's story, is figured as the testimony of a speaking corpse, we need to take into account the presence of the body, not just the limits of its speech. The novella, which began by presenting its readers with a speaking corpse, ends by depicting a corpse that is silenced, hermetically sealed to its mirror image in the novel's closing gesture. But its body remains, and that body poses a crucial challenge to the text's community of readers, who are required to reenact the dilemma posed by Moshe to the people of Sighet without, however, the opportunity to "listen."[20]

François Mauriac's foreword to the novella differs from most critical commentary on *Night* because he focuses on this body. Describing his impression of *Night*'s author, Mauriac refers to "a Lazarus risen from the dead . . . still a prisoner within the grim confines where he had strayed, stumbling among the shameful corpses" (ix).[21] Unlike Semprun's Allied officers and their silent, silencing gaze, Mauriac responds to this body with speech—a speech, however, that is posited as unspeakable, something Mauriac could *not* say to Wiesel:

Zion has risen up again from the crematories and the charnel houses. The Jewish nation has been resurrected from among its thousands of dead. It is through them that it lives again. We do not know the worth of one single drop of blood, one single tear. All is grace. If the Eternal is the Eternal, the last word for each one of us belongs to Him. *This is*

*what I should have told this Jewish child. But I could only embrace him,
weeping.* (xi; emphasis mine)

If the speaking corpse with which *Night* opens charges his audience to
"listen," the silent corpse in the novella's final pages propels us, its readers,
to speak. It does so, however, without offering anything ethically comfortable to say—a point painfully demonstrated by Mauriac's violent wrenching
of Holocaust horror into an expression of his own Christian faith.[22] By rendering this speech unspeakable—what Mauriac should have, but felt he
could not, tell the "Jewish child"—silence masquerades as a responsible acknowledgment of this ethical dilemma, rather than a dissociation from it.
Thus, despite the symbolic embrace that seems to affirm the corpse's physical presence, Mauriac's foreword offers a reading of *Night* that not only
posits the testimony itself as unspeakable but excludes the witness who
bears it from the very community that, as Avni stresses, must appropriate its
story. In this way Mauriac's foreword is not dissimilar to the conclusion of a
videotaped testimony that Langer describes in which the survivor, gazing directly into the camera, asks, "Am I a part of that human community? I don't
think so" (*Holocaust Testimonies* 52–53). Langer comments that "he [the sur-
vivor] is convinced that what was done to them [the victims] represented a
consensus, through a combination of active participation and passive
indifference, of the world at that time," and notes that "his interviewers greet
his question with silence" (52–53). Remaining, in this discussion, with the
silence of the interviewers, Langer, like Mauriac, addresses his readers, figuring the question (and its not-so-subtle accusation, from which Langer distances himself, and us, by implying that this accusation refers—merely—
to "the world *at that time*") as answerable only by silence.

Making an Order with Things: Figuring the Material in *Maus*

In *Night's* representation of Holocaust testimony, testimony is condemned
to fail, a reading enhanced by the critical tendency to focus not on the body
but on its speech, speech that Wiesel figures as silenced, incoherent, dismissed, or denied. This emphasis on language's limits, together with the
text's ellipses, gaps, and minimalist aesthetic, contributes to the construction of the Holocaust as unspeakable—a position that Wiesel has consistently and urgently reinforced. My own reading of *Night* attempts to avoid

this emphasis by focusing on the text's evocation of the survivor as silent, or silenced, but *there*. Though the witness's speech may be met with silence or even disbelief, her body remains; *Night's* movement from a speaking corpse in the opening pages to a silenced one at the end of the book is, then, both a compelling gesture toward silence and an eloquent foregrounding of the corporeal.

In Art Spiegelman's *Maus: A Survivor's Tale,* the distinction between the body and its speech is less easy to maintain, since the text presents us with a visual figuration of both. It is this visual figuration—accentuated by the animal motif—that generated the initial controversy around *Maus.* This controversy focused on two issues: the inadequacy of the visual format of the comic book to express the immensity of Holocaust horror, and Spiegelman's use of the animal motif (Jews are mice, Nazis are cats, Poles are pigs, Americans dogs, French frogs, etc.), which seems to echo essentialist structures of racism associated with Nazi Germany. In response to these issues, Stephan Tabachnik and Spiegelman himself have argued that the limitations posed by the medium's reductive format actually enable a more effective response to the subject. In these aesthetic justifications of *Maus,* the unspeakable is evoked to counter both the specter of racism and the stricture of *Bilderverbot:* the animal motif, like the comic-book format, uses its own inadequacy to emphasize the incommunicability of what it fails to represent.[23]

But though the Holocaust is posited here as unspeakable, testimony to it is not. Testimony and its representation are inseparable in *Maus,* which leads critics to address testimony *as* representation, rather than a challenge *to* it, and to focus on how, as Young puts it, the relation between the father's historical experience and the son's imaginative account of this experience generates "a new story unique to their experience together" ("The Holocaust" 31). But if, as Huyssen observes of *Maus, "Bilderverbot* and mimesis are no longer irreconcilable opposites, but enter into a complex relationship" (76), what has happened to the unspeakable, that which exceeds or challenges mimesis? For Huyssen and Young—as for many other readers of *Maus*—the unspeakable takes the form of an absent, silenced, untold story: Anja's story.[24] Anja is Art's mother and Vladek's first wife; her diaries, lost in Poland and rewritten in the United States, are destroyed by Vladek after her suicide. "After Anja died I had to make an order with everything," confesses Vladek. "[T]hese papers had too many memories so I BURNED them" (159).[25] Art's response to this information is to call Vladek a "murderer" (*Maus I* 159).

Who, precisely, does Vladek murder? Most critics assume that by destroying Anja's diaries, Vladek also destroys her self, reflecting a tendency to align human beings with texts that Hungerford terms personification. It is, Hungerford writes, "as if the destruction of Anja's record of her experiences at Auschwitz were somehow equivalent to the kinds of destruction that took place at Auschwitz," an equation that she calls "at best hyperbolic" (73), but one that works in a broader context to posit culture as "the most common site on which we relocate the pathos that ordinarily belongs to the human victim" (76). Hungerford's reading makes sense of the kinds of emphases on silence, absence, and loss that characterize critical approaches to this scene and to *Maus* as a whole, according to which the absence of Anja's story reflects the unspeakable quality of the stories that are told. "By making the recovery of the story itself a visible part of *Maus*," writes Young, referring to the destruction of Anja's diaries, "Spiegelman can also hint darkly at the story not being recovered here, the ways that telling one story always leaves another untold" ("The Holocaust" 34). According to this logic, Spiegelman's decision to include the absence of Anja's story in *Maus* enacts that inevitable gesture toward representation's limits so common among representations of the Holocaust.

Read not in the context of the millions of murders that occurred during the Holocaust but in the context of the text of *Maus*, "murderer" works slightly differently. In "Prisoner on the Hell Planet," Art's depiction of Anja's suicide, the destruction of body is explicitly aligned with the absence of text: "In 1968, when I was 20, my mother killed herself. . . . She left no note! (*Maus I* 100).[26] And here, too, the absence of text produces an accusation of murder: "Well, Mom, if you're listening," the "Art" on Hell Planet apostrophizes, "you've committed the perfect crime. . . . You MURDERED me, Mommy, and you left me here to take the rap!!!"(103). Given that the absence of Anja's "note" evokes the accusation of murder in "Prisoner on Hell Planet," we might read the absence of her diaries at the end of *Maus I*, and the subsequent accusation that *this* absence produces, in the same way: the murder victim is not the (absent) text's author but its (intended) recipient, not Anja but Art—a reading that may appear counterintuitive but that

effectively evokes both the mortal blow that the Holocaust is commonly assumed to have inflicted on artistic endeavor and the endurance of the aptly
named Art who relates, in both volumes of *Maus,* the story of his death.

Reading Art as a speaking corpse enables us to read Anja's missing diaries
without recourse to the unspeakable. Like the murdered bodies, the absent
text is posited as the condition of possibility for both the survivor's *presence* and for his *speech*—a point eloquently conveyed in *Maus II* as Art describes his discomfort with *Maus*'s critical and commercial success while
surrounded by dead bodies (referring, again, to Anja's missing note). The
absence of Anja's texts—the note and the diary—does not just haunt Vladek
and Art, it lends them substance and form, in-forming their relationship
and interactions. Read thus, Vladek's destruction of Anja's diaries is not a
reenactment of her death in Auschwitz but a gesture toward his own life, his
own survival in Rego Park, which is predicated on "mak[ing] an order with
everything" (*Maus I* 159). Art echoes Vladek's "order" in his own need to "get
[the story] straight," a need that forces chronology onto Vladek's narrative.
"WAIT! Please, Dad, if you don't keep your story chronological, I'll never get
it straight," says Art, to which Vladek replies by ceding his story to the listener: "Okay. I'll make it so how you want it," he says (*Maus I* 82). The product of this process—the text of *Maus*—is the result of Art's appropriation
and retelling of Vladek's story, just as Anja's story, in *Maus,* is appropriated
and told by Vladek: "I can tell you," Vladek says to Art, "She [Anja] went
through the same what me: TERRIBLE!" (*Maus I* 158). As Vladek recounts
Anja's story as his own, and Art does the same with Vladek, the stories of the
living do not stand for the absent stories of the dead, they *are* the stories of
the dead.

Reading *Maus* via the image of the speaking corpse foregrounds how Art
consistently separates Vladek's life *after* the Holocaust from his survival *of* it,
despite Vladek's repeated attempts to connect the past with his life in the
present, especially his unhappy relationship with Mala, whom he married
after Anja's suicide, and his future (he constantly frets about what he feels
to be Mala's designs on his money, which he wants to leave for Art). Art
constantly silences Vladek at these moments: "Auschwitz, Pop. Tell me
about Auschwitz," he says (*Maus II* 25), or even "ENOUGH! Tell me about
AUSCHWITZ!" (*Maus II* 47). Foregrounding Art's persistent disavowals
of Vladek's life after Auschwitz, Spiegelman poses Vladek as a bearer of

From *Maus II: A Survivor's Tale/And Here My Troubles Began* by Art Spiegelman.
(Copyright © 1986, 1989, 1990, 1991 by Art Spiegelman. Used by permission of Pantheon Books,
a division of Random House, Inc., and the Wylie Agency)

testimony while denying him identity as a survivor. "In some ways," Art says of Vladek, "he DIDN'T survive" (*Maus II* 90). As if to confirm Art's words, the final volume of *Maus* ends with the completion of Vladek's story, as he is reunited with Anja, juxtaposed with a tombstone in which the names of both are inscribed.

Echoing *Night's* closing image of Eliezer facing the corpse, or himself, in the mirror, *Maus* concludes by conflating the living with the dead, the speaking corpse with the silent one, as Vladek confuses Art with Richieu, Vladek and Anja's other child, who perished in the ghetto. "[L]et's stop, please, your tape recorder," murmurs Vladek, ". . . I'm tired from talking, Richieu, and it's enough stories for now . . ." (*Maus II* 136). Michael G. Levine's reading of the end of *Maus II* implicitly identifies this scene as a reenactment of Art's murder at the end of *Maus I:* "While Art is symbolically killed by his father's slip of the tongue, Richieu is revived as the addressee of his father's last words," writes Levine. "This role reversal suggests that Vladek's testimony will have been addressed not merely to the living and the dead, but to the living *as* the dead" (338).

My discussion of *Night* focused on the tension the text produces between body and speech, each of which poses crucial challenges to testimony's audience both within the text and outside it. In *Night*, the recipients of testimony can harbor the former while dismissing the latter (as the people of Sighet harbored Moshe's body while dismissing the story of his death), or embrace one while silencing the other (as Mauriac does with Wiesel). In *Maus*, however, the body and its speech are inextricable: testimony cannot be detached from its representation, an approach common to second-generation survivors for whom, as Young puts it, "to leave out the truth of how they came to know the Holocaust would be to ignore half of what already happened" ("The Holocaust" 42). In its depiction of the body as inseparable from its speech, *Maus* denies us the luxury of refusing, as the people of Sighet refused, to listen. It does so by extending the image of the speaking corpse from the text's content to its form, uniting the object of representation with representation as object, as the visual medium imbues the narrative with a degree of corporeality that prohibits the kind of dissociation of survivor from speech, and the dismissal of the latter as unspeakable, that characterizes *Night's* encounters with the speaking corpse. Read thus, *Maus* forces us to confront the complicity that the unspeakable is generally evoked to evade: here, the complicity of body with text.

The implications of this complicity are rendered palpable in the "Time Flies" section of *Maus II* (41). On the opening page of this section, Art's personal dates, facts, and figures echo, and are echoed by, the past. While initially posed as ironic ("Vladek started working as a tinman in Auschwitz in the spring of 1944 . . . I started working on this page at the very end of February 1987"), these juxtapositions do not retain their temporal and thematic integrity and, like the juxtaposed words "time" and "flies," collapse into a single phrase and image: "time flies (when you're having fun)" is, equally, the contiguity of *time* (Art's reflection on the passage of time and the disparities between his dates and his father's) and the *flies* with which he is surrounded (attracted by the pile of rotting corpses at his feet). This disruption of linguistic reference by the visual image is reinforced by the cameraman's voice calling "Alright, Mr. Spiegelman . . . We're ready to shoot": the words are positioned directly beneath the concentration camp watchtower visible through the window. Thus, the work of representing testimony to atrocity is figured as polluting contemporary temporality with the ugly past—hence the flies surrounding Art as he sits at his drawing table, and the visual hint of corpses in the trash on the New York City street that Art shuffles through on his way to his therapist. Significantly, this section of *Maus* ends with a scene in which Art and Françoise, discussing Vladek and their reluctance to be responsible for him, pointlessly gas some insects. The similarity between their behavior and the Nazis' is inescapable. Complicity between past and present, word and action, image and text is figured by the fly that punctuates this section like the period at the end of a sentence, extending this complicity to text as corporeal being, itself rotting and corrupted.[27] In *Maus,* notes Levine, "the multiple layers of verbal and visual narrative . . . repeatedly bleed into and through one other" (318). "My father bleeds history," reads the subtitle of *Maus I,* and as the product of this corporeal history, artist and subject are mutually implicated: the subtitle of the second volume reads, "And here my troubles began."

From Image to Incarnation: Claude Lanzmann's *Shoah*

Reading representations of Holocaust testimony through the image of the speaking corpse that insists on telling "the story of my death" has led us away from silence, absence, and the limits of speech and toward the presence of the body and the problematic negotiations with that presence that

Time flies...

From *Maus II: A Survivor's Tale/And Here My Troubles Began* by Art Spiegelman.
(Copyright © 1986, 1989, 1990, 1991 by Art Spiegelman. Used by permission of Pantheon Books,
a division of Random House, Inc., and the Wylie Agency)

the body demands. The image of the speaking corpse has also enabled us to rethink the relation between representation and its object, as *Night's* depiction of Holocaust testimony *represented* a speaking corpse (the mirror image that closes the novella foregrounds its mimetic function) and *Maus's* explicitly visual medium traced, on several levels, the "murders" that accompany the process of *becoming* a speaking corpse, extending the challenge that the speaking corpse embodies from the object of representation to representation as object. In this section I will focus on that object, tracing a movement from image to text through reading some scenes from Claude Lanzmann's monumental film *Shoah*, Felman's seminal essay on the film in *Testimony*, and Lanzmann's own commentary on the film as text in the introduction to *Shoah: An Oral History of the Holocaust*. In this movement, the trajectory from the unspeakable to corporeality culminates in the production of speaking corpses and the injunction of a responsibility toward them. Such a responsibility, predicated on presence rather than absence, does not rely on respectful gestures toward the limits of comprehension, and the concurrent gestures toward the inviolability of history, that have come to characterize Holocaust testimony and its representation.

For Lanzmann, the Holocaust is, quite simply, unspeakable, inimitable, and antithetical to the hubris of the aesthetic. At a Yale seminar devoted to a discussion of the film Lanzmann reacts with outrage to the suggestion that a "minimalist esthetic" is operating in the film: "You say esthetic? How dare you. How do you dare to talk about esthetic?" ("Seminar" 97).[28] But Lanzmann's investment in the unspeakability of the Holocaust causes him some ethical discomfort about his own work of interviewing witnesses and survivors, eliciting testimony and directing the film's evocative scenes, work that sits uneasily with his refusal of "illustration" (97). As a result, he spends a considerable amount of the Yale seminar agonizing over his "insincerity" in "staging" some of the scenes of testimony, or of "acting" in such scenes, and ultimately defines his "purpose" in *Shoah* as "transmission":

For instance, Simon Srebnik. I didn't understand one word of what Srebnik was telling me. Srebnik was a boy thirteen and a half years old. He went through the most horrible things, which I have purposely not put in *Shoah*, because they were so horrible for this boy that I thought people would think that this was only a matter of sadism, that the killers were sadistic people and nothing else. The degree of horror was so high that this would have destroyed my purpose. My purpose was the transmission. (93)

With "my purpose was the transmission" Lanzmann responds to what he perceives to be unspeakable by simultaneously assuming and relinquishing agency: his "purpose" is to be a medium through which information is transmitted. But it is impossible to be both agent and medium, an impossibility that is reflected in his disingenuous assertion "I didn't understand one word of what Srebnik was telling me." This is clearly not meant literally (though Srebnik speaks in Polish); rather, it poses Srebnik's testimony as containing some quality that eludes understanding, that is unspeakable, beyond the limits of Lanzmann's comprehension and—one would assume—of the viewers'. But Lanzmann's following statement—that what was so horrible *for Srebnik* would produce the conclusion that "the killers were sadistic people and nothing else"—does away with these limits, implying that Lanzmann understands not only what Srebnik was telling him but also some element in Srebnik's own experience that was too horrible for Srebnik himself. Further, Lanzmann assumes that this element, if it were included in *Shoah,* would produce *too much* comprehension in the viewer, who would reach the (presumably inaccurate) conclusion of sadism. Ultimately, the contradiction between what Lanzmann says he doesn't understand and his assumption of the very specific conclusions that the film's viewers would draw articulates his agenda in *Shoah:* Lanzmann says that his "purpose was the transmission," but what he "transmits" is—purposely—constructed as unspeakable.

In light of his conviction of the unethicality of Holocaust representation, illustration, and aesthetic, Lanzmann's definition of his purpose as "the transmission" works to efface his own aesthetic predilections and to evade the ethical implications of representing what he is convinced is unrepresentable. In "The Return of the Voice: Claude Lanzmann's *Shoah,*" Felman expands and articulates Lanzmann's position. Describing his triple function in the film (he is interviewer, narrator, and inquirer), Felman emphasizes that "Lanzmann's rigor as a narrator is precisely to speak strictly as an interviewer (and as an inquirer), to abstain, that is, from narrating anything directly in his own voice" (217), identifying the *presence* of Lanzmann in *Shoah* as the articulation of an *absence*. His voice in the film, says Felman, is "the voice of the inquirer and of the interviewer, not of the narrator. As narrator," she adds, "Lanzmann does not speak but rather, vocally recites the words of others, *lends his voice*" (217).

One such recitation occurs in the Ruhr scene that concludes the first half of *Shoah*. Lanzmann reads a letter written by a Nazi officer detailing necessary alterations to Sauer vehicles in order to render their function as gas vans more efficient. The letter is shocking in its clinical terms and impassive rhetoric, and the reading of the letter, in French translation, is presented in voice-over as the camera pans across an ugly, polluted industrial zone. The scene's closing shots are of a present-day Sauer vehicle, the camera slowly zooming in on the Sauer logo on the front of the van, followed by a cut to the company's name on the mudguard of the back wheel. Felman describes the letter as "an extraordinary document which might be said to formalize Nazism as such (the way in which the most perverse and most concrete extermination is abstracted into a pure question of technique and function)." She adds that "we witness Lanzmann's voice modulating evenly—with no emotion and no comment—the perverse diction of this document" (218).

But in her emphasis on Lanzmann's absence as narrator, and on the absence of an emotional response to the document he is reading, Felman misses the extent to which he employs his own voice in particular, and sound in general, to render emotion not absent but present. For example, Lanzmann reads the section regarding the difficulty in maintaining the vehicle's proper balance while the "merchandise aboard" (the Jews inside) is so unstable. As he reads, he pauses strategically so that the noise of passing cars will not interfere with the reading of the document; however, he deliberately reads "merchandise aboard" over the noise of a passing bus:

> The manufacturers told us during a discussion that reducing the size of the van's rear would throw it badly off balance. The front axle, they claim, would be overloaded. In fact [pause as car passes] the balance is automatically restored [pause as car passes] because the *merchandise aboard* [stressed in order to be heard over noise of passing bus] displays during the operation a natural tendency to rush to the rear doors, and is mainly found lying there at the end of the operation. So the front axle is not overloaded.

Ostensibly speaking over the noise, Lanzmann's voice lends "merchandise aboard" a crucial emphasis that, had a bus not been passing, would have seemed manipulative and contrived (hence it is important that he reads the French translation of the document rather than the German original; this crucial timing would be lost in the subtitling). Both the impression of objective impassivity (reading a document) and the ostensive neutrality of what we see and hear (present-day traffic) camouflage the staged quality of the scene, which is designed to elicit a specific emotional response.

While Lanzmann emphasizes that the film is not at all representational and defines his purpose as "the transmission," the Ruhr scene in *Shoah* demonstrates how the mutual imbrication of past and present extends to representation and its object, the work of transmission and the imposition of aesthetic. By constructing and presenting the object of representation as unspeakable and by defining his role as one who does not represent but, rather, transmits, he renders this work of representation transparent. Herein lies the appeal of *Shoah:* by rendering representation transparent, Lanzmann foregrounds the immensity of the film's subject matter and lends immediacy to its testimonies, effectively generating the impression the film is not a *representation* of Holocaust testimony but a *presentation* of it. Hence he facilitates the conclusion, endorsed in Felman's essay, that *Shoah* does not *represent* Holocaust testimony; it *is* Holocaust testimony.

By rendering the work of representation transparent, *Shoah* raises crucial questions about whether representation can ever be entirely done away with. To represent something as unrepresentable is still to represent it; to *present* something unrepresentable does away with the kinds of qualifications and impositions that cause Lanzmann to react with horror at the thought of "illustration." Further: if, as Felman suggests, *Shoah* does not represent Holocaust testimony but, in fact, *is* Holocaust testimony, the film should offer crucial hints to the relationship between the body and its speech that, as I outlined in the beginning of this chapter, inform current approaches to testimony and to its representation. The question becomes, then: is representation present in, or absent from, *Shoah?* The answer, I submit, is that representation is both present *and* absent: like a ghost, representation haunts the film.

My reference to ghosts in this context relies on a discourse of spectrality that Jacques Derrida outlines in *Specters of Marx.* "If there is something like spectrality," writes Derrida,

there are reasons to doubt this reassuring order of presents and, especially, the border between the present, the actual or present reality of the
present, and everything that can be opposed to it: absence, nonpres-
ence, noneffectivity, inactuality, virtuality, or even the simulacrum in
general, and so forth. There is first of all the doubtful contemporaneity
of the present to itself. Before knowing whether one can differentiate
between the specter of the past and the specter of the future, of the past
present and the future present, one must perhaps ask oneself whether
the *spectrality effect* does not consist in undoing this opposition, or even
the dialectic, between actual, effective presence and its other. (39–40)

Derrida's discourse of spectrality enables a reading of the movement from
film to text and from cinematic performance to critical commentary, a movement that gives rise to crucial tensions between presence and absence, the
present and that which is of "doubtful contemporaneity" with it. The transition between mediums (from film to text) and contexts (from cinematic
performance to critical commentary) generates a space from which ghosts
emerge. More importantly, in responses to the film (Lanzmann's own comments and Felman's discussion in *Testimony*) these ghosts are incarnated as
speaking corpses.

Felman's textual account of Simon Srebnik's return to Chelmno (which
opens and ends the first half of the film) emphasizes the ghostliness of Srebnik's image on the screen and his presence in the village. As Felman puts it,
Srebnik

is himself rather a ghost of his own youthful performance, a returning,
reappearing ghost of the one-time winner of chained races and of the
boy singer who moved the Poles and charmed the SS, and who, like
Scheherazade, succeeded in postponing his own death indefinitely by
telling (singing) songs. Thus, if Srebnik on the screen at forty-seven, in
the scene of Chelmno of today, embodies a return of the dead, his improbable survival and his even more improbable return (his ghostly
reappearance) concretizes allegorically, in history, a return of the (missing, dead) witness on the scene of the event-without-a-witness. (257)

Describing Srebnik as absent, missing, and dead—yet present in Chelmno,
and alive—Felman dissociates the body from its speech, metaphorically

killing the former in order to celebrate the latter (this chapter is titled "The Return of the Voice"). "When Srebnik saw all that, he was not really a (living) witness," writes Felman. "It is therefore only now, in returning with Lanzmann to Chelmno, that Srebnik in effect is returning from the dead (from his own deadness) and can become, for the first time, a witness to himself" (258). A similar paradigm is in effect in the scenes with the historian Raul Hilberg, whom Lanzmann interviews about Adam Czerniakow's diary of the Warsaw ghetto. Felman quotes Lanzmann's statement that Hilberg is there "to incarnate a dead man" and rephrases: "[t]he historian is there to embody, to give flesh and blood to, the dead author of the diary," adding that "[u]nlike the Christian resurrection . . . the vision of the film is to make Czerniakow *come alive precisely as a dead man*. His 'resurrection' does not cancel out his death" (216). Hilberg both embodies and is a witness to the dead witness Czerniakow, and Srebnik (returning from his own deadness) is "a witness to himself" (his formerly dead self). In Felman's reading of *Shoah,* the witness's death is unequivocal; it does not, then, present the living with the impossible imperative of welcoming a corpse. Further, Felman enacts the dissociation of speech from the body that, as I discussed in the opening pages of this chapter, is so prevalent in discussions of representations of Holocaust testimony. While Srebnik's body is present in Chelmno, his voice, as Felman repeatedly notes, is not; while Czerniakow's voice may be articulated by Hilberg (who reads sections of his diary), his body remains in Poland (the section devoted to his testimony ends with a camera close-up on a tombstone bearing Czerniakow's name). It is the dissociation of spoken word from material image that maintains the living Srebnik and the dead Czerniakow in the realm of the spectral, enabling their testimony to be articulated and rearticulated without confronting the dilemma posed by the figure of the speaking corpse.

What has happened, then, to the speaking corpse? What becomes of its disturbing corporeality in *Shoah's* spectral space? Who can—or cannot—listen to its impossible testimony? The answer lies in the movement of the film from screen to text, from the ephemerality of the visual and the aural to the relative materiality of the written word. Lanzmann traces this movement in his introduction to the text of *Shoah* as he focuses on the subtitles of this multilingual film. Curiously, he distinguishes *Shoah's* subtitles from its "words": the first enigmatic sentence of the introduction reads, "Here is the complete text—words and subtitles—of my film *Shoah*" (vii). The first paragraph of the introduction emphasizes the names of the translators and the languages from which they translate, evoking a multiplicity of presences: the nationalities echoed by the languages (Polish, Hebrew, Yiddish, French, German, English), the individual translators, the witnesses, the spectators, Lanzmann himself. Translation—so prominent a part of the film—is foregrounded in the introduction to the text which is, itself, a translation (into either French or, for the American edition, English). This work of translation, as Felman noted, opens up a temporal space which performs a "cinematic testimony" (212). The presence of the subtitle erases this space, and in the movement from the film to the text this temporal space of cinematic testimony is lost.

The terms in which Lanzmann treats the subtitle in the introduction evoke, by echoing, this loss. In his terms, the subtitle's relation to the image in the film is one of "incarnation": "[T]he faces of those who are speaking, their mimicry, their gestures, in other words, the image itself is the natural support of the subtitle, its *incarnation,* for the subtitle ideally must not precede or follow the spoken word but coincide exactly with it, flashing at the very instant the word is uttered . . . in other words, the subtitle becomes, as it were, invisible" (vii; emphasis mine). Significantly, the subtitle's "incarnation," determined by the image, the physical exigencies of space and time on which speaking relies, is also its demise:

On the screen the subtitle appears and disappears barely born, followed immediately by another one which lives in the same way its short life. Each of these flashes under our gaze, goes back to nothingness as soon as it appears, and it is the number of spaces allowed both by the time of reading and by the shift from one shot to another that determines the length of the sentence, the final cut, frequently violent, *because it is the uninterrupted cascade of words that brutally pronounces the death of the subtitle."* (viii; emphasis mine)

The text of the film reincarnates the subtitle, returning it from ephemerality and invisibility to physical and visible presence. While "on the screen," says Lanzmann, "subtitles are unessential."

Bringing them together . . . in this book, engraving on page after page the succession of sheer instances that in the film maintain the rhythm imposed by their sequence, having then pass from the inessential to the essential, suddenly gives them another status, another dignity, as it were, a seal of eternity. They have to exist by themselves, to justify themselves without any indication of what is happening, without any image, without any face, without any of the countryside, without a tear, without a silence, without the nine and a half hours of film that constitute *Shoah*. (viii)

This reincarnation of the subtitle in the text of the film is a movement from the visual, the temporal, the physicality of the work of translation to the relative corporeality of words on a page. Lanzmann describes this incarnation as corpselike: "naked and bloodless." At the same time, though, this text "lives its own life." As he writes, "I read and reread this naked and bloodless text. A strange force seems to have filled it through and through, it resists, it lives its own life. It is the writing of disaster, and that for me is another mystery" (viii).

Lanzmann's concluding reference to Blanchot's *Writing of the Disaster* re-evokes the spectrality that Derrida posed as a crucial way to assume responsibility to the presence of the past. The writing of the disaster takes place, for Blanchot, in the realm of a negativity that, like Derrida's spectrality, precludes dichotomies of presence/absence, speaking/silence, writing/not-writing. "Not writing is among the effects of writing; it is something like the sign of passivity, a means of expression at grief's disposal" (Blanchot 11). This concept of passivity, with its connotations of subjection and negation (*pas*), is, for Blanchot, spectral: "Passivity is measureless: for it exceeds being; it is being when being is worn down past the nub—the passivity of a past which has never been, come back again. It is the disaster defined—hinted at—not as an event of the past, but as the immemorial past (*Le Très-Haut*) which returns, dispersing by its return the present, where, *ghostly*, it would be experienced as a return" (17; emphasis mine)."[29]

Writing of the disaster requires, however, an engagement of thought in the spectral realm of passivity. Concerning what he calls "a passive that is thought" (33), Blanchot emphasizes the closeness of thought to representation and to presence: thought "cannot make itself present, or enter into presence, and is still less able to be represented or to constitute itself as a basis for a representation" (33). In the writing of the disaster, an "absent meaning" is "formed" (41).[30] Within the context of passivity and thought, this "absent meaning" must be welcomed: "[T]o write is perhaps to bring to the surface something like absent meaning, to welcome [*accueillir*] the passive pressure which is not yet what we call thought, for it is already the disastrous ruin of thought" (41).

Blanchot is positing the writing of the disaster in terms of welcoming, or offering hospitality to, an "absent meaning" that is generated by the process of thinking about the disaster in the spectral realm of passivity. What Blanchot seems to be hinting at here is that the writing of the disaster takes the form of welcoming ghosts. And Derrida, in the final pages of *Specters of Marx*, poses hospitality to ghosts as the only method by which to reconcile *effectivité* and *idéalité*, to come to terms with history: "Only mortals, only the living who are not living gods can bury the dead. Only mortals can watch over them, and can watch, period. Ghosts can do so as well, they are everywhere where there is watching; the dead *cannot do so*—it is impossible and they must not do so" (174–75). Derrida concludes that in order to keep the dead from burying the dead, to keep the memory of the dead present in a history that must yet move beyond them, we must be hospitable to ghosts: "to grant them the right, if it means making them come back alive, as *revenants* who would no longer be *revenants*, but as other *arrivants* to whom a hospitable memory or promise must offer welcome" (175).

To return to the introduction to the text of *Shoah:* If representation haunts the film that Lanzmann describes as "not at all representational" ("Seminar" 97), its ghost is incarnated as a speaking corpse as the film moves from ephemeral image to textual presence. Lanzmann's brief evocation of the speaking corpse is quickly referred to the spectral realm of Blanchot's "writing of the disaster." Within this realm, Derrida's emphasis on hospitality to ghosts imagines a representation of Holocaust testimony that poses less forbidding a threat to its audience than does the speaking corpse: if we cannot listen to the speaking corpse's testimony, perhaps we could extend a welcome or promise to *revenants*. But Derrida's recognition that ghosts can come back alive, not as *revenants* but as *arrivants*, once again resurrects the potentially destructive image of the speaking corpse, whose testimony presents us with a crucial responsibility toward future and past, but whose corrupting corporeality poses a very real threat to existence in the present.

In this, its final incarnation, the speaking corpse, produced through and against the spectral, echoes—albeit faintly—the survivor's confrontation with the limits of language and of representation in her attempt to articulate her experience, a confrontation that a rhetoric of the unspeakable consistently foregrounds. Throughout the wide variety of contexts, images, and frameworks in which her testimony is figured, these representations of testimony inevitably retain some ghostly image of this initial challenge. The unspeakable, with its emphasis on the limits of representation, of comprehension, and of speech, cannot effectively address the crucial, material challenge to representation that the speaking corpse enacts. Further, as I will discuss in the following chapters, such rhetoric's implicit privilege of the semantic occludes the troubling presence of the body and the significant disruption of language's limits that the body's corporeality both forces and performs.

Chapter 4

**Nat
Turner's
Key**

The previous chapters' exploration of the relationship between historical fact and cultural artifact moved from the limits of representation—the extent that the historical fact in question (the Holocaust) inevitably eludes the cultural artifact that represents it (like a Hollywood film)—to the dissociation of body from speech (in *Night*) and the reconstitution of that relation in the visual/textual dimensions of *Maus*. Turning to the film *Shoah*, I demonstrated how the imagery in Lanzmann's and Felman's discussions of the film renders the body spectral, and Lanzmann's introduction to the published subtitles of *Shoah* ascribes corporeality to text. In the unspeakable's urgent evocation of language's limits, then, insists an underlying dynamic of body and text—specifically, the evocation of the former in, and by, the latter.

This chapter initiates the move of *Against the Unspeakable* from one atrocity commonly imagined to be unspeakable—the Holocaust—to another: American slavery. Though most of my discussion will focus on William Styron's controversial 1967 novel *The Confessions of Nat Turner*—a controversy in which the unspeakable was evoked as the indicator of racial identity, racial difference, unfathomable atrocity, and history—I open with a discussion of the final pages of Styron's 1979 novel about the Holocaust, *Sophie's Choice*. In these pages, text is invested with a corporeal dimension that critical emphases on the unspeakable tend to elide. My reading of the final pages of *Sophie's Choice* will outline an approach to *Confessions* in which the relation of body to text, and not speakable to unspeakable, is key.

As the focus shifts from the Holocaust to American slavery, I should remind the reader that *Against the Unspeakable* is not a comparative analysis of two historical events but an interrogation of how the unspeakable operates in narratives about each. If, as I argued earlier, the unspeakable's implicit privileging of the semantic (*language*'s limits) facilitates a certain dissociation from the speaker's physical presence and from her act of articulation, this dissociation weds epistemology and ontology, designating the limits of our language as the limits of our world, and implicitly evades the complexities of physical action as material differences are consigned to the unspeakable's immaterial realm. The unspeakable's eschewal of reference facilitates the relocation of identity from body to text, implicitly designating the latter as a morally comfortable space for identity's articulation, a speech without the (racialized, politicized, body of the) speaker. As the previous chapter demonstrated, though, this body cannot be ignored or denied: in its function as a locus of historical verity it haunts the spaces, both conceptual and material, that its absence lays waste.

From *Sophie's Choice* to *The Confessions of Nat Turner:*
The Speaking Corpse as Pre-text

In the final pages of *Sophie's Choice,* the narrator Stingo returns to his journal—"the record," he says, "of myself" (595). The journal details the story of Sophie, the beautiful and doomed Polish survivor of Auschwitz; of Nathan, her American Jewish lover; and of Stingo himself, a thinly disguised youthful version of the mature narrator whose attraction to Sophie and fascination with her story makes up most of the novel. In "a spectacular backyard auto-da-fé" (595) the younger Stingo had consigned this record to the flames. A few pages are selected to survive, though, and from these, just three lines the mature Stingo considers to be worth preserving. These lines, and the mature Stingo's commentary on them, conclude *Sophie's Choice*.[1]

The first sentence: "*Someday I will understand Auschwitz*" (596). Reviewing this sentence, the mature Stingo pronounces it "brave . . . but innocently absurd," because, as he puts it, "no one will ever understand Auschwitz" (596). So the mature Stingo amends the text to reflect the genesis of the novel and, perhaps, of himself as a writer, offering a potential interpretation (and justification) of *Sophie's Choice*. The revised sentence reads: "*Someday I will write about Sophie's life and death, and thereby help demonstrate how absolute evil is never extinguished from the world*. Auschwitz itself," he concludes, "remains inexplicable" (596). By replacing "will understand" with "will write," and by revising "Auschwitz" to read "Sophie's life and death," the mature Stingo rescues Auschwitz from the innocent absurdity of his earlier words, designating it, in his more authoritative adult prose, unspeakable.

Following the trajectory traced by the revision of this sentence, critical work on the novel tends to read *Sophie's Choice* in terms of fiction's encounter with its limits. "It is," as Richard G. Law puts it, "as if the novel accepts its subject as a challenge: if *Sophie's Choice* can provide a medium in which Auschwitz can, in some meaningful sense, become known, then literature can treat anything; no subjects are off-limits; no veils may be drawn across any area of human experience" (236–37). For some of the novel's critics, Styron has succeeded in rising, as Law puts it, to the challenge of his subject matter; for others, he has failed. But for the novel's earliest reviewers as well as for many of its later readers, much of Styron's success or failure lies in the extent to which the novel makes good on the mature Stingo's revision of the statement about Auschwitz in these final pages. In a 1979 review, John Gardner refers to this passage, wonders whether "Styron's scaled-down goal is not as innocently absurd as the earlier goal," and concludes that Styron "has not succeeded, quite, in doing what he set out to do" (177). For Pearl K. Bell, also in 1979, *Sophie's Choice* does succeed in honoring Stingo's vow: "[I]t is an extraordinary act of the novelist's imagination, which recreates Sophie's ordeal in Auschwitz and beyond through a wealth of immediate, dramatic detail" (183). Five years later Michael Kreyling reads *Sophie's Choice* as a meditation on language and silence, the body and speech—all of which Auschwitz, the unspeakable, radically challenges; regardless of whether or not he succeeds, Kreyling concludes that "we must acknowledge Styron's huge gamble in flinging himself at the monolithic and inscrutable sign of the time, Auschwitz, with good faith, sincere emotion, and the English language" (199). And

Law, writing in 1990, identifies the recognition of Auschwitz's unspeakability as testimony to the narrator's mature recognition of the limits of his art, applauding the gesture toward language's limits: "Sophie's encounter—and the mature narrator's re-encounter—with [. . .] the nature of things beyond our language for it, paradoxically affirms the need for speech, for coherence and meaning, and therefore for art, at the same time that it demarks their limitations and acknowledges their frailty" (251).

It appears that whether the novel does or does not rise to the challenge of its subject is less to the point than that this challenge is acknowledged and respected; in other words, these readings of Stingo's statements (both as mature narrator and as youthful protagonist) about Auschwitz are read as gestures toward the unspeakable.[2] The prominence and institutional verification accorded to the unspeakable is a key player in the critical reception of the novel, published in 1979, months after the NBC miniseries *Holocaust* was aired and during a period of widespread concern, generally linked with the appearance of that miniseries, over the trivialization of Jewish suffering under the Nazis and the appropriateness of certain media for Holocaust representation.[3] Despite some reservations about Styron's decision to cast a non-Jew as his main character, the novel's gestures toward the unspeakable in its final pages importantly contributed to the urgent construction of the Holocaust as a "uniquely inexplicable" event at the time (Novick 212).

This may be why, despite Styron's controversial representations of women and of Jews, his repeated analogies between the Holocaust and slavery, his pervasive sexual imagery in representations of violence, his realistic depiction of life inside Auschwitz, his conflation of victim and perpetrator in the figures of Sophie, Nathan, and Stingo himself, *Sophie's Choice* did not generate the kind of acrimonious and impassioned debate as did Styron's earlier novel, *The Confessions of Nat Turner,* published in 1967.[4] Critical responses to *The Confessions of Nat Turner* identify a range of racial and political agendas that are overt or covert in Styron's aesthetic choices: his decision to narrate the novel from Nat Turner's point of view was perceived as a perpetuation of the blackface tradition; his amendments to Thomas Gray's 1831 document about the rebellion and its leader (Styron has Nat Turner grow up on a plantation under the fond tutelage of a kind owner; he kills off Nat Turner's father and grandmother and inserts a homoerotic encounter with another young slave) were understood as an attack on black history, sexuality, and community; the protagonist's sexual fantasies, vivid religious visions, and dismissive attitude toward his fellow slaves were not perceived as a representation of a psyche damaged by oppression but as a deliberate distortion, evidence of ingrained racism in a self-avowed liberal.[5]

Kenneth Greenberg, Daniel Ross, and most importantly Ashraf Rushdy have all addressed how the timing of the publication of *The Confessions of Nat Turner* is linked to its reception, focusing on the configurations of power into which the novel entered and which the novel's critical reception either confirmed or revised (most memorably with John Henrick Clarke's edited collection *William Styron's Nat Turner: Ten Black Writers Respond*). But unlike *Sophie's Choice*, *The Confessions of Nat Turner* did not so much confirm the unspeakability of its subject matter as it precipitated the need for such a discourse in the fraught context of race relations in the 1960s United States. Within this context, the novel's critics worked to generate a discourse of unspeakability by evoking a "real" Nat Turner who eludes Styron's novelistic capture, effectively rendered unspeakable by Styron's first-person narrator (a narrator described by Lerone Bennett Jr. as "a neurasthenic, Hamlet-like white intellectual in blackface" [5]).

The difference in the reception of the two novels, then, invites crucial questions about the role played by the unspeakable in each. If *The Confessions of Nat Turner*, like Steven Spielberg's *Schindler's List*, raised critical ire by virtue of its representational gestures toward a presumably unrepresentable reality, does *Sophie's Choice* represent this unrepresentable reality more accurately, responsibly, or thoughtfully by inscribing these gestures, and their inevitable limits, into the text? Or does the difference lie not in the presence or absence of gestures toward the unspeakable but in the object determined to be unspeakable, with the gesture toward the unspeakable in Styron's novel about the Holocaust, and the absence of such a gesture in his novel about slavery, reflecting the Holocaust's role as the paradigm for all suffering, a paradigm under which slavery presumably falls short? Perhaps the difference has to do not with the object determined to be or not to be unspeakable but with the speaking subject, with the first-person narration of *The Confessions of Nat Turner* identifying the novel with its subject in a way that *Sophie's Choice*'s multiple dissociations do not, a distinction that aligns evocations of the unspeakable not with the object of representation but with the racial, national, or religious identity of the speaker? Or does the difference lie in such speech's addressee, for whom a discourse of unspeakability needs to be established or confirmed?

This chapter will address the multiple manifestations of the unspeakable in *The Confessions of Nat Turner*'s production, reception, and text. But first I want to return to the final lines of *Sophie's Choice*. The sentence about Auschwitz is, remember, only the first of three sentences the mature Stingo considers worth preserving. The second sentence, "*Let your love flow out on all living things*" (596), identifies the movement of Auschwitz away from comprehension as a movement toward text. The mature Stingo recalls the process of writing this sentence, describing it as a corporeal manifestation of an eternal, universal truth. While the words of the sentence bear a crucial particularity and materiality (they are, he comments, "remarkably beautiful, strung together in their honest lumplike English syllables"), what they refer to "springs from the universe and is the property of God, and the words have been intercepted—on the wing, so to speak—by such mediators as Lau-tzu, Jesus, Gautama Buddha and thousands upon thousands of lesser prophets, including your narrator, who heard the terrible truth of their drumming somewhere between Baltimore and Wilmington and set them down with the fury of a madman sculpting in stone" (596).

But Auschwitz continues to haunt this statement about writing; it remains, for the mature Stingo, a cipher, a demonstration of "the words' truth—or, if not their truth, their impossibility" (596–97): "For did not Auschwitz effectively block the flow of that titanic love, like some fatal embolism in the bloodstream of mankind? Or alter the nature of love entirely . . . in a world which permitted the black edifice of Auschwitz to be built?" he wonders, concluding, as he did in his revision of the first sentence, with an affirmation of comprehension's limits: "I do not know" (597). Both as comprehension and as text, the spectral presence of Auschwitz's unknowability—it persists even under erasure—turns the mature Stingo's attention to his own spectrality, his uneasy simultaneity as both present and past: "[A]s I see them [the words] now on the ledger's page, the page itself the hue of a dried daffodil and oxidized slowly by time into near-transparency, my eyes are arrested by the furious underlining—*scratch scratch scratch*, lacerations—as if the suffering Stingo whom I once inhabited, or who once inhabited me . . . was trying physically to excavate from that paper the only remaining—perhaps the only bearable—truth" (596).

By the questions and doubts it raises, "Auschwitz" forces a revision of Stingo's "truth" into the mature Stingo's "fragile . . . hope" (597). Initially designated as unspeakable, then, Auschwitz returns to haunt the text—

specifically, a text imagined as written on a body: "*scratch scratch scratch,* lacerations" (596)—which the present and past Stingos alternately inhabit, haunt, or possess: the narrator is no longer able to distinguish between "the suffering Stingo whom I once inhabited, or who once inhabited me" (596).

If the first statement and its quick revision initiated a movement from Auschwitz to the unspeakable, and the context provided for the second statement establishes the spectral body as the locus of this unspeakability's "truth," in the third statement text and body, past and present unite: the words are inscribed not on the page but on Stingo's *mind;* this is also the only sentence of the final three left to stand unrevised, without commentary. Awaking from dreams characterized by "helplessness, speechlessness," of being "a living cadaver" (598), Stingo "bless[es his] resurrection" (599). "It was then," recalls the mature Stingo, "that in my mind I inscribed the words: *'Neath cold sand I dreamed of death/but woke at dawn to see/in glory, the bright, the morning star*" (599).

The closing lines of *Sophie's Choice* trace a number of trajectories. On the one hand, they describe the destruction, by fire, of a text that the mature Stingo explicitly aligns with his self (the journal is, he writes, "the record . . . of myself" [559]) and the resurrection of a body on which words are, literally, inscribed: the production of a textual, if not a speaking, corpse. These lines also trace a trajectory from the unspeakable (identified as Auschwitz), to the act of writing, to the reconciliation of body with text. In the course of this movement the distinction between the youthful Stingo and the mature one falls away, as each is haunted by the other. Finally, the novel's closing reference to "*the bright/the morning star*" echos the closing lines of *The Confessions of Nat Turner:* "Oh how bright and fair the morning star . . ." (428). These trajectories, then, offer a point of entry into the debate around *Confessions,* a text that, notoriously, both forces and prohibits questions about, as Ross puts it, "the appropriateness of subject matter, about the legitimate (or illegitimate) uses of history in fiction, and about an author's unconscious intentions" (*Critical Responses* 6–7).

The critical attention to the relationship of *Sophie's Choice* with its subject matter—the extent to which the novel does or does not recognize the limits of language and of art—has privileged the statement about Auschwitz over the context in which this statement appears. Read in context, the movement from the first to the last of these three sentences traces a process of identifying the body with its speech, the present with its past, an identification that reanimates the image of the speaking corpse discussed in the previous chapter. This movement also offers a paradigm through which we can productively revisit this complex relationship of representation with its object in terms of body and text, and points toward *The Confessions of Nat Turner* as a space in which this relationship might be explored. Read thus, the final lines of *Sophie's Choice* provide a key to *Confessions of Nat Turner*, and in this chapter I want both to describe this key and employ it, revisiting the novel's fraught and painful critical reception through the mutual implication of body and text that the conclusion of *Sophie's Choice* provides.

"Unparalleled and Inhuman": Reading the Rebellion

In the early hours of August 22, 1831, six rebel slaves entered the house of Joseph Travis, a wheelwright in Southampton, Virginia. Led by Nat Turner, a local preacher and a slave belonging to the family, the rebels murdered Travis, his wife Sally, and three children, initiating forty-eight hours of ferocity and vindictiveness that terrified the young nation. "It was hardly in the power of rumor itself, to exaggerate the atrocities which have been perpetrated by the insurgents: whole families, father, mother, daughters, sons, sucking babes, and school children, butchered, thrown into heaps, and left to be devoured by hogs and dogs, or to putrify on the spot," reported a witness. "What strikes us as the most remarkable thing in this matter is the horrible ferocity of these monsters," read the *Richmond Enquirer*. "They remind one of a parcel of blood-thirsty wolves rushing down from the Alps; or, rather like a former incursion of the Indians upon the white settlements." "A bloodier and more accursed tragedy was never acted, even by the agency of the tomahawk and scalping knife," added the *Constitutional Whig*. "Throughout this affair the most appalling accounts have been given of the conduct of the negroes, the most inhuman butcheries the mind can conceive of, men, women, and infants, their heads chopped off, their bowels ripped out, ears, noses, hands, and legs cut off, no instance of mercy shown," reflected John Floyd, governor of Virginia at the time (qtd. in Greenberg, *Confessions* 64, 67, 75, 106).

Aligning the rebels with forces of destruction (monsters, savages, bloodthirsty wolves), these early accounts of the Turner rebellion exclude its agents from a community that identifies itself as civilized, Christian, and humane. The violence of the rebels' actions is posited as something better left unspoken precisely in order to keep this community intact.[6] Such strategic emplotments and exclusions enable early accounts of the Turner rebellion to set up a number of distinctions that reinforce the social order against which the rebellion directed itself. The rebels, identified as uncontrollable, irrational forces of nature, are distinguished from their victims, the white citizens of Virginia. That state's repression of the rebellion—the lynchings, summary executions, torture, and mutilations that yielded far more black victims than the fifty-five white victims of the rebellion itself—is rhetorically aligned with the operations of civilization against which the uncontrollable, irrational forces of nature are arrayed. The public trials (themselves hardly examples of due process) of the rebels and their associates served the function of further distancing white Virginians from the slaughter, reinscribing state violence into the logic of the community from which it emerged. If "the brutality generated by the initial reaction to the rebellion exposed the ugly force and violence which lay behind the power of the ruling group," writes Greenberg, "the trials should be seen as an attempt to recover from that exposure" (*Confessions* 22).[7] In this exposure and recovery the violence of the rebellion remains, as Thomas R. Gray puts it, "unparalleled and inhuman" (55): unclaimed, unreconciled with the civilized, Christian and humane community whose symbolic order it set out to destroy.

For present-day scholars of the rebellion, this exclusion of the rebellion's violence from the symbolic is a source of significant rhetorical and ethical power. That which is "unparalleled and inhuman" for apologists for slavery in 1831 becomes, by the end of the twentieth century, the grounds from which these apologies, and the narratives that informed and sustained them, can be historicized, analyzed, and dismantled.[8] More than 150 years after the rebellion, Stephen Howard Browne will muse on the force and challenge of this exclusion, which he calls a "crisis of representation": "Violence on the order of Turner's rebellion," says Browne, "calls into question the capacity of language to render coherent that which is inexplicably destructive" (310). The point of Browne's discussion is not to reconcile the rebellion with the symbolic but rather to emphasize the rebellion's exclusion from it, an emphasis that enables him to pose "significant questions as to how violence on this scale gets represented and what kind of cultural work such depictions are made to do" (310).

Browne's motives are, of course, very different from those of the nineteenth-century accounts and, to a contemporary reader's eye, far more palatable.

But in focusing on the rebellion's challenge to representation, and not on the rebellion itself, Browne is engaged in a similar pursuit. The 1831 accounts of the rebellion excluded the rebels and their actions from representation, comprehension, and speech in order to justify the white community's brutal suppression of the rebellion and to establish that community as civilized, righteous, and humane. Present-day readings of those accounts actively assume this exclusion and use it in order to trace the ideological and political agendas that determined how violence was to be represented in 1831. Both approaches to the rebellion evince a significant investment in maintaining this exclusion as such, and the focus of this investment is Nat Turner, "the leader of this ferocious band" (Gray 40), whose body, actions, and speech, as problematic as they are compelling, are the wellspring of impassioned debate about representation and appropriation, ethics and aesthetics, narrative, experience and possession of the "real."

Nat Turner remained at large for about six weeks after the rebellion; he was arrested on October 30, 1831, and conveyed to the Southampton county jail for trial and execution. There he was interviewed by Thomas R. Gray, a local lawyer and slave owner, who published the results of the interview as "The Confessions of Nat Turner" in November 1831. Posited as "a faithful record of his confessions" (Gray 40), "an authentic account of the whole insurrection" (39), with "little or no variation" from Nat Turner's "own words" (40), the "Confession" was also designed to further Gray's explicit political agendas—"to demonstrate the policy of our laws in restraint of this class of our population . . . [and] to see that they are strictly enforced" (41)—and implicit financial ones (which may contribute to the sensationalistic and voyeuristic quality of the narrative, designed to be a best seller). Present-day readings of "Confessions" analyze Gray's text with an eye toward the cultural work this representation of violence was designed to enact, tracing its rhetorical performance of containment and control, of transforming the fifty-five opened and bleeding white bodies that the rebellion produced into a narrative that, by "removing doubts and conjectures from the public mind" (Gray 42), enacts their symbolic closure.

But as a crisis of representation merges with a politics of commemoration, the inevitable exclusions and inclusions inherent in both these forms of cultural work and rhetorical control come to the fore. What gets represented, and how? What is commemorated, and by whom? What gets represented as unrepresentable, and do such evocations command memory or oblivion? Greenberg's characterization of "Confessions" as "a joint production—with many of the major decisions in the hands of local lawyer and slave owner Thomas R. Gray," and his assertion that "any reading of the 'Confessions' must begin with some understanding of Thomas Gray and his motives" (*Confessions* 8) are axioms for present-day readings of the pamphlet, which engage these questions by focusing on the tension between Thomas Gray and Nat Turner. The lawyer and the preacher, the scribe and the speaker, the free white slave owner and the condemned black captive were enmeshed in a series of power relations that must have informed and directed their interaction, and present-day readings of "Confessions" trace those relations while keeping in mind a range of agendas that inform the pamphlet's production, of which the need to pacify yet tantalize the public, to offer an authentic report and to produce a lucrative account, to transform scattered rumors into a coherent and definitive narrative, and to reconcile the violence of the insurrection with a version of slavery as a benevolent institution are but a few. In crucial counterweight to these agendas is the figure of Nat Turner, whose actions precipitated this text and inform its operations.

Present-day readings of "Confessions" tend to highlight Thomas Gray's attempts to silence and manipulate Nat Turner's voice, detailing where and how Nat Turner emerges from—or despite—the white man's version of the events. Inevitably, they produce an account of how Nat Turner's silenced agency forces the limits of Gray's authorial control. Such attempts to identify traces of Nat Turner in Gray's text, or to distill Gray's motives from Nat Turner's tale, evince a certain resistance to closing the text, to assigning it coherence, reference, and a unilateral "meaning." This resistance takes the form of identifying competing discourses, incommensurate narratives, or innumerable interpretations. Rather than detailing, say, the conquest of world by word, the relegation of experience to narrative, the silencing of black action by white text, present-day readings of "Confessions" wield the limits of representation in order to dramatize the collision of world *with* word, tracing the limits of narrative control in the context of experiential unpredictability to determine the circumscription of speech by silence. Keeping in the forefront of these dramatizations the power relations that compose and determine them, such readings refuse resolution into a single coherent "meaning." Browne, for example, reads "Confessions" "to identify mutually authorized discourses striving for rhetorical presence in a text incapable of resolving one into the other" (315), reflecting the text's inability to "control," as he puts it, the "meaning" of Nat Turner (324).[9] That "meaning," William Andrews adds, "is perpetually postponed and relative, a function of the innumerable alignments of the two Nat Turners produced by a text that always keeps one partially eclipsed by the other" (77).

Thoughtful, complex, and sophisticated such readings are. But the question persists: what purpose do *they* serve? *Why* insist that this text remain, as Browne puts it, "open, available to interpretations not specified by the pamphlet's author" (312)? What agenda underlines this emphasis that one meaning, one discourse, one "Nat Turner" inevitably eludes the other? Answers to these questions reflect the political and ethical implications of negotiating the unspeakable into and out of speech. By claiming to present, explain, and explicate the rebellion, Thomas Gray attempts—literally—to "close the book" on history; despite his assertion that the account is Nat Turner's "own words," Gray substitutes his words for Nat Turner's: the text is, after all, an attempt to conquer and subdue Nat Turner's actions, his presence, and his voice. Critical readings of "Confessions," therefore, evoke the limits of representation in order to maintain the presence of what they claim Gray's narrative fails to contain. They refuse closure, decry substitution, condemn conquering, and argue that Nat Turner's voice is unspeakable by Thomas Gray's text. And the unspeakable is, as we have seen, a formidable force.

It is this formidable force that motivates the critical work of identifying and detailing the text's silences and absences and of delineating the ideological confrontations that "Confessions" contains, evokes, but refuses to resolve. By engaging in such critical work, present-day readings of "Confessions" evoke the stubborn presence of Nat Turner's voice, actions, and experience in, through, and around Gray's narrative. Here the resistance to closure takes the form of an emphasis on the literary's failure to contain and control experience, as readers of "Confessions" identify spaces of silence, absence, and incommensurability which they align with Nat Turner's "voice." This "voice," argues Greenberg, appears in the *absence* of Thomas Gray's agency (in the details of "Confessions" which Gray "would have had no reason to create or distort") and in the "*silences* in [the] text" (*Confessions* 10–11; emphasis mine). Greenberg goes on to align Gray with the "literary" aspects of the pamphlet (both in his description of the rebellion and in his literary tweaking of what he presents as Nat Turner's verbatim confession), distinguishing between Nat Turner's "voice" and Gray's editorial insertions, distortions, and manipulations. In present-day readings of the 1831 "Confessions," then, a rigorous insistence on meaning's instability takes the form of tracing the contours of the unspeakable. Readers of the pamphlet evoke the unspeakable to distinguish between the literary and the historical, representation and experience, Thomas Gray's text and Nat Turner's silenced voice. Given the inherent injustice of the racial politics that informed the pamphlet's production and the subsequent alignment of sympathies this injustice is expected to generate in present-day readers, these distinctions take on a political cast, enabling readers to participate in what they perceive as the rebellion's historical and ethical stakes. Nat Turner eluded his pursuers for six weeks, and he was the last of the rebels to be captured. To demonstrate that "Confessions" fails to "capture" Nat Turner's voice is to extend those six weeks to infinity.

By reading "Confessions" in terms of Gray's inability to contain and control Nat Turner, present-day readings of the 1831 pamphlet evoke the limits of representation in order to celebrate the stubborn presence of what this representation fails to contain. At stake is the interrelation of the literal and the literary, experience and representation, silence and speech, and the ethical investment in rendering one inaccessible to the other—an investment that animates the historical document with a literary quality and keeps the text perpetually political. "To the extent," writes Browne, "that ['Confessions'] continues to resist closure . . . it must remain as disturbing and deeply relevant in our time as in its own" (310–11). Browne's imperative—"it must remain"—embues the presence of the unspeakable with an ethical dimension and situates these ethics in the political context in which the 1831 pamphlet is read. To abandon the unspeakable is to assume Nat Turner's accessibility by Thomas Gray's text, subsuming the black man's experience to the white man's prose. Given the ethical and political currency with which the unspeakable is endowed, this is a hazardous project and a costly one, as William Styron's *Confessions of Nat Turner* reveals.

"The Real Nat Turner": Reading the 1960s Controversy

The Confessions of Nat Turner, which appeared in 1967 to considerable acclaim (the novel was awarded a Pulitzer Prize), elicited serious criticism

from some African American critics who identified Styron's "own private attempt as a novelist to re-create and bring alive" Nat Turner (Styron, "This
Quiet Dust" 14) as a literal as well as a literary appropriation. For many of
these critics—I am referring here to the novel's critics in the 1960s, primarily but not exclusively the authors of the essays included in Clarke's edited
volume *William Styron's Nat Turner: Ten Black Writers Respond*—Styron's
novel was less of a "meditation on history," as its author claimed ("Author's
Note" to *Confessions*), than an illustration of the inability of white imagination to access black experience, and the subsequent effacing and silencing
of that experience and that history—a silencing of literal suffering with a literary work. The stakes of this silencing are revealed in the context of the debate, as assertions of historical fact merge with the authority assumed by a
history of suffering to produce a reality claimed as a crucial constituent of
identity: the critics charged Styron with stealing "our Nat," with replacing
the heroic revolutionary with a series of white racist stereotypes, and with
deliberate distortion of historical fact.

In order to do so, many of the novel's critics referenced Gray's 1831 pamphlet as the origin of this history, assigning a factual quality to the document
while recognizing its bias. Styron's depiction of Will's role in the Turner rebellion, for example, "contradicts *the facts* as established by the Thomas Gray
'Confessions'" (Bennett 13; emphasis mine). Vincent Harding contrasts Styron's *Confessions* with Gray's, conflating Gray and Nat Turner in what he
refers to as Nat Turner's "*own* 'Confessions'" (27; emphasis mine). Herbert
Aptheker locates the "realities of the Turner rebellion" (191) in Gray's text
(which he calls the "actual 'Confessions'" [192]), and scolds Styron for omit-
ting Nat Turner's reply, when asked if he was mistaken in conceiving and
directing the rebellion, "was not Christ crucified?" (Gray 48). This "direct,
simple and great flash" from Gray's "Confessions" is absent from Styron's
novel, one of many discrepancies between "the *realities* of the Turner rebellion and Mr. Styron's rendition thereof [which] form . . . a pattern amount-
ing to consequential distortion" (191–92; emphasis mine).

The rhetoric employed by these critics has been denigrated as mean-
spirited, ad hominem, slanderous, insulting, and bitter. More sympathetic
readers of these critics characterize the essays as unsophisticated in their
concepts of race and counterproductive in their enactment of politics.
Rushdy's detailed account of the controversy in *Neo-slave Narratives* focuses
on the tensions between the novel's "critics" (whom he identifies as Black

Power intellectuals) and defenders (whom he calls "respondents"). At stake, for Rushdy, is the relation between historical accuracy and cultural representation, and the controversy itself reveals a great deal about what gets enshrined as valid historical evidence and whose readings of this evidence are deemed acceptable. While respondents worked hard to establish a concept of history as "objective," they missed, Rushdy says, "the critics' most important and most ignored claim—the claim that what Styron produced was less a 'meditation on history' than it was an appropriation of a slave's voice, a slave's life's meaning, and an important piece of slave testimony" (58).

But Rushdy's reading misses the fundamental stakes of the debate: the ethical and political investment in producing and maintaining Nat Turner *as unspeakable*. In order to do so, the 1960s critics posit Thomas Gray's "Confessions" as a strategic foil to Styron's novel. Bennett, exploring "the difference in tone between the *Confessions* of Gray, the racist, and Styron, the white liberal" concludes that "the two *Confessions* demonstrate how white Americans see black Americans, no matter what we do" and that "[t]he prophet who died in the Jerusalem of America . . . still awaits a literary interpreter worthy of his sacrifice" (16). Harding, who describes "Confessions" as "the basic historical document" (24) uses this document to demonstrate Gray's superiority to Styron in both honesty and acumen, in comparison to whom "it is almost embarrassingly obvious that Styron is unable to comprehend Nat Turner's real stature and meaning" (25). Respondents (to follow Rushdy's terminology) read this strategy as historical naïveté (the critics conflated a historical document with historical fact) or ideological strategy (they eschew conceptual nuance in favor of political expedience). But aligning Gray's "Confessions" with history enabled the novel's critics to read Styron's *Confessions* as a misrepresentation of history, and to subsequently condemn *Confessions* as an attack on reality. This reality is compellingly posited as absolute and extratextual, a gesture that situates Nat Turner beyond the cultural and political agendas of Thomas Gray's *or* William Styron's text. "The *real* Nat Turner," writes Bennett, in a typical such move,

> was a virile, commanding, courageous figure. Styron rejects history by rejecting this image of Nat Turner. In fact, he wages literary war on this image, substituting an impotent, cowardly, irresolute creature of his

own imagination for the *real* black man who killed or ordered killed *real* white people for *real* historical reasons. The man Styron substitutes for Nat Turner is not only the antithesis of Nat Turner; he is the antithesis of blackness. (5; emphasis mine)[10]

"History, Politics and Literature: The Myth of Nat Turner," published in 1971, is the seminal defense of Styron's novel from these accusations. The essay's authors, Seymour L. Gross and Eileen Bender, challenge assertions of "truth" and "facts" by the critics, pointing out that much of what the critics pose as "truth" is the product of Gray's editorial decisions. But while drawing distinctions between what Gray wrote and what Nat Turner might have said, Gross and Bender make a strange move: they, too, evoke a "real" Nat Turner.

> Considering Turner's rhetorically matter-of-fact method of recounting the murders, it is jarring to come upon stock locutions which italicize in the manner of sentimental fiction. It is difficult to conceive of Turner speaking of sending Richard Whitehead "to an untimely death," or crying out "Vain hope!" in response to a door shut by a white family against the invaders, or declaiming that Mrs. Reese's "son awoke, but it was only to sleep the sleep of death." Equally unbelievable is Turner's goth-icized self-portrait of himself as viewing "the mangled bodies . . . in silent satisfaction." *The real Nat Turner*, or even the Nat Turner who cold-bloodedly narrates the details of the slaughter, may indeed have felt something like this, but the language is as clearly Gray's as is its intention. (497; emphasis mine)

If the novel's critics' repeated references to "the real Nat Turner" evoked a "reality" that Styron (wittingly or not) appropriates or ignores, Gross and Bender counter by referring to a "real Nat Turner" who is as inaccessible to Styron's opponents as he is to Styron himself. They are not unique in this move. Revisiting the controversy in 1983, James M. Mellard applies the same logic to Thomas Gray. Praising Gross and Bender's characterization of Gray's "Confessions" as "a political document in the most basic sense of the word" (159), Mellard evokes a "*real* Gray" whom he describes as "a crafty rhetorician who never gave his best ploys away" (160; emphasis mine).

Rushdy's reading of the controversy in *Neo-slave Narratives* emphasizes the extent to which the respondents (he mentions Gross and Bender specifically) "miserably failed to take up most of the major issues raised by the critics, since they did not listen to the critics but instead contested and repressed both the emergent discourse on slavery and the Black Power intellectuals who mobilized it" (57). The respondents' refusal to "listen," Rushdy continues, reflects the problematic position of African American subjectivity in the United States. Quoting June Jordan's observation that black people have always "been speaking as subjects, as first persons" and repeating her urgent question, "is anyone, anyone white, preparing to listen?" Rushdy concludes that the controversy around *The Confessions of Nat Turner* reveals that "the answer to that question was, no, the time for listening had not yet arrived" (56); later he adds that "the critics' comments were simply not heard" (62). The refusal to "listen" is, for Rushdy, both an active silencing of a political reality and a failure to interpret silence as such: "[T]he respondents . . . *lacked the capacity to interpret the silences* the social conditions of slaves forced them to inscribe" (61; emphasis mine).[11]

This emanation of "the real Nat Turner" from both sides of the controversy realizes both the stakes of the controversy itself and the similarity of these stakes to present-day readings of Thomas Gray's pamphlet. Indeed, the debate around the novel sets the stage for present-day readings of the pamphlet, informed, as they are, by an ethical investment in Nat Turner's evading the ideological imposition of Thomas Gray's prose. Participants in the 1960s controversy over *Confessions* and present-day readers of the 1831 "Confessions" are engaged in the same project: generating a space of unspeakability against which all representations (Gray's as much as Styron's) can be held up, and to which all representations must come up short. It is this mandate that drives the novel's critics to evoke a "reality" which they claim Styron ignores, and which drives its defenders to evoke a "reality" which, they argue, is as unspeakable by Styron as it is to the critics. Both "realities" are characterized as inaccessible to the narrative that attempts to capture, to render commensurable, and to communicate. As Greenberg puts it, "[T]he dispute was really about a clash of worldviews so profound that it did not lend itself to conversation. William Styron's defenders and his critics spoke different languages based on radically different racial, political, and literary assumptions. They lived in parallel worlds of meaning separated by a gap of silence" ("Epilogue" 247). As the concentric circles of silence extend from the rebellion itself, to the controversy around *Confessions*, to readings of "Confessions" and readings of the controversy, what remains consistent is a commitment to maintaining the resistance of experience and silence to representation and speech. If this resistance cannot be maintained, it must be produced; in either case, the rhetorical performance of identifying the presence of the unspeakable masquerades as ethical practice—a vicarious and belated participation in the shriek of defiance that was the Southampton slave rebellion of 1831.

Nat Turner Speaks

"The major complaint," writes Mary Kemp Davis, "was apparent from the book's first sentence: How dare a white man write so intimately of the black experience, even presuming to become Nat Turner by speaking in the first person?" (235). Charles Joyner agrees with Davis that Styron's choice to narrate the novel from Nat Turner's point of view was perceived by his critics as "without question the most offensive of Styron's faults" (213), the manifestation of "unspeakable arrogance" (212). By writing from Nat Turner's point of view, Styron's first-person narrator "speaks" what the 1831 "Confessions" deemed unspeakable, and condemnations of the novel evince their own ethical agendas by evoking the unspeakable in their responses to it. Thus Greenberg describes the novel as generating silences that divide its readers along racial lines and that no language can traverse, "silences that signified a breakdown in the ability of language to transmit meaning across a deep cultural divide. No voice seemed able to speak words understandable to all participants in the controversy" ("Epilogue" 246). It is in this light that we may understand Mike Thelwell's statement about the novel: deploring the absence of slaves' "real language," Thelwell concludes that "Mr. Styron's Nat speaks . . . in no language at all" (80–81).

But it would be more accurate to say that Styron's narrator speaks so many languages in the novel that there is no language he can claim for his own.[12] Early in *Confessions*, the fictionalized Nat Turner deliberately chooses "nigger talk" in order to manipulate Kitchen, the white boy who works in the jail, thinking, "Big talk will fetch you nothing but nigger talk might work" (*Confessions* 9). "Maybe you could fetch me just a little piece of pone," he says to Kitchen, "just a little bitty piece of pone. . . . Please, young mastah. I'm most dreadful hungry" (9–10). Nat's "nigger talk" to Kitchen contrasts sharply with the deferential, but more authoritative, prose that he uses in his conversations with the fictionalized Thomas Gray: "Last night," he says to Gray, "after they carried me up here from Cross Keys and I sat here in the dark in these chains, I tried to sleep. And as I tried to sleep, the Lord seemed to appear to me in a vision" (15). Similarly, Nat's attempt to prepare his friend and fellow slave Hark for the work of killing takes the form of evoking and parodying these different languages, aligning "nigger talk" with submission. Responding to Hark's eagerness to serve a white visitor, Nat recalls, "I began to mimic him, hoarsely, beneath my breath. 'Red bar'l, massah! Dat's de bar'l wid de gennlemen's cidah! I fix de brandy fo' you, massah!'" (56). Emerging from this parodic "nigger talk" to address Hark directly, Nat confronts him with "How come you make with that kind of talk . . . You a *fool*, Hark. How'm I goin' to teach you?" (57). This early association of rebellion with rhetoric is strengthened as Nat's first glimpse of his "divine mission" that "the whole world of white flesh would someday founder and split apart upon my retribution, would perish by my design and at my hands" (307) produces, significantly, his first sermon. In rhythmic vernacular he addresses the crowd: "'Come closer!' I commanded . . . 'This here is no time for laughin'! This is a time for weepin', for *lamentation*! For rage! You is *men*, brothers, men not beasts of the field. You ain't no four-legged dogs! You is *men*, I say! Where oh where, my brothers, is yo' pride?" (307). Musing on his speech, Nat notes: "My language was theirs, I spoke it as if it were a second tongue" (308).

"My language was theirs, I spoke it as if it were a second tongue": these words indicate a simultaneous appropriation and disavowal of a mother tongue, or language indelibly associated with the subjectivity of its speaker.[13] The language of his fellow slaves both *is* and *is not* Nat's. This simultaneous appropriation and disavowal generates an inherent ambiguity that problematizes the very notion of an "originary" or "authentic" language, situating Nat at one remove from *any* language he uses. The implications for this dissociation are dual: it renders Nat's subjectivity literally unspeakable, and it identifies the literary, dispassionate, twentieth-century prose in which much of the novel is written (prose that seems indistinguishable from that of Styron's less controversial narrators) as no more Nat's "own" language than the "nigger talk" with which he addresses Kitchen or the parody of servility with which he confronts Hark. If Styron does speak the unspeakable in *Confessions*, he does so via a narrator who can claim no language as his own.

Indeed, Nat's choice of language is a strategic ploy determined by the context in which he speaks—a context inevitably informed by the racialized relations of his world—and the complex, evocative prose of the interior monologue needs to be understood as an equally strategic ploy: not a naive expression but a rhetorical address. *Confessions*, like "Confessions," is a self-conscious construction with a specific reader in mind. It is this reader whom Nat addresses self-consciously, occasionally deferential ("do not consider me impertinent," he coaxes [168]), occasionally perplexed ("Does it seem a hopeless paradox [. . .]?" he muses [342]), always aware of the conclusions this reader is likely to draw ("do not think me overly cautious," he cautions [61]), and ever alert to the effect of his story: "do not consider me altogether heartless," he implores (59). Thus, as when Nat distinguishes that which is, he says, "impossible to explain" from information "without which you cannot understand" (69–70), Styron extends the cultural and political work of "Confessions" to the cultural and political world of *Confessions*, and responses to the novel that distinguish its language from its subject refuse, as Rushdy puts it, to "listen." Philip Rahv, for example, distinguishes "the language" of the novel, which he identifies as "unmistakably Styron's," from "the set of mind, the emotions, and the pathos," which, he states, "are entirely Turner's" (129); less sympathetic readers condemn *Confessions's* language as "inauthentic," or the novelist as having "appropriated" Nat Turner's "voice." Such readings of *Confessions* as a (mis)representation of the rebellion's *leader* miss its function as an address to the novel's *reader*, and these condemnations of Styron's aesthetic choices work to efface the reader's role. It is this role, and the structures of complicity it generates and reflects, that are articulated when *Nat Turner* speaks.

"You're the Key": "Confessions" and *Confessions*

"A moral imperative of every white Southerner," wrote Styron in 1965, is "to break down the old law, to come to *know* the Negro." Acknowledging that "the Negro may feel that it is too late to be known, and that the desire to know him reeks of outrageous condescension," Styron describes his "search for Nat Turner, [his] own private attempt as a novelist to re-create and bring alive that dim and prodigious black man," as "at least a partial fulfillment of this mandate" ("This Quiet Dust" 14). *The Confessions of Nat Turner* is the result of this "search" and of Styron's self-proclaimed "moral imperative" to "know." The novel takes Thomas Gray's "Confessions" as its primary historical source, and the relation between the two texts yields some important realizations about the stakes of the dichotomy of speech and silence, experience and narrative, with which present-day readings of the pamphlet and of the novel are concerned.

In the opening pages of the novel, Nat and Gray engage in a series of negotiations about "Confessions." This section (titled "Judgment Day") opens on the day of Nat's trial, and Nat and Gray spend the hours of that morning reviewing the text of "Confessions," with Gray reading, commenting, and pausing for clarification. Interjected into this scene is a flashback to Nat's first encounter with Gray. Nat's strategic silences bridge the two, working as both context and cause for the appearance of the historical "Confessions" on the literary scene:

> "Mornin', Reverend," [Gray] said finally. *When I made no reply,* he reached inside his waistcoat and took out a sheaf of papers, unfolding and flattening them against his lap. He said nothing more for a bit as he held the papers close to the lantern, shuffling them in and out, humming to himself, pausing from time to time to stroke his mustache, which was gray and indecisive, a faint shadow. His jaw was in need of a shave. With such an empty feeling in my stomach the oversweet smell of him almost made me puke as I sat there watching him, saying nothing.[. . .]
>
> *For I had said nothing* when first I laid eyes on him. (12; emphasis mine)

Gray's production of "Confessions" (the "sheaf of papers" he extracts from his waistcoat) seems linked to Nat's silence: the text makes its appearance "when [Nat] made no reply." This interrelation of text and silence on the day of the trial echoes the dynamic of Nat and Gray's first meeting, when Nat "said nothing" as he "first laid eyes" on Gray. In that first meeting, Gray introduced himself to Nat with a series of not-so-veiled threats designed to break this silence and compel the rebel to speak—a speech that will provide

Gray with the contents of "Confessions." Responding to Gray's harangue with silence, Nat catapults Gray into a misreading that ultimately works to Nat's benefit:

> For the first time I spoke, and his voice abruptly ceased. He was of course working up to the idea that if I did not tell him everything, he would find a way of getting at me through some sort of villainous monkey business with Hark. But he had misjudged everything. He had at once misinterpreted my silence and unwittingly anticipated my most nagging, immanent need: to scratch my back. If I was to be hung come what may, what purpose could be served by withholding a "confession," especially when it might augment in some small way my final physical relief? Thus I felt I had gained a small, private initial victory. . . . White people often undo themselves by such running off at the mouth, and only God knows how many nigger triumphs have been won in total silence. (14)

Nat describes his confession as the production of knowledge: "Mr. Gray," he avers, "I'll swear that the Lord came to me in a vision. And the Lord said this to me. The Lord said: *Confess, that all the nations may know. Confess, that thy acts may be known to all men.*" He adds, "For a brief instant I thought the falsity of these words would reveal itself, but Gray was lapping it up" (15). The "knowledge" that Nat is conveying to Gray is posited not only as a lie but as language detached from subjectivity—it is the "falsity of these words" and not the speaker's duplicity that Nat fears may "reveal itself"—a detachment enhanced by Nat's insistence, as Gray amends Nat's words to include the phrase "Confess your sins," that "[t]here was no *your sins* at all" and his tenacious alignment of the act of confession with the production of knowledge: "Not confess your sins, sir," I replied. "He said confess. Just that. Confess. That is important to relate. There was no *your sins* at all. *Confess, that all nations may know* . . ." (15). Nat's first words to Gray are an attempt to thwart the convention of the confession, to distinguish his subjectivity from the knowledge that he is proffering—an attempt that is informed by precisely that ethical imperative evinced by present-day readings of "Confessions" and the 1960s debate: the dissociation of black experience from white text. As Nat puts it, "[T]here were matters which had to be withheld even from a confession, and certainly from Gray" (34).

But Styron represents this exchange in a manner designed to counteract Nat's attempt to dissociate the confession from the subjectivity it is presumed to generate. Delighted by Nat's willingness to speak, Gray conflates Nat's speech with his self: "All over America," Gray says,

the people have asked theirselves: How could the darkies get organized like that, how could they ever evolve and promulgate not to say coordinate and carry out such a *plan?* But the people didn't know, the truth was not available to them. They were in the profoundest dark. Them other niggers didn't know. Either that or they were too dumb. Dumb-assed! Dumb! *Dumb!* They couldn't talk. (17)

As Gray slips from one referent of "dumb" ("them other niggers didn't know") to another ("they couldn't talk"), he conflates speech with knowledge. Nat, Gray intimates, is "dumb" in neither sense of the word: Nat's speech will simultaneously break a significant silence *and* produce the knowledge that Gray needs. Gray images this knowledge and speech as a "key": "Nat and Nat alone had the key to all this ruction," he says. But the conflation of speech and knowledge in the image of the key extends to a conflation of Nat with Thomas Gray's text of "Confessions," the purpose of which is to "[gratify] the public curiosity" and "[remove] doubts and conjectures" ("Confessions" 42). In this conflation of speech with knowledge, Nat does not merely *possess* the key—he *embodies* it: "[Gray] paused again, then said in a voice almost a whisper: 'Don't you see how you're the key, Reverend?'" (*Confessions* 17–18).

With "don't you see how you're the key," the relation between the rebel slave speaker and the white man's text, the unspeakable and speech, becomes one of *embodiment.* Nat both possesses and embodies the key—in both its metaphoric sense as that which yields understanding or explanation and its relation to a cluster of literal meanings which may wander from the material to the symbolic; from the key to unlock the "web of chain" (*Confessions* 26) in which Nat is ensconced to the "key" to the textual artifact in which Nat searches ceaselessly for coherence in an incomprehensible world ("In the woods I prayed often and searched ceaselessly in my Bible *for some key*" [288; emphasis mine]). The key conflates knowledge, possession, and embodiment, extending their inextricability to sentience and literacy, being and reading, body and word (both sacred and profane; Nat is, after all, a preacher).

In the course of this discussion, we will see how this relation of language and body permeates the novel. The scene with Gray is, in fact, yet another step in a process that began in Nat's childhood, when he learned to read by recognizing the words painted on the barrels and kegs in the cellar of the Turner mansion where he grew up. Hence his hunger—itself a recurring motif—is both literal and literary. Nat recalls poring over *The Life and Death of Mr. Badman*, a book he has stolen from the Turner library, and "press[ing] on in despair, *searching for the key*, hunting for the soft and sweetly familiar, SUGAR, GINGER, CAPISCUM, CLOVES" (144; emphasis mine). As Nat is searching for the "key" to his stolen book, his mother, in the kitchen, is singing,

Bow low, Mary, bow low, Martha,
For Jesus come and lock de do'
An' carry de keys away. (145)

The "key" Nat craves is absent, removed from the world by an equally absent deity, and Nat will subsequently identify physical hunger pangs (as he tries to read the stolen book, he "feels [his] insides churning with hunger" [139]) with his craving for communication with God. This fusing of physical and psychic hunger torments the condemned man in his cell: musing over his first encounter with Gray, Nat recalls, "I wondered if he would get them to bring me some food, after they took off the manacles and chains. I also wondered if I could persuade him to bring me a Bible, which I had begun to hunger for far down inside me with a hunger that made me ache" (28). Finally, as if confirming the myth that Nat Turner sold his body to the physicians for dissection and spent the money on ginger cakes, Styron's Nat proffers his confession in exchange for relief of his physical craving: "I'll be in a better fix for that confession if I had a little somethin' on my stomach," he says to Gray (25).

"Bow low, Mary, bow low, Martha": *Confessions* and Complicity

If what emerges from both sides of the debate around *The Confessions of Nat Turner* is a series of concerns around the relation of representation to its object, we can further characterize this relation as one of *fidelity*. The 1960s controversy, with its emphasis on "the real Nat Turner," prescribed gestures

Against the Unspeakable

toward the unspeakable as the most appropriate enactment of this fidelity; in the wake of the controversy, present-day readings of the pamphlet and the novel reiterate this fidelity by affirming and reaffirming representation's limits. In other words, when the object of representation is presumed to elude representation, evoking the unspeakable works to enshrine the self-proclaimed inadequacies of representation as the only possible manifestation of fidelity to its (inaccessible) object.

But to assume that representation bears some responsibility to its object is to forget that fidelity is read into or out of representation by critical work, work that is itself informed by a variety of ethical and political agendas. Sympathetic to these agendas we may be, but to forget that they are agendas is to conflate critical work with the politics that inform it—a conflation that enables condemnations of the novel to masquerade as condemnations of racism per se.[14] This complex interrelation of agency and ethics inheres in the assumption of representation's responsibility to its object, an assumption that paradoxically posits that object as both in and out of representation's reach: "the real Nat Turner," like the women of Nat's fantasies, simultaneously invites and eludes violation. This tantalizing, so-near-yet-so-far quality of Nat's sexual objects reflects, in its structure, the relation of representation to its object, and nowhere is this clearer than in Nat's (imagined) encounter with Mrs. Ridley, an encounter that identifies the unspeakable as a space where violation can be simultaneously appropriated and undone.

Mrs. Ridley is a Northerner and a newcomer to Southampton. She appears to have lost her way, and in a scene Nat witnesses, she asks Arnold, a free black man, for directions. Arnold and Mrs. Ridley have difficulty understanding each other, and Mrs. Ridley's inability to comprehend Arnold's speech (Nat describes it as "blue-gum country-nigger talk at its thickest, nearly impenetrable" [262]) precipitates her collapse:

"But—but—" the woman began to stammer, "I don't seem to know what—" And she halted, her expression now full of chagrin, sorrow, something even more disturbing—perhaps it was horror, but it seemed even more to be akin to pity . . . the woman said nothing more, simply stood there while her arm went limp and the parasol clattered to the road, then raised her clenched fists to her face as if she were striking herself—an angry, tormented gesture—and burst into tears. (263)

Nat's sexuality—his recurring fantasies of raping a white woman and his homoerotic experience with his friend Willis—has generated a great deal of discomfort for the novel's readers. It was this issue, Joyner writes, and the white racist ideology it manifested, that was "the most controversial component of Styron's *Confessions*, the component that infuriated his critics more than anything else, the component that called forth their most unmeasured epithets of contempt" (206). Nat's reaction to Mrs. Ridley's collapse is a paradigm of the sort of scene that precipitates this response:

I had risen in the meantime with my Bible clasped between my hands, and as I drew nearer to the edge of the gallery I was seized by a hot convulsive emotion that I had never known so powerfully before—it was like a roaring in my ears. For what I had seen on this white woman's face was pity—pity wrenched from the very depths of her soul—and the sight of that pity, the vision of that tender self so reduced by compassion to this helpless state of sobs and bloodless clenched knuckles and scalding tears, caused me an irresistible, flooding moment of desire. And it was, you see, pity alone that did this, not the woman herself apart from pity. . . . It was as if, divesting herself of all composure and breaking down in this fashion—exposing a naked feeling in a way I had never seen a white woman do before—she had invited me to glimpse herself naked in the flesh, and I felt myself burning for her. Burning!

And even as I stood there trying to dominate and still this passion, which I knew to be abominable to the Lord, I sensed that my thoughts had already run galloping beyond control, and in a swift fantasy I saw myself down on the road beginning to possess her without tenderness, without gratitude for her pity but with abrupt, brutal, and rampaging fury, watching the compassion melt from her tear-stained face as I bore her to the earth, my black hands already tearing at the lustrous billowing silk as I drew the dress up around her waist, and forcing apart those soft white thighs, exposed the zone of fleecy brown hair into which I drove my black self with stiff merciless thrusts. (263–64)

Condemnations of the sexual and racial implications of this description miss the role that speech and language play in this scene, and the further implication that the unspeakable is the site where agency, like language, can be simultaneously appropriated and disavowed. For if it is the encounter with the incomprehensible that causes Mrs. Ridley to burst into tears, it is her active assumption of the incomprehensible that enables her to regain her composure:

> "I don't understand!" I heard the woman cry. "Oh God, I don't understand!" And then she raised her head from her hands, and at that instant it was as if my hot vision and her sudden seizure had simultaneously dissolved, vanished. She shook her head in a quick furious motion, paying no attention to Arnold, her pale and beautiful face tear-streaked yet no longer haggard with pity but quite proud, with a kind of buried exultancy, and angry; and as she said it again now—"Oh, no, I *just don't understand!*"—her voice was calm with a flat emphatic outrage and she reached down and retrieved her parasol from the road then turned and strode very briskly but with stately and composed steps up the street, the resplendent silk of her dress making a slippery swishing as she disappeared, erect and proud, past the corner of the market. I later learned that soon she left town and never came back. (265)

This uneasy coexistence of agency and its abnegation, responsibility and its relinquishment, fidelity and betrayal, characterizes the women in Nat's life and ultimately comes to inform his fantasies. These complex issues, like the image of the key, are instilled in Nat early on, when as a child he witnesses his mother's rape by the white overseer. Nat, hidden beneath the house, is trying to read his stolen book. Meanwhile, in the kitchen, his mother Lou-Ann is singing:

> Bow low, Mary, bow low, Martha,
> For Jesus come and lock de do'
> An' carry de keys away. (145)

The absent key, as I mentioned above, figures the inaccessibility of salvation. Submission to this situation ("Bow low, Mary, bow low, Martha") is figured as inevitable—as inevitable as Lou-Ann's submission (a broken bottle to her neck) to the Irish overseer McBride. But as Lou-Ann becomes a willing partner in the sexual act, her transformation from victim to participant causes a crucial reversal of power roles between slave and overseer. At the closing of this scene, the song is repeated with the reference to submission ("Bow low, Mary, bow low, Martha") omitted (150).[15]

Ross calls this moment the "primal scene" of the novel; Nat's witnessing his mother's rape, Ross argues, informs the violent cast of his sexual fantasies, which find expression in the rebellion. But Ross's reading omits the crucial role *language* and *text* play in this violence, as instigator, conduit, and medium. After witnessing his mother's rape, Nat's fantasies of a "nameless white girl . . . her lips half open and whispering," are still characterized by "tenderness and desire" (173), and it is not until after he witnesses Miss Emmeline's sexual encounter with her cousin that he begins to think of sex as a violent act, characterized not by desire but by defilement. Here it is important to note that what shocks Nat and precipitates the violence is not the *sexual* nature of this action but, rather, its quality as a *verbal* performance:

> It was not the loud whisper of her voice that shocked me so much—though I instantly distinguished it—but the Lord's name in her mouth, uttered in a frenzy, the first time in my life I had heard blasphemy on a woman's tongue. *And so astonished was I by the words that as I stood there rooted in the dark it did not just then occur to me to consider the event which occasioned them.* (180; emphasis mine)

The fact of blasphemy, not the act of sex, catapults Nat into an uneasy recognition of his own embodiment and of the relation of that embodiment to knowledge: "This is what comes of being a nigger. . . . If I wasn't a nigger I wouldn't find out about things I don't want to find out about" (181). Finally, Emmeline's profanity, which Nat links to his racial subjugation, echoes that of McBride, who leaves Lou-Ann's kitchen repeating *"God blast!"*—a profanity that generated, in the young Nat hiding under the kitchen, "a sense of my weakness, my smallness, my defenselessness, my *niggerness* invading me like a wind to the marrow of my bones" (150).

Emmeline's response to the sexual act is the mirror image of Lou-Ann's: while Lou-Ann reconfigured her violation as consent, Emmeline reconfigures her consent as violation. For both Lou-Ann and Emmeline, the voluntary embrace of their own submission—a powerful abnegation of agency that, like Mrs. Ridley's, effaces the distinction between dominance and submission—is a significant source of power, and language (specifically

Against the Unspeakable

speech) is the arena in which this power is exercised. Emmeline declares her willingness to "go back to Maryland and become a whore again, and allow the only man I ever loved to sell my body on the streets of Baltimore. Get your God damned hands *off* me," she adds, "and don't speak another *word* to me again!" (182). Couching her violation as verbal and physical inaccessibility, Emmeline echoes Lou-Ann, whose calm, controlled voice, "unperturbed and serene as before," is in stark contrast to McBride's and Nat's emasculation—McBride leaves the kitchen disoriented (Ross describes him as "a veritable toddler" ["Things" 86]) and Nat, "like something shriveled," withdraws back into his hiding place (*Confessions* 150). Hence, when Emmeline replaces the earlier "innocent" girl of Nat's fantasies, "sobbing 'mercy, mercy, mercy' against my ear, allow[ing] me to partake of the wicked and godless yet unutterable joys of defilement" (193), it is her speech, rather than her self, that will inform all of Nat's subsequent sexual fantasies in the novel, fantasies that are virtually identical in language and structure—each ends with a long sentence that builds up to the release of "warm milky spurts of defilement"—and which reverberate with the same rhythmic profanity that Nat witnessed as Emmeline builds to and descends from climax: "oh Jesus . . . oh Christ . . . oh Christ . . . oh yes, *now!* . . . Oh mercy . . . mercy . . . mercy" (181).[16]

If Emmeline, in rhythm and language if not by name, resonates throughout Nat's psyche, the image of his mother's rape reemerges only once, when Samuel informs Nat of his plans to set him free. The centrality of food in the scene of his mother's rape, and his alignment of hunger for literacy with literal hunger, make Nat associate freedom with famine: "Thinking now of my mother's words long ago . . . *Druther be a low cornfield nigger or dead than a free nigger. Dey sets a nigger free and only thing dat po' soul gits to eat is what's left over of de garbage after de skunks an' dogs has et . . .*" (194). Styron situates this scene in ironic contrast with the slave coffle that Nat and Samuel meet that day. Here Nat encounters Raymond, whose white blood gives him, Nat reflects, "a certain shabby yet subtle prestige" and a modicum of "meager authority" in the form of folk wisdom, much of which Nat contemptuously dismisses. Raymond accosts Nat—in a voice described as "sweet and low, high-pitched" (201)—with flattery, calling him "sugah," "sweet," and "honey chile," and repeated requests for food: "Pretty please, honey chile," he persists, "isn't you got a nice sweet potato for ole Raymond? Or a tiny ole piece of bacon?" (199).

Awash with memories of his mother's rape in the kitchen and the fear of hunger evoked by his own impending freedom, Nat's response to Raymond's servile persistence is the entirely inappropriate "my mastah's goin' to set me free in Richmond" (200). The association of text and sex informs his response to Raymond's flattery. When Raymond turns his attention to the "pretty bag on dat saddle" ("I bets dey's all kinds of nice things to eat in dat bag," Raymond suggests), Nat's response—"Dey's on'y a Bible in dat bag!" (200)—is an attempt to redirect the unwanted attention from body to book, the vehement denial implicitly confirming the subtle eroticism of Raymond's insinuations. As Nat flees the scene, Raymond's parting words emphasize Nat's inescapable corporeality: "Yo' shit stink too, sugah. Yo' ass black jes' like mine, honey chile" (201).

The hints of eroticism in Nat's encounter with Raymond become explicit in the scene that immediately follows: Nat's homoerotic encounter with Willis, an encounter driven by a "hungry tenderness" (204) galvanized by blasphemy and characterized by violence. To Willis's exclamation, in response to a pricked finger, of "fuckin' Jesus!" Nat responds by striking him "sharply across the lips, drawing a tiny runnel of blood. 'A filthy mouth is an abomination unto the Lord!' I said" (204). Willis, who responds by lightly touching his mouth, unknowingly mimics McBride's gesture as he leaves Lou-Ann's kitchen ("[McBride] runs his fingers over his mouth—a curious, tentative motion almost of discovery, as if touching his lips for the first time" [149]), and the sight of the moccasin fangs that Willis wears around his neck may well remind Nat of Raymond, whose authority rested in such folk remedies (at the conclusion of their encounter, Nat will replace these fangs with a cross). As the erotic cast of Raymond's entreaties becomes, with Willis, an explicit sexual encounter, Nat's attempt to counter Raymond's eroticism with "dey's on'y a Bible in dat bag" takes the form of reformulating the encounter in biblical terms: only after he narrativizes his sexual pleasure as the story of David and Jonathan can he move to confront the implications of his actions for his body and Willis's and, declaring them "unclean," baptize them both.

Unable to violently relinquish comprehension, like Mrs. Ridley; unwilling to reinscribe consent as violation, like Emmeline; unlikely—given his fidelity to the biblical text—to follow Lou-Ann's example of subtly rewriting a given narrative (her omission of "Bow low, Mary, bow low, Martha" after her encounter with McBride is a subtle refusal of the directive to submit), Nat repeatedly counters corporeality with text, wielding one (in the case of Raymond) to silence the other, or using one (in the case of Willis) to control the other. Evoking a biblical narrative as a means to subdue, control, and render bodies docile, Nat echoes Richard Whitehead's sermon in the early pages of *The Confessions of Nat Turner,* the Mission Sunday sermon, where Whitehead, as Margaret puts it, *"preaches to the darkies"* about slavery's justification by God (95; emphasis in the original). Nat spends the sermon planning the rebellion—itself a confrontation of precisely that narrative that Richard Whitehead is expostulating with the corporeality it attempts to control.

As a rebellious slave who murders his owner, Nat signifies the limits (literal and metaphorical) of the slave system, a signification that must be negotiated back into the system itself. As a result of the rebellion, Nat finds himself in the position of the inexplicable that must be narrativized, and—more poignantly—his own narrative (in the form of the "Confessions") is co-opted to work against him. Hence his trial, the outcome of which is fore-ordained—Nat, says Gray, will "be tried next Sattidy . . . And hung by the neck until dead" (22)—and in which the issue of guilt or innocence is irrelevant: "What difference does it make, Reverend? Prosecution, defense, it don't make a hair's difference one way or the other . . . your goose is cooked already . . . I mean—well, to call a spade a spade . . . I mean—Hell, you know what I mean" (29). Gray's stuttering, his tautology, and his final turn to Nat to acquiesce in what he ultimately cannot articulate, demonstrate a system confronted with its own collapse, its meaning-making mechanism turned tautological and performative, instantiating itself with the same violence as Gray's triumphant cry *"Justice. Justice! That's how come nigger slavery's going to last a thousand years!"* that replaces, for Nat, the absent voice of God (25, 41).

Nat Turner's Key

"Historians," notes Greenberg, "do not readily accept the idea that their knowledge of the past may be limited. They are too often subject to the hubris common among men and women who . . . believe that they can reconstruct a dead world from the shards of a pot, or that they can reconstruct the life of a slave from a few marks on a page" ("Name" 3). Turning to the available historical information about Nat Turner, focusing on the complexities of slave names, physical descriptions, and the fate of Nat Turner's corpse (reportedly delivered to doctors for dissection), Greenberg concludes with a bleak list of the facts that are doomed to elude historical investigation: "We do not know the name of Nat Turner. We do not know what he looked like. We cannot find his body." In the face of this elusiveness, Greenberg advocates "[h]umility, deep humility about the limits of our knowledge" ("Name" 22–23, 3).[17]

Greenberg's emphasis on knowledge's limits and the necessity of facing them with humility reiterates the ethical injunction, evinced by present-day readings of "Confessions," against collapsing the distinction between experience and narrative, voice and text, the black man's and the white man's account. But like the temple on the hill that haunts Nat throughout *The Confessions*—"white inscrutable paradigm of a mystery beyond utterance or even wonder" that is inextricable from the blackness of its windowless interior, "dark as the darkest tomb" (422)—Styron's text explicitly enacts what Gray's text attempts: the collapse of these distinctions into their mutual embodiment, a corruption of representation by corporeality. Attempts to deny this inextricability are attempts to abstract the object of representation from representation itself, instantiating the former as unspeakable by the latter; and the urgent designation, by the participants of the controversy, of this unspeakability as "real" is echoed by Greenberg, for whom historical reality is the product of the unspeakable's ethical imperative: the necessity of humility when faced with comprehension's limits.

But the image of the key, to which this chapter repeatedly returns, casts the production of "Confessions" in terms of the incarnation of a problematic body as a textual artifact. Simultaneously possessed by Nat and possessing him, the key to the rebellion that Gray evokes in *Confessions* translates Nat's experience into Gray's text, producing Nat *and* "Confessions" as an object of knowledge—both for the white community of 1831 and for the Styron who fulfills his "moral imperative" to "*know* the Negro" in 1965 ("This Quiet Dust" 14; emphasis in the original). The resulting complicity of body with text—initiated by Lou-Ann, for whom the absent key that Jesus "carr[ies] away" opens a space in which power relations can be strategically negotiated—informs Nat's much-criticized sexual fantasies, saturated as they are with the complicity of sex with text, body with blasphemy, desecration with description, corporeality with curse. *Nat Turner's* key, then, explicitly defies Greenberg's exhortation, rendering it impossible to extract unspeakability from the novel's representation of the rebellion's leader (hence, perhaps, Styron's much-criticized decision to narrate the novel from Nat Turner's point of view: when the object of representation represents itself, its quality as unrepresentable is severely depreciated).

If present-day readers of the 1831 text emphasized the *collision* of word and world, narrative and experience, silence and speech, Styron's vision of their mutual embodiment precipitates the collapse of these dichotomies; they no longer collide, they collude. The relation of representation to its object is not one of fidelity (to the object or, most crucially, the object's inaccessibility) but complicity (with the object's inevitable distortion by representation). Tracing this complicity in the previous section revealed the imbrication of sex and text, body and word, in Styron's representation of (what the novel's critics perceive as) Nat's problematic sexuality—an imbrication that extends to Nat's equally problematic identity as a slave. In the opening pages of the novel, Nat responds to Gray's conflation of the text Nat will produce with Nat's own body in "don't you see how you're the key, Reverend?" (18) by turning his attention to the fact that he will stand trial, and not, as he had expected, be lynched:

An image came to mind like an explosion of light: myself, the day before, hurried toward Jerusalem along the road from Cross Keys, the booted feet thudding into my back and behind and spine and the fierce sting of the hatpins in my shoulders, the blurred infuriated faces and the dust in my eyes and the gobs of their spit stringing from my nose and cheek and neck . . . and, above all, one anonymous wild voice high and hysterical over the furious uproar: "Burn him! Burn him! Burn the black devil right here!" And through the six-hour stumbling march my own listless hope and wonder, curiously commingled: I wish they would get it over with, but whatever it is they're going to do, burn me, hang me, put out my eyes, why don't they get it over with right now? (18)

The reason, Gray explains, lies in Nat's value, not merely as the repository of knowledge (the "key" to the rebellion) but as a slave: "the rights of property" (19). Nat not only possesses knowledge but is himself a possession—a nightmarish species of logic, "the quintessence of white folks' talk . . . totally implausible yet somehow wholly and fearfully real" (22). Like the key, which works both literally (something Nat possesses) and metaphorically (possessing the key, Nat is it) the rights of property collapse Nat's value as subject and object, rendering him the embodiment of his own possession. The reference to Cross Keys is especially telling, combining, as it does, the image of the key with the concept of crucifixion. This combination confirms the identity of body and text that Gray instantiates with "don't you see how you're the key, Reverend?" as a motif of incarnation: word made flesh.[18]

Given this alignment of narrative authority with the corporeal it should not be surprising that one of the most problematic aspects of Styron's Nat is, precisely, his *body:* his obsession with white women ("page after page of squirming white buttocks," as Bennett puts it [6]), his habit of masturbation (again, to visions of "milky-white legs and arms" [qtd. in Bennett, 6, 12]) and his encounter with Willis, which led one of the novel's critics to mourn the emasculation of Nat, "half man half faggot" (Killens 35). Styron's Nat, whose ultimate salvation is imaged through sexual union with the only white woman he manages to kill, is as disturbingly carnal as it is ideologically destructive—literally embodying a wealth of racist myth. The charge of complicity with such embodiment is leveled not only at the novel itself; it is extended to the novel's author (Styron ruefully reflects that "my problem was less that of my work than that of my color" [454]) and, in such extension, is reflected back onto the novel's—generally identified as black—critics. Thus, the problematic body generated by Styron's text renders other bodies (the bodies that engage with this text) equally problematic. George Steiner may have sensed this when, after a laudatory review of the novel, he asks, "[W]ould a Negro recognize Nat Turner for one of his own, would he find Mr. Styron's fiction authentic to his own experience?" ("Fire" 124). In an equally laudatory review, Rahv noted that "only a white Southern writer could have brought it [the novel] off. A Northerner would have been too much outside the experience to manage it effectively; and a Negro writer, because of a very complex anxiety not only personal but social and political, would have probably stacked the cards, producing in a mood of unnerving rage and indignation, a melodrama of saints and sinners" (128). As if to confirm Steiner's and Rahv's sense that Styron's novel is somehow a catalyst for the articulation of racial, ethnic, or regional identity, Harding describes feeling "black and increasingly anguished" as he experienced "Styron's audacious attempt to recreate his own Nat Turner out of the sparse materials of history and out of the strangeness of his creative dreams" (24). This effect found expression in much of the attack on the novel from self-identified black critics, many of whom felt the need to catapult the novel's problematic

Against the Unspeakable

bodies out into the context of social violence and upheaval that characterized the period of its publication, rendering one as the embodiment of the other: "Let me speak plainly," writes Killens. "Every black American, then and now, was and is, a potential Nat Turner. . . . There are thousands of Nat Turners in the city streets today" (37, 43). Harding adds that Styron lacks comprehension of "the profound and bitter depths through which America continually moves towards the creation of a thousand Nat Turners more real than his could ever be" (23). And as Roy Swanson puts it, "Styron's Nat Turner is just too white. There is a preponderance of whiteness in the combination of white William Styron as black Nat Turner as white Nat Turner: black Nat Turner proves to be William Styron in blackface: the spirit is willing but the flesh is white" (163).[19]

But if Styron's novel highlighted the interrelation of the terms of this dichotomy (flesh and spirit, world and word, body and speech), contemporary discussions of the novel and of the debate tend to focus on the strategic rhetorics and the historical contexts through which the controversy was articulated, effectively eschewing the issues of embodiment that the original controversy urged—issues that remain a crucial constituent of contemporary identity politics in the United States. Denigrations of the controversy as "emotional" and "vituperative" (Stewart 182), "some of the most vicious and strident attacks ever launched at a modern author" (Bryer and Friedman 419), and informed by "racist understructures dictated by individual whim and political and economic concerns" (Fabricant 361) may well be expressions of discomfort with these identity politics and the racial and racialized embodiments they evoke. In any case, following Gross and Bender's defense of the novel (which attempted "to free Styron's novel from the coffle of propagandistic criticism masquerading as historicity" [517]), these readings tend to posit a distinction between the novel and history in order to focus on the rhetorical situation of the novel in history, the specific historical moment in which the novel appeared, the role the novel played in that moment, and the implications of the political configurations that formed around and against it—hence Mellard's reference to the novel as "a cultural Rorschach test" (165). But if *The Confessions of Nat Turner* calls, as Harding puts it, for a history that needed to be "fleshed out" and "spoken from the bowels of our blackness" (32), attempts to avoid complicity in such configurations of embodiment drive scholars to dissociate themselves from Styron, from the 1960s critics of the novel, and from the controversy.[20] Thus, a text that catapults its writer and readers into the corporeal produces interesting patterns of flight away from corporeality, as scholars of the controversy attempt to distance themselves from the identity politics that such focus on corporeality entails: their flight from the body is, ultimately, a flight from their selves.

Charles Hamilton, in his response to Styron's novel, noted that "the white liberal feels that rhetoric and good intentions are sufficient to relieve him of responsibility. He is sadly mistaken. To him, the problem is abstract, academic. To us, it is real, tangible" (77). If the unspeakable facilitates the masquerade of rhetorical performance as ethical practice, Hamilton's attention to the discrepancy between rhetoric and responsibility, intentionality and tangibility, "us" and "them," identifies this problem both in the text of the novel and in the controversy it generated. But when we focus our critical eye on these discrepancies, the multiple configurations of embodiment that both the novel and the controversy perpetuate and confront disappear. It is these configurations that need to be the focus of our attention: the cultural and political implications of rendering representation complicit with materiality, discourse with corporeality, that have too long been masked by urgent gestures toward the unspeakable. "Nat Turner," writes Mellard, "presents (indeed, even embodies) a version of history" (161); "the study of history," William Styron adds, "is not intended to make us feel good" ("More Confessions," 223).

)

Chapter 5

The One Word That Mattered

Beloved, Complicity, and the Corporeal

But if, as Styron ruefully concludes, "the study of history is not intended to make us feel good" ("More Confessions" 223), the past does make us feel, and the limits of language play a crucial role in evoking and wielding this emotional clout. Beyond these limits, though, crucial distinctions must be maintained, and evocations of the unspeakable in the context of different "pasts" speak to equally crucial distinctions in how these pasts are studied, remembered, represented, and repressed. If *Sophie's Choice*, complete with its gesture toward the incomprehensibility of Auschwitz, contributed to the establishment of a discourse of unspeakability that rose to prominence after the airing of the NBC miniseries *Holocaust*, *The Confessions of Nat Turner* highlighted the *absence* of such discourse surrounding American slavery at the time, and offered critics like the "ten black writers" the opportunity to determine the limits of Styron's imagination, comprehension, and representative abilities. Such urgent gestures toward "the real Nat Turner" demonstrate the unspeakable's utility as a vehicle for political empowerment: the body that eludes text, the silence that eludes speech, the truth that eludes history—all are spaces in which the limits of representation are vested with potent, because incalculable, effect. As I move from Styron's novels to Morrison's monumental *Beloved*, the opportunities that the unspeakable opens up for the articulation of identity, and the price of such articulations, will move to center stage.

Sixty Million and More

Since its publication in 1987, Toni Morrison's dedication of *Beloved* to "sixty million and more" has elicited stern admonitions from the novel's readers and critics. Amy Schwartz writes for the *Washington Post* that "the book's dedication page brings up echoes of another experience entirely: 'Sixty Million, And More,' it says," adding wryly that "the echo has not gone unnoticed." This ellipticalness informs other, more critical responses to the dedication: "Sixty is ten times six, of course," Stanley Crouch informs us, "and that is very important to remember" (67). While "the figure bears no relation to any scholarly estimate," writes Peter Novick, "it is, of course, ten times six million" (194). And as Emily Budick bluntly states, "[I]n the American context this dedication cannot, especially to a Jewish readership, but recall the 'six million' of the Holocaust" (161).

In each of these responses, an emphasis on the "obvious," the "of course," and the "cannot but recall" implicitly reiterates the assumption that the Holocaust holds a certain centrality in Western literature and history, a centrality that goes without saying, as obvious and as unquestionable as six times ten. In light of this assumption, six million, unlike "sixty million and more," appears inarguable, irrefutable—this despite Raul Hilberg's official estimate that the number of Jews murdered in the Holocaust is closer to five million.[1] "Six million" is posited as the standard against which Morrison's figure requires explanation, justification, and recourse to such official sources as scholarly estimates. "I take it to be incontrovertible that the number of Jews who lost their lives owing to the Holocaust was six million or thereabouts," writes Laurence Thomas. "On the other hand, estimates of the number of blacks who lost their lives during the voyage from Africa to the United States—the Middle Passage, as it is traditionally called—have gotten wildly out of control" (*Vessels* 9).

"Wildly out of control"—the rhetoric is disquieting, suggestive of the need for some kind of restraint on these uppity scholars and their numbers game.[2] The issue of comparative atrocities is a thorny one, of course, and it is, at best, misguided to suppose that a writer of Morrison's critical and political acumen could be so naive as to assume that she could evoke this figure without generating such responses. And yet, having invited discussion—"you haven't asked about the 60 million," she reminds an interviewer—Morrison refuses to engage in it (Clemons 75). In interviews following the publication of *Beloved*, Morrison has repeatedly emphasized that the dedication of the novel to "sixty million and more" has nothing to do with the Holocaust but is rather a guess (and guesses, given the paucity of documentation, are necessary) as to the number of slavery's victims. At the same time, her own accounts of the figure vary radically. Speaking to *Newsweek* on September 28, 1987, Morrison explained that the figure of sixty million is "the best educated guess at the number of black Africans who never even made it into slavery—those who died as captives in Africa or on slave ships" (75). One week later, speaking to the *Washington Post*, she stated: "I asked some scholars to estimate for me the number of black people who died in 200 years of slavery . . . those 60 million are people who didn't make it from there to here *and through*" ("Toni Morrison's"; emphasis mine).[3]

There is, however, a significant difference between those who never made it into slavery, on the one hand, and those who died in Africa and on slave ships in addition to the victims of slavery itself, on the other. So drastic a revision of the figure's referent within so short a space of time itself attests to the significant absence of adequate documentation of the atrocities perpetrated by slaveholders, slave traders, and the institution of American slavery: "[S]lavery itself," writes Karla Holloway, "defies traditional historiography. The victim's own chronicles of these events were systematically submerged, ignored, mistrusted, or superceded by 'historians' of the era" (68). Unlike the Holocaust, where the presence of documentation is overwhelming, it is the absence of proper documentation that contributes to slavery's horror. Morrison's figure and the slippage of its referents, therefore, eloquently emphasize how, in light of such significant absence of historical documentation, the numbers themselves are clearly not the point. Human suffering is.

Why, then, would Morrison choose to evoke the Holocaust's emblematic six million in her novel about slavery in the United States? What do the two have in common? The answer is the debate's *American* context, a context that highlights the rhetoric of commemoration while obscuring the historical and cultural distinctions between these atrocities, their perpetrators, and their victims. Putting the Holocaust in dialogue with slavery in America neglects the different methods and manners of these genocides, the ideologies under which they were conceived, and the means by which they were carried out, and elides the crucial fact that slavery, unlike the Holocaust, was perpetrated by American citizens on American soil. The dedication itself and the debate arising from it are no more about slavery and the Holocaust then they are about whether "sixty million and more" is an accurate estimation of those who perished; rather, "sixty million and more" and the responses it evokes raise the complex implications of African Americans and Jewish Americans comparing the extent, degree, and clout of their respective victimizations.[4]

In this specifically American context, then, Morrison's dedication of *Beloved* to "sixty million and more" is deliberately posited as a vague approximation that serves the purpose of evoking a vast array of dead bodies rather than counting and accounting for the bodies themselves. It demonstrates the extent to which numerical figures (not to mention figures of speech) cannot account for so vast and devastating a disaster. Evoking this figure works to efface the figure's referent, to challenge the very concept of numerical accuracy, and to foreground the inevitable insufficiency of scholarly appraisal while demonstrating the inherent unreliability of language when confronted with overwhelming mass suffering. Finally, Morrison's emphasis on the referent's instability enables her to posit herself as ethically invested in the principle of inclusiveness over and above the notion of historical accuracy: "Some people told me 40 million, but I also heard 60 million, and I didn't want to leave anybody out" ("Toni Morrison's" 12).

To say that Morrison is "appropriating" the Holocaust by citing the figure of sixty million (and, perhaps, upping the victimization ante by adding "and more") is, then, inaccurate. In dedicating *Beloved* to "sixty million and more" she is utilizing the unspeakable in order to establish that slavery shares, with the Holocaust, a quality of unspeakability: like Auschwitz, slavery "lies outside speech as it lies outside reason" (Steiner, "K" 123); in its wake, like in the wake of the Holocaust, "the human imagination [. . .] is simply not the same as it was before" (Rosenfeld, *Double Dying* 13). By evoking this quality of unrepresentable horror, Morrison is foregrounding suffering under slav-

Against the Unspeakable

ery in the context of a historical narrative usually imagined as "after Auschwitz" and, more importantly, granting this suffering a certain degree of legitimacy by defining it in terms derived from the unspeakable's venerable
association with the Holocaust. At the same time, though, this rhetoric also
enables her to avoid the issue of comparative atrocities by strategically situating herself above and beyond the possibility of comparison per se. To
Stanley Crouch's now-infamous description of *Beloved* as "a holocaust
novel in blackface . . . written in order to enter American slavery into the
big-time martyr ratings contest, a contest usually won by references to, and
works about, the experience of Jews at the hands of the Nazis" (67), Morrison has replied, "The game of who suffered most? I'm not playing that
game. That's a media argument. It's almost about quantity. One dead child
is enough for me. One little child . . . who didn't make it. That's plenty for
me" (C. Brown 466).[5]

No Bench by the Road

Morrison has described *Beloved* as a novel "about something the characters don't want to remember, I don't want to remember, black people don't
want to remember, white people don't want to remember" (qtd. in Rushdy,
"Daughters" 39). For Morrison, this reluctance to remember is reflected in,
if not embodied by, the absence of memorials:

> There is no place you or I can go, to think about or not think about, to
> summon the presences of, or recollect the absences of slaves; nothing
> that reminds us of the ones who made the journey and of those who did
> not make it. There is no suitable memorial or plaque or wreath or wall
> or park or skyscraper lobby. There's no 300 foot tower. There's no small
> bench by the road. There is not even a tree scored, an initial that I can
> visit or you can visit in Charleston or Savannah or New York or Provi-
> dence or, better still, on the banks of the Mississippi. And because such
> a place does not exist (that I know of), the book had to. ("A Bench by the
> Road," qtd. in McKay 3)

So broad a definition of "memorial" (from a 300-foot tower to a small bench
by the road, from a skyscraper lobby to an initial on a tree) and so expansive a description of the work of memory (thinking and not thinking,

summoning presence and recollecting absence) rephrases Morrison's statement about not wanting to remember as an expression of the inability to commemorate. The implicit assumption performed by this emphasis on suitable memorialization is this: no memorial can ever be sufficiently "suitable" or compelling, no monument can be grand enough or mean enough to contain such limitless suffering.

When *Beloved* stands for the absence of suitable memorial spaces, then, it is not so much rendering absence present but rather articulating the paradoxical inextricability of absence and presence, memory and forgetting, the unspeakable and speech. Critical writing on *Beloved* tends to stress these paradoxes: "[Morrison's] themes revolve around the wish to forget and the necessity to remember, to reject and to reclaim, and to elide the boundaries between past and present," writes Nellie McKay (12). Rafael Pérez-Torres notes that "the interplay between presence and absence, accepting and rejecting, appearing and disappearing, repeats and resurfaces throughout the course of *Beloved*" ("Knitting" 93). Barbara Hill Rigney says that "the history of slavery itself, Morrison writes in *Beloved,* is 'not a story to pass on,' but rather is something that is 'unspeakable,' unconscionable, unbearable" (142–43).[6]

But when considering these paradoxes, we need to keep in mind that silence and forgetting are as much a strategic and self-conscious gesture on the part of the subjugated as they are the product of the subjugating culture's demands and requirements. On the one hand, absence and silence have been imposed—there is indeed no "bench by the road"—but at the same time, absence and silence are assumed: there are, in fact, plenty of benches by roads, but none of these, Morrison declares, can adequately serve as a suitable memorial for slavery because there can be no suitable memorial for the unspeakable. In order to speak the unspeakable, then, it is necessary to posit what you are speaking as unspeakable in the first place. Doing so involves a double effacement: something must be silenced in order to be rendered unspeakable, and the unspeakable must be forgotten in order to be commemorated as such. In light of these multiple silencings and effacements, negotiating the unspeakable into language is a hazardous undertaking, and the novel opens with precisely such a negotiation: Sethe's purchase of a tombstone for her murdered child.

Despite some critics' confusion,[7] Beloved is not the name of the baby Sethe murdered in the shed. In fact, her first daughter remains nameless throughout the text, referred to only as Sethe's "crawling already?" baby girl. Since all her other children do have names, and Denver refers to the baby's "given name," the fact that we never learn Sethe's third child's name is the result not of the child's being nameless but rather of a general reluctance or refusal, on the part of the novel's characters and narrator, to speak it. The baby's given name is posited as unspeakable, and its confrontation with, or negotiation into, the realm of language is both violent and violating:

> "For a baby she throws a powerful spell," said Denver.
> "No more powerful than the way I loved her," Sethe answered and there it was again. The welcoming cool of unchiseled headstones; the one she selected to lean against on tiptoe, her knees wide open as any grave. Pink as a fingernail it was, and sprinkled with glittering chips. Ten minutes, he said. You got ten minutes I'll do it for free. (4–5)

It is Sethe's statement about the *way* she loved her baby, an expression so potent that it rivals the ghost's persecution of the inhabitants of 124, that conjures up this moment of "rememory." The inscription on the tombstone is less about the murdered baby than it is about Sethe and her own "rough choice" (180). Hence when the young woman who walks out of the water assumes the name "Beloved" upon her arrival at 124, she embodies the replacement of her own name and identity with the word on the tombstone. In 124 she slowly spells B-E-L-O-V-E-D, identifying herself as a process of inscription (letter by letter) rather than by her given name (52). It is by this process of inscription that Denver recognizes her: "[W]hen she came back I knew who she was too. Not right away, but soon as she spelled her name— *not her given name, but the one Ma'am paid the stonecutter for*—I knew" (208, italics mine).

As the murdered baby's given name is replaced by "the way" Sethe loved ↓ her, Sethe speaks the unspeakable: not by naming that which has no name, but rather by replacing an existing name silenced by a community's reluctance to utter it with an expression of her (Sethe's) personal response to this silencing. Further, Sethe's actions reveal the extent to which *performing* her relation to this silencing—the inscription is not an expression of her love but a description of her loving, the *way* she loved—renders her position vis-à-vis this unspeakability even more complex. The "way" Sethe loved posits her as an active agent, a far more problematic position than that of helpless victim. If we, like Paul D, assume that Sethe "lived with 124 in helpless, apologetic resignation because she had no choice," we, like Paul D, are "wrong" (164). As an active agent with her own disturbing "way" of loving, Sethe's actions challenge the paradoxes stressed by Morrison's critics—presence and absence, memory and forgetting, the unspeakable and speech—by introducing the problematic issues of agency, responsibility, and volition. Sethe assents to and participates in her own violation by the stonecutter: this is prostitution, not a rape.

> Ten minutes for seven letters. With another ten could she have gotten "Dearly" too? She had not thought to ask him and it bothered her still that it might have been possible—that for twenty minutes, a half hour, say, she could have had the whole thing, every word she heard the preacher say at the funeral (and all there was to say, surely) engraved on her baby's headstone: Dearly Beloved. But what she got, settled for, was the one word that mattered. (5)

"The one word that mattered" locates Sethe's own agendas, priorities, and agency at the center of this act of memorialization. Crucial to Sethe's rememory of this moment is her recollection of "every word she had heard the preacher say *at the funeral.*" Sethe never attended her child's funeral, since she was in prison at the time.[8] When wondering why Sethe claims to remember words she hears spoken at the funeral, a ceremony she never attended, we need to keep in mind another ceremony she never attended: a marriage ceremony. Sethe recalls "how bad I felt when I found out there wasn't going to be no [marriage] ceremony, no preacher. Nothing" (58). The words she remembers from the "funeral" is a phrase that commonly opens a marriage ceremony—"Dearly Beloved"—and the merging of two missed ceremonies in Sethe's memory indicates the extent to which it is her own (unconscious?) motives and agendas that dictate her speaking what has been posed by the community to be unspeakable. Thus, when Sethe claims that "Beloved" is "the one word that mattered," begging the question, mattered to whom? the answer is, mattered to Sethe: this word serves as her response to the community that condemned her; it is her own answer to "one more preacher, one more abolitionist and a town full of disgust" (5). Speaking the unspeakable, then, says more about the speaker herself than about what had been rendered unspeakable in the first place—"Dearly Beloved, which is what you are *to* me," Sethe recalls (184)—and Sethe's "answer" to the community, her choice of "the one word that mattered," figures in this scene as an unsettling economy, reflecting commemoration's exacting toll:

> Counting on the stillness of her own soul, she had forgotten the other one: the soul of her baby girl. Who would have thought that a little old baby could harbor so much rage? Rutting among the stones under the eyes of the engraver's son was not enough. Not only did she have to live out her years in a house palsied by the baby's fury at having its throat cut, but those ten minutes she spent pressed up against dawn-colored stone studded with star chips, her knees wide open as the grave, were longer than life, more alive, more pulsating than the baby blood that soaked her fingers like oil. (5)

The act of speaking the unspeakable replaces and effaces what had been determined—overtly or covertly—to be unspeakable in the first place, propelling the speaker into complicity with this silencing, since she is the one replacing and effacing her murdered daughter with the word on the tombstone. It is this complicity that most disturbs her: having to "live out her years in a house palsied by the baby's fury" is, ultimately, less of an ordeal than having to live with the way her acquisition of the engraving on the tombstone, her commemoration of the baby's death, replaced that death with a life defiled and defined by concentric degrees of violation: "those ten minutes . . . were longer than life, more alive, more pulsating than the baby blood that soaked her fingers like oil."

In the context of this complicity, the tension between language and its limits resurfaces. As the inscription becomes less about the nameless baby and more about Sethe and her own motivations and agendas, the engraving's appropriation of the murdered baby's identity is reflected, in Sethe's rememory of the moment, by language's appropriation of perception. Sethe's description of the tombstone moves from simile and adjective ("pink as fingernail" and "glittering chips") to metaphor ("dawn-colored" and "star chips"), as the images of her recollection replace its objects. In this movement from simile to metaphor, from asserting resemblance to creating identity, the figurative language in this scene renders the external world an expression of Sethe's own mind, a translation enacted in the subtle transition from "*any* grave" to "*the* grave" (5).

As Sethe names, unnames, commemorates, forgets, and silences, the fact remains that "Beloved" is not the name of Sethe's murdered baby. It names Sethe's own frustrations and desires, and it is precisely these frustrations and desires that come back to haunt her, rendering language simultaneously superfluous and crucial, and positing the relation between speech and the unspeakable as the crux of the novel. This relation originates in the problematic negotiation in and out of language in the tombstone scene and remains an integral part of the interactions of Beloved, Denver, and Sethe. Denver, fearful of losing Beloved, is "careful to appear uninquisitive about the things she was dying to ask [her]" (119). And Sethe, identifying Beloved as her elder daughter, aligns this recognition with a respite from speech: "Thank God I don't have to rememory or say a thing because you know it. All," thinks Sethe. "I know you don't need me to do it. To tell it or even think over it. You don't have to listen either, if you don't want to" (191, 193). But despite Denver's caution and Sethe's disavowals of the necessity of telling or saying, their deteriorating relationship with Beloved is defined by the inevitability of speech and its attendant destruction: "[E]ven when Beloved was quiet, dreamy, minding her own business, Sethe got her going again. Whispering, muttering some justification, some bit of clarifying information to Beloved to explain what it had been like, and why, and how come" (252).

Sethe's memorialization and Morrison's are, then, very different. In her discussion of "no bench by the road," Morrison posits an absence of memorial spaces that "had to" be addressed by the presence of the book, implicitly situating the literary space of *Beloved* as an arena where absence of physical space can be addressed, but concurrently eliding the uncomfortable negotiations involved in selecting, say, one bench, one tree, one initial (whose?) over another. Absent here are Morrison's own agency and volition, the implications of her own gesture of memorialization that, like Sethe's, silences as it articulates. In other words, while Morrison's description of why the book "had to" exist posits her as responsibly addressing a crucial and painful absence while excluding her from the problematic *performance* of such an address, the fictional depiction of Sethe's performance actively challenges and problematizes such responsibility: speaking what had been determined to be unspeakable propels Sethe into complicity, forcing her into actions that force us to question the uneasy distinctions between presence and absence, memory and forgetting, the unspeakable and speech.

Against the Unspeakable

The violent effacements and appropriations that Sethe performs as she purchases the inscription on the tombstone raise the issue of language, names,
identity, and the complexities of their interactions. The novel is inconclusive
about whether Beloved—the spoken word, its inscription, and its fleshy
manifestation—embodies, expands, or replaces the identity of Sethe's baby
girl, whose own name remains unspeakable. "Beloved, whose birth name
we never learn, takes her identity from the single word on her tombstone
and from the love her mother bears her, the paradox of which is reflected in
the novel's epigraph from Romans," writes Rigney, concluding that "finally,
Beloved has no identity other than that merged with the 'Sixty Million and
more' of the dedication, all those who suffered the outrage of enslavement"
(146). Critics have used the instability of Beloved's identity to reflect on the
inherent insufficiency of language to convey identity, especially in the context of atrocity. "*Who, what is Beloved?*" agonizes James Phelan. "*Yes, Sethe's
murdered daughter. And—or?—a survivor of the Middle Passage.* Labels, not
understanding" (226).

This vexed relation with language informs much critical writing on
Beloved, and what lies beyond language's limits—specifically, silence—
becomes a crucial common denominator for a wide variety of critical approaches to the text. Pérez-Torres writes, "Given sociohistorical conditions
compelling it toward silence, African-American literary production questions not what distinguishes itself from other forms but rather how it manages to speak at all. Language at once masks and reveals the social and political structures from which it arises and which it creates. The link between
language and ideology presents black writers with a quandary: how to speak
when compelled to silence?" ("Between Presence" 179). Dwight McBride
puts it thus: "[T]he language of the African American text itself stands as an
emblem of the Herculean struggle to represent an experience that the language is not intended to accommodate. Such texts constitute the attempt
to write the seemingly unwritable, the unspeakable" ("Speaking" 150). And
Rigney, in an oft-quoted passage, notes:

All of Morrison's works are about silence as well as about language,
whether that silence is metaphysical or physically enforced by cir-
cumstance. All African Americans, like a great many immigrants to

America, write and speak in a language they do not own as theirs. Historically, the dominant culture has enforced black silence through illiteracy, through the metaphoric and the actual insertion of the bit in the
mouth . . . Morrison indicates in each of her novels that images of the
zero, the absence, the silence that is both chosen and enforced, are ideologically and politically revelatory. (142–43)

I quote these critics in order to highlight the central role that language's
limits play in their theories of what constitutes African American identity (a
point to which I will return in the conclusion). Given this central role, the unspeakable facilitates the articulation of an identity that, precisely by its refusal of language, may be imagined as enabling, liberating, positing—to
borrow Henry Louis Gates's terms—a "black self" that is free from the
Western languages that subjugated, enslaved, and effaced it ("Criticism" 7).
Kimberly W. Benston, analyzing this "topos of (un)naming", focuses on
language's power to appropriate, identifying the refusal of the name as a crucial mode of empowerment in slave narratives in particular, and in African
American identity in general: "Language—that fundamental act of organ-
izing the mind's encounter with an experienced world—is propelled by a
rhythm of naming: it is the means by which the mind takes possession of
the named, at once fixing the named as irreversibly Other and representing
it in crystallized isolation from all conditions of externality" (152). Refusing
the name implies significant authority and power, and enables a subjugated
individual to establish an identity separate from the hegemonic discourses
that he or she confronts:

The refusal to be named invokes the power of the Sublime, a transcendent impulse to undo all categories, all metonymies and reifications,
and thrust the self beyond received patterns and relationships into a
stance of unchallenged authority. In short, in its earliest manifestations
the act of unnaming is a means of passing from one mode of representation to another, of breaking the rhetoric and "plot" of influence, of
distinguishing the self from all else. (153)

For Benston, then, "unnaming" forges a self that is imagined as unique,
individual, and grants that self an authority that, precisely by virtue of its
heterogeneity to language, remains "unchallenged": who could articulate

such a challenge? how would such a challenge be worded? By emphasizing the liberatory potential of "unnaming," Benston is positing identity-as-unspeakable as efficacious resistance to subjugation, and unnaming as an empowering assertion of identity and individuality.

But in *Beloved* names, like language, cannot be easily extricated from identity, and Morrison challenges Benston's privileging identity-as-unspeakable as an efficacious response to subjugation. Characters in *Beloved* grapple with the relation of names in particular, and language in general, to subjugation. At the same time, names are crucial both for memory (Sethe says to Stamp Paid, "I wish I knew your name so I could remember you right" [91]) and for community (Sethe recalls her twenty-eight days of unslaved life as "days of company: knowing the names of forty, fifty other Negroes" [95]) and cannot be easily abandoned. Hence the characters in *Beloved* do not easily assume the dubious privilege of "distinguishing the self from all else" (Benston 153), and have little, if any, recourse to the liberatory implications of unnaming and of the notion of identity-as-unspeakable.

Stamp Paid is the only character in the novel who deliberately abandons his slave name, Joshua, and renames himself Stamp Paid, replacing a biblical narrative with an assumption of debtlessness: "he didn't owe anybody anything" (185). But not owing anybody anything "didn't seem much of a way to live and . . . brought him no satisfaction" (185). So Stamp Paid "extended this debtlessness to other people by helping them pay out and off whatever they owed in misery. Beaten runaways? He ferried them and rendered them paid for; gave them their own bill of sale, so to speak." Hence his identity as Stamp Paid resurrects the biblical narrative that he has presumably abandoned—Joshua, too, led the Chosen People (themselves runaway slaves) across the river (the Jordan) and into the (however ironic) Promised Land. Rather than unnaming or renaming, then, it is the *conflation* of the slave name (Joshua) and the free name (Stamp Paid) that enables Stamp Paid to claim a community identity—ironically articulated by the very economy from which he had fled: "[T]he receipt [to their own bill of sale] was a welcome door that he never had to knock on" (185).[9]

Paul D, whose name identifies him as one of a series of Pauls, is plagued by an inability to imagine a self outside slavery, which takes the form of an inability to imagine a self outside language.[10] As a fugitive and an ex-slave, Paul D retains a vexed relation to his manhood, a term conferred by Garner, through most of the text. "Garner called and announced them men—but only on Sweet Home, and by his leave. Was he naming what he saw or creating what he did not?" ruminates Paul D (220). This inability to imagine an identity outside the master's language is itself the condition of the Pauls' enslavement—it prevents Paul D and his brothers from easily acquiescing to Sixo and Halle's escape plan, because the Pauls are literally fettered by words: "Suppose Garner woke up one morning and changed his mind? Took the word away. Would they have run then? And if he didn't, would the Pauls have stayed there all their lives?" (220). This linguistic fettering defines Paul D's life not only as a slave but also as an ex-slave, in the form of his inability to claim a sense of "manhood"—a term that, for him, stands for ontological existence as well as physical performance: "Is that where the manhood lay? In the naming done by a whiteman who was supposed to know?" (125). "Oh, he did manly things, but was that Garner's gift or his own will?" he thinks, wondering further, "Did a whiteman saying it make it so?" (220).

It is Baby Suggs, though, who performs the most complex negotiation of names, identity, and language, addressing their implications for selfhood—both physical and psychic. As Baby Suggs, borne across the border by Mr. Garner, moves from servitude to freedom, the necessary redefinition of self that such movement requires is introduced precisely by the issue of her name:

> Baby Suggs thought it was a good time to ask him something she had long wanted to know.
> "Mr. Garner," she said, "why you all call me Jenny?"
> "'Cause that what's on your sales ticket, gal. Ain't that your name? What you call yourself?"
> "Nothing," she said, "I don't call myself nothing."
> Mr. Garner went red with laughter. "When I took you out of Carolina, Whitlow called you Jenny and Jenny Whitlow is what his bill said. Didn't he call you Jenny?"
> "No, sir. If he did I didn't hear it."
> "What did you answer to?"
> "Anything, but Suggs is what my husband name."
> "You got married, Jenny? I didn't know it."
> "Manner of speaking."
> "You know where he is, this husband?"
> "No, sir."

Against the Unspeakable

"Is that Halle's daddy?"

"No, sir."

"Why you call him Suggs, then? His bill of sale says Whitlow too, just like yours."

"Suggs is my name, sir. From my husband. He didn't call me Jenny."

"What he call you?"

"Baby." (142)

With the distinction between what she calls herself ("I don't call myself nothing"; I answer to "anything") and her name ("Suggs is my name, sir. From my husband."), Baby Suggs articulates slavery's violent erasure of individual identity, on the one hand, and the complexities of reclaiming that identity, on the other. Hence she qualifies the term "marriage," a social structure from which she, as a slave, was excluded, as (merely) a "manner of speaking," though she retains the word "husband" when presenting this relationship to her former owner.[11]

Like Stamp Paid, who identifies himself as debtlessness and, in order to establish himself in a community, extends this self-definition to the services he renders the community, Baby Suggs's identity and the function she performs for and within this community are indistinguishable: "Baby Suggs, holy, loved, cautioned, fed, chastised and soothed" (87) mingles noun, verb, and adjective. Unlike Stamp Paid, though, Baby Suggs does not attempt to unname herself. When she rejects "some bill-of-sale name," she is not doing so to establish an individual identity separate from slavery, figuratively—as Paul D imagines—sloughing off language's shackles; rather, she recognizes herself as a linguistic entity, one who exists in terms of being called and claimed by a predominantly linguistic community: "Baby Suggs was all she had left of the 'husband' she claimed. . . . Now how could he find or hear tell of her if she was calling herself some bill-of-sale name?" (141). It is this community formed by call, by claim, and by hearing tell that excludes the wandering loneliness of the epilogue: "[E]veryone knew what she was called, but nobody anywhere knew her name. Disremembered and unaccounted for, she cannot be lost because no one is looking for her, and even if they were, how can they call her if they don't know her name? Although she has claim, she is not claimed" (274).[12]

In *Beloved*, "calling" is a physical act of articulation that merges identity (who is being called), language (her name), and community (that which "claims"). Thus calling—especially in the context of its origin in the oral tradition of Call-and-Response[13]—merges linguistic and physical performance. It is Baby Suggs's performance in the Clearing, where she Calls and speaks the Word, that enables Sethe, together with the other ex- or fugitive slaves, to "claim herself": "Freeing yourself was one thing; claiming ownership of that freed self was another" (95). Here Sethe's psychic claim of her "freed self" will be sadly qualified by Schoolteacher, who enters 124 in order to physically claim Sethe's "freed self" under the Fugitive Slave law.

Baby Suggs's Call, and the vision of self-claim that she articulates, introduce physical exigencies into the work of language: self-claim can only exist in a "here" that is not "yonder" ("Here . . . in this here place, we flesh. . . . Yonder they do not love your flesh. They despise it" [88]) and is informed by the necessary distinction of "we" from "they." The importance of such physical exigencies becomes clear in the explicitly spatial violation that the white men's trespassing at 124 performs. Significantly, it is this spatial violation, rather than Sethe's infanticide, that Baby Suggs stresses to Stamp Paid as they discuss why, as Stamp Paid puts it, she "quit the Word":

> "You saying the whitefolks won? That what you saying?"
> "I'm saying they came in my yard."
> "You saying nothing counts."
> "I'm saying they came in my yard."
> "Sethe's the one did it."
> "And if she hadn't?"
> "You saying God give up? Nothing left for us but pour out our own blood?"
> "I'm saying they came in my yard." (179)

Baby Suggs's emphasis on this *spatial* trespass indicates that the work of language in self-articulation is not itself sufficient for a community that requires space, time, and bodily integrity for the articulation of identity. Gates notes that "to think oneself free simply because one can claim—can utter—the negation of an assertion is not to think deeply enough. . . . It is to take the terms of one's assertion from a discourse determined by an Other" (7), and Kathleen Brogan adds that the "community's ability to reject the master's language . . . provides no model for speaking the unspeakable" (87). But "discourse," "utterance," "language," and "speaking" are complicated in *Be-*

loved by the exigencies of space and place, where physical trespass ("they came in my yard") is equally a psychic one, a violation not only of the victim's identity but of her ethical integrity and her potential for agency. Stamp Paid realizes, too late, why Baby Suggs abandoned the Clearing: "The heart that pumped out love, the mouth that spoke the Word, didn't count. They came in her yard anyway and she could not approve or condemn Sethe's rough choice. One or the other might have saved her, but beaten up by the claims of both, she went to bed" (180).

Language's complicity with subjugation has been well noted by *Beloved's* critics. Brogan writes that in *Beloved* "language itself has in a sense been sullied by its disastrous uses and has become so intertwined with violence that the creation of a counternarrative to white domination is not, at this point, fully conceivable for the novel's characters," adding that "*Beloved* works to detach writing from this appropriation of black bodies, while at the same time dramatizing how difficult it is to redeem a language so deeply implicated in a history of oppression" (87). But Brogan's assumption that writing can be detached from its appropriation of black bodies somewhat more successfully than language can be detached from oppression does not sufficiently take into account that bodies, too, can be complicit in language and in history. In *Beloved* it is the body, marked by slavery, that articulates language's complicity with oppression. Baby Suggs's colloquial speech—"in this here place, we flesh"—is informed by the crucial absence of the ontological verb "are," linguistically fusing body ("flesh") to community ("we"), and Baby Suggs ends her sermon by performing the identity of body, community, and speech: "Saying no more, she stood up then and danced with her twisted hip the rest of what her heart had to say while the others opened their mouths and gave her the music" (89).

Benston's notion of a free, autonomous identity that is capable of distinguishing itself from language's appropriation is, then, strongly qualified in *Beloved,* not only by the necessity of being called and claimed by a community, but by the inextricability of the slave's body and slavery's discourse—most crucially for slave women like Sethe, Sethe's Ma'am, and Baby Suggs, whose children were considered the slave owners' property. Sethe recalls that as a slave in Kentucky "maybe I couldn't love em [her children] proper . . . because they weren't mine to love" (162). Sethe's term "love em proper" reflects the difficulty of loving property—bodies that belong to someone else. Further, as property that produces more property, the slave woman's body becomes the means by which the institution of slavery is perpetuated and maintained—both physically and discursively—as the slave woman is forced into complicity with her own subjugation. When Sethe mourns to Paul D, "He couldn't have done it if I hadn't made the ink," she is painfully aware of how her physical subjugation perpetuates the subjugating discourse of slavery, grotesquely figured by the recurring image of the schoolteacher's nephews suckling her as he documents the scene "in ink she herself had made" (98).

In stark contrast to much of the slave-narrative genre, in which the acquisition of literacy, the production of texts, and the power of speech are figured as powerfully liberating forces, words offer no such recourse in *Beloved,* especially for the female characters, whose bodies as well as their language are appropriated by slavery's pervasive and all-encompassing discourse—both material and immaterial. While names can be changed, assumed, relinquished, called, claimed, and reclaimed, an appropriated body can claim no identity other than its own appropriation. Sethe recalls that her mother "had the bit so many times she smiled. When she wasn't smiling she smiled, and I never saw her own smile" (203). Sethe identifies her mother's disfigured face with the fake smiles of the slaughterhouse prostitutes: "They said it was the bit that made her smile when she didn't want to. Like the Saturday girls working the slaughterhouse yard" (203). Sethe's replacement of her murdered daughter's name with the word on the headstone reenacts this appropriation: "Working a pig yard. That has got to be something for a woman to do, and I got close to it myself when I got out of jail and bought, so to speak, your name" (204), and while Sethe describes herself as "able to smile on my own like now when I think about you," Beloved has a "smile . . . under her chin" (239) where Sethe drew the handsaw. While obscuring identity and expression, then, the appropriated body remains identity's only expression, and the disembodied voice of the middle section expresses and identifies itself as appropriation: "her smiling face is the place for me   it is the face I lost   she is my face smiling at me" (213).

This interrelation of a complicit speech with a complicit body both invites intimacy and renders it unsustainable. Sethe's mother identifies herself by her brand but slaps Sethe's face when Sethe replies, "mark the mark on me too" (61), and Sethe's own "mark" initially attracts and then repels Paul D. Finally, Baby Suggs, who "speaks" by dancing with her twisted hip, presents a

Against the Unspeakable

vision of community that is irrevocably marked by the bodily violation that is its history. Perhaps it is Baby Suggs's suspicion that her words, like her body, cannot be distinguished from this violation that causes her to couch her physical abandonment of the Clearing and her withdrawal from the community in terms of speech's betrayal: "Baby Suggs, holy, proved herself a liar . . . Baby Suggs, holy, believed she had lied" (89).

Not a Story to Pass On

The characters' inability to extricate language—and its attendant complicity with subjugation—from their own bodies and actions extends to their rhetorical performance of storytelling by which the narrative unfolds. Speaking, telling, and passing on stories are crucial for the characters in *Beloved*. And yet, the traumatic experiences of slavery's survivors curtails this storytelling. "One of *Beloved*'s strengths lies in Morrison's powerfully compelling representation of the tortured internal world of those traumatized by slavery," writes Brogan (79), and the many stories Sethe tells in the course of the novel are abruptly curtailed by the limits of language associated with traumatic experience. Significantly, these limits are expressed in physical and spatial terms: "the single slow blink of the eyes; the bottom lip sliding up slowly to cover the top; and then a nostril sigh, like the snuff of a candle flame—signs that Sethe had reached the point beyond which she would not go" (37). For Sethe and Paul D, whose relationship to their past and to each other determines the narrative's momentum, speaking the unspeakable has uncomfortable implications for their physical as well as their psychic integrity—implications that propel them both toward and away from each other, toward and away from language, toward and away from complicity, toward and away from silence.

Early in the novel, life under slavery is determined to be unspeakable—a point on which Sethe and Baby Suggs "had agreed *without saying so*" (58; emphasis mine). Sethe and Baby Suggs enter into a conspiracy of silence, the articulation of which is unbearable, but which is itself crucial for "the day's serious work of beating back the past" (73). Thus throughout *Beloved*, Sethe's stories are informed as much by her silence as they are by her speech. But the possibility of a future, of a community beyond the haunted realm of 124, and of "some kind of tomorrow" (273) propels Sethe and Paul D to try to render their traumatic experiences in words.

Sethe envisions her future with Paul D in terms of a single story, and sharing that story involves speaking their shared past to themselves and to each other: "Her story was bearable because it was his as well—*to tell, to refine and tell again,*" Sethe thinks (99; emphasis mine). She perceives her future with Paul D as a process of learning to speak to each other what, at present, they both find unspeakable: "The things neither knew about the other—the things neither had word-shapes for—well, it would come in time: where they led him off to sucking iron; the perfect death of her crawling-already? baby" (99). Sethe's vision of a community and of a future depends, then, on rendering their respective traumas as stories to tell and to retell. In the course of the novel, however, Sethe's and Paul D's attempts to speak about their respective traumas, to tell "the things neither had word-shapes for," forces the realization of complicity, a realization that drives them apart, rather than together.

For Paul D, "where they led him off to sucking iron" marks the limit of what he can tell Sethe. Significantly, what is unspeakable for Paul D is not what happened to him in Alfred, Georgia, but rather his response to it—the absence of his "red heart":

Paul D had only begun, what he was telling her was only the beginning when her fingers on his knee, soft and reassuring, stopped him. Just as well. Just as well. Saying more might push them both to a place they couldn't get back from. He would keep the rest where it belonged: in that tobacco tin buried in his chest where a red heart used to be. Its lid rusted shut. He would not pry it loose now in front of this sweet sturdy woman, for if she got a whiff of the contents it would shame him. And it would hurt her to know that there was no red heart bright as Mister's comb beating in him. (73)

In the shed behind 124, Beloved entreats Paul D to "touch me on the inside part and call me my name" (116), urging Paul D to confront the "shame" of his heart's absence by opening that tobacco tin and, by calling her, to perform the inseparability of a history of atrocity from his own identity: "She [Beloved] reminds me of something," Paul D confesses to Stamp Paid. "Something, look like, I'm supposed to remember" (234). Paul D, fearing precisely that memory and the implications of such a call, rejects Beloved: "If he trembled like Lot's wife and felt some womanish need to see the nature of the sin behind him; feel a sympathy, perhaps, for the cursing cursed, or want to hold it in his arms out of respect for the connection between them, he too would be lost" (117). When Beloved begs him to "please call it [my name], I'll go if you call it," he says "Beloved," but she does not go.

Regardless of whether Beloved is, in fact, her name, what Paul D "said" is ultimately less important than the fact that she responds to a *call*. Whatever "it" refers to (the girl, the ghost, the word on the tombstone, the murdered baby with its "spite") is rendered irrelevant in light of the act of calling that is—as Baby Suggs's Call in the Clearing demonstrates—itself a physical performance that generates community and enables self-claim. In the context of this performance, the notion of language's limits is irrelevant. Therefore, if Paul D's initial investment in the limits of language had presumed that silence safeguards from shame, that what he doesn't *hear* is what he doesn't *know* ("She moved closer with a footfall *he didn't hear* and *he didn't hear* the whisper that the flakes of rust made either as they fell away from the seams of his tobacco tin. So when the lid gave *he didn't know* it" [117; emphasis mine]), the call that Beloved responds to removes this safeguard. Thus, when Paul D reaches that "inside part" that is both Beloved's and his own, inside and outside, body and word, dream and reality merge: "What he knew was that when he reached the inside part he was saying, 'Red heart. Red heart,' over and over again. Softly and then so loud it woke Denver, then Paul D himself. 'Red heart. Red heart. Red heart'" (117).

It is this merging of speech with action, and the subsequent identification of body with word, that force Paul D to question his manhood, its relation to language, and the extent to which it is a word that may or may not perform identity on his body: "Was that it? Is that where the manhood lay? In the naming done by a whiteman who was supposed to know?" he wonders. Paul D's manhood is conferred linguistically—an act of naming—but is challenged as he realizes that, like a slave woman, the integrity of his body is subject to violation: "If schoolteacher was right [that slaves are not men] it explained how he had come to be a rag doll—picked up and put back down anywhere any time by a girl young enough to be his daughter. Fucking her when he was convinced he didn't want to" (126). Paul D's vexed relation with his manhood, a "name" conferred and withheld by Garner (his figurative father) and ultimately challenged by "a girl young enough to be his daughter," is the reason he cannot confess his sexual relationship with Beloved to Sethe: "He could not say to this women who did not squint in the wind, 'I am not a man'" (129). Rather than confess his doubts about his manhood, he suggests inscribing ("documenting") his manhood onto Sethe: "I want you pregnant, Sethe. Would you do that for me?" he asks her, realizing that "it was a solution: a way to hold on to her, document his manhood and break out of the girl's spell—all in one" (128).

As Sethe attempts to tell Paul D about the death of her baby girl, to speak what is, to her, unspeakable, she is keenly aware of language's inability to convey what she is trying to say: "[S]he knew that the words she did not understand hadn't any more power than she had to explain" (161). Sethe posits her infanticide within the same conspiracy of silence that enabled her and Baby Suggs to "[beat] back the past": "Sethe knew that the circle she was making around the room, him, the subject, would remain one. That she could never close in, pin it down for anybody who had to ask. If they didn't get it right off—she could never explain" (163). In this way Sethe assumes that only in acquiescence to the event's unspeakability can true understanding occur. The very attempt to speak or to explain renders the subject unspeakable.

In her discussion of *Beloved,* Sally Keenan points to "a remarkable absence of an adequate discourse that could address slave women's forms of resistance to slavery on the one hand and the meanings women attached to motherhood within slavery on the other" (50). Both issues are central to the novel, where motherhood, co-opted by slavery, becomes the site of both resistance and complicity. Both Sethe and her mother destroy their children "without names," and Ella "delivered, but would not nurse, a hairy white thing, fathered by 'the lowest yet'" (259). Sethe's version of mother love forces the conflation of identity and appropriation—"when I tell you you mine, I also mean I'm yours. I wouldn't draw breath without my children" (203)—and it is this conflation that determines her act of infanticide: "She just flew. Collected every bit of life she had made, *all the parts of her* that were precious and fine and beautiful, and carried, pushed, dragged them through the veil, out, away, over there where no one could hurt them. Over there. Outside this place, where they would be safe" (163; emphasis mine). Brogan notes that this murder "'repeats' the original trauma of slave experience in two fundamental ways: in its violence against blacks and in the magnitude of Sethe's claim to own, and therefore to have the right to dispose of, her children,"[14] adding that it is "this usurpation of the master's right to own and destroy" that "scares" Paul D (75). But I would add that this repetition of a traumatic experience is, in its murderous consequences, equally a complicit

Against the Unspeakable

(re)enactment of slavery's destruction. Finally, it is Sethe's love and the re-sistance it dictates that confirm the Sheriff's racist assumptions: "[A]ll testi-mony," he thinks, "to the results of a little so-called freedom imposed on people who needed every care and guidance in the world to keep them from the cannibal life they preferred" (151).[15]

Rather than attempting to tell Paul D her story—informed, as it is, by multiple levels of complicity—Sethe performs multiple circles around the story as well as around the room, physically demarcating the space of the unspeakable. Recognizing that her circling, literal and figurative, echoes her inability to "close in, pin it down" (163), she pauses to concentrate on the fence that used to encircle the yard. The fence is a border that separates outside from inside, and while it can be crossed ("there was a gate that someone was always latching and unlatching in the time when 124 was busy as a way station" [163]), it operates as a line distinguishing "124" from "not-124"; and the white men's trespasses are the beginning of a series of boundary disruptions that culminate in Sethe's murder of her baby. Sethe's memory re-creates these disruptions: "When she got back from the jail house, she was glad the fence was gone. That's where they had hitched their horses—where she saw, floating above the railing as she squatted in the gar-den, schoolteacher's hat. By the time she faced him, looked him dead in the eye, she had something in her arms that stopped him in his tracks. He took a backward step with each jump of the baby heart until finally there were none" (163–64).

It is Sethe's *act*, rather than anything she can *say*, that disrupts the discourse that authorized the power balance between herself and School-teacher: "she had something in her arms that stopped him in his tracks." These disruptions, while beyond Sethe's ability to articulate, are performed by the language employed to describe them: Schoolteacher's receding steps and the baby's dying merge; "there were none" can refer equally to the back-ward steps and to the baby's heartbeats, lending special weight to Sethe's gaze as she looks Schoolteacher "dead in the eye."

At the core of this multiple disruption of boundaries, Sethe tries, to the best of her ability, to put her act into words: "'I stopped him,' she said, star-ing at the place where the fence used to be. 'I took and put my babies where they'd be safe'" (164). Displacing what is, for her, unspeakable into its pur-pose and result, Sethe lends her actions a figurative tone that, by its multiple plays on the word "safe," dissolves the referential power of language, both forcing and enforcing the limits of speech as an adequate form of communication. The word "safe" has been destabilized; we, like Paul D, no longer know what it means: "This here Sethe," thinks Paul D, "talked about love like any other woman; talked about baby clothes like any other woman, but what she meant could cleave the bone. This here Sethe talked about safety with a handsaw" (164).

This violation of description with performance, in the discrepancy between words and what they mean, emphasizes, like Beloved's actions in the shed, language's inadequacy and dissolves the distinction between the speakable and the unspeakable in the form of a violation of presence with absence, present with past, reality with fantasy. As Sethe speaks these words, she "[stares] at the place where the fence used to be," evoking, by her gaze, this dissolution of dichotomies. Staring at where the fence used to be calls up the fence's presence while emphasizing its absence. It dissolves the border between what is there and what is not. It injects the present with the past, violates reality with fantasy. Finally, it radically challenges the possibility of a coherent identity that can be defined in the context of an identifiable community or a comprehensible language, a challenge demonstrated by this section's deterioration of reference: the Sethe Paul D "knew" in the past is rendered unrecognizable by the present, "new" Sethe—a Sethe not defined in reference to Halle (presumably, for Paul D, a known quantity), but rather a Sethe external to any and all referential contexts: "The prickly, mean-eyed Sweet Home girl he knew as Halle's girl was obedient (like Halle), shy (like Halle), and work-crazy (like Halle)," thinks Paul D. "This here Sethe was new. . . . This here new Sethe didn't know where the world stopped and she began" (164).

Paul D's response to "this here new Sethe," and to the multiple dissolution of coherence that her act realizes and forces him to realize, is to evoke the animalistic discourse that is so poignant an instrument of racial subjection: "You got two feet, Sethe, not four," he says (165). By doing so, he aligns himself with Schoolteacher, whose instructions to "put her human characteristics on the left; her animal ones on the right" (193) propelled Sethe to get her children away from Sweet Home at any cost, and propelled her to murder them rather than send them back: "[N]o one, nobody on this earth, would list her daughter's characteristics on the animal side of the paper. No. Oh no" (251). Paul D implicates Sethe with this rhetoric, suggesting that she cannot imagine an "other way" (165).

Against the Unspeakable

Significantly, Paul D's accusation of Sethe's complicity is propelled precisely by a disturbing sense of his own: "Later he would wonder what made him say it. The calves of his youth? or the conviction that he was being observed through the ceiling? How fast he had moved from his shame to hers. From his cold-house secret to her too-thick love" (165). This mutual sense of complicity forces silence between them—"right then a forest sprang up between them, trackless and quiet" (165)—and their mutual reluctance to speak the word "goodbye" reinforces their mutual retreat from language. Paul D, unwilling to hurt Sethe further by telling her he is leaving, merely informs her he will be late getting back; Sethe, rueful and amused by his strategy, nonetheless acquiesces to his retreat from her story as well as from her self, and collaborates with him in the silent "forest" that separates the two: "'So long,' she murmured from the far side of the trees" (165).

Paul D and Sethe's reunion in the novel's penultimate scene takes the form of reconciling themselves to the silences that Sethe had been so sure "word-shapes" (99) would be found for. The future envisioned here is one sustained by maintaining silence, rather than trying to speak the unspeakable. But after the exorcism of Beloved, Paul D and Sethe are left in very different relations to language, identity, and community. On his way to 124, Paul D encounters Denver, who is looking forward to a future, and he deliberately refrains from warning her that her future may be contaminated by his past: "When he asked her if they treated her all right over there, she said more than all right. Miss Bodwin taught her stuff. He asked her what stuff and she laughed and said book stuff. 'She says I might go to Oberlin. She's experimenting on me.' *And he didn't say,* 'Watch out. Watch out. Nothing in the world more dangerous than a white schoolteacher'" (266; emphasis mine).

Paul D's ability to choose silence, to consciously refrain from warning Denver, embodies his vision of "some kind of tomorrow" with Sethe (273), a future that is made possible through silence, not speech. Looking at Sethe, he relocates his manhood in Sethe's *silence* about his "neck jewelry" (273)— "she never mentioned or looked at it, so he did not have to feel the shame of being collared like a beast. Only this woman Sethe could have left him his manhood like that" (273). For Paul D, then, silence not only relieves him of the complex relationship of his masculinity to speech but also relieves him of his "shame." It is through this silence, rather than speech and its attendant complicity, that Paul D envisions his future with Sethe: rather than telling and retelling a shared story, "he wants to put his story *next to* hers" (273; emphasis mine).

But Paul D's assumption that both he and Sethe possess a story that can be placed in proximity disregards Sethe's profound sense of loss for both her mother and her child, each of whom can be the referent for "she left me," and "she was my best thing" (272). Not only does this loss of her "best thing," and hence of a significant part of herself, result in a fractured subjectivity whose ability to tell or to possess a "story" is highly questionable; it also reinforces Sethe's exclusion from stories and from the ability to tell and retell that—figured by Baby Sugg's Call in the Clearing—perform community in *Beloved*. Earlier in the novel, Sethe recalled the death of her mother, an abandonment couched as an exclusion from speech, to which she can return only when she sees Halle, her children's father: "Nan snatched me back," she recalls, "before I could check for the sign. It was her all right, but for a long time I didn't believe it. *I looked everywhere for that hat. Stuttered after that. Didn't stop it till I saw Halle*" (201; emphasis mine). Looking at Paul D, Sethe recalls this exclusion ("her ma'am had hurt her feelings and she couldn't find her hat anywhere"), so that when she confesses that "she left me . . . she was my best thing," the conflation of her mother and her daughter as possible referents for "she" posits Sethe herself, as mother and daughter, the embodiment of that abandonment, both physical and linguistic. Hence Sethe does not possess the agency, as Paul D does, to silence the past by refraining from speech, nor can she locate her identity in her equally fractured body: "There's nothing to rub now and no reason to. Nothing left to bathe" (272). Instead, she can only articulate the forced complicity that has destroyed her: "I made the ink, Paul D. He couldn't have done it if I hadn't made the ink," she tells him (271). It is this complicity that forces a fragmentation of her identity—both physical ("if he bathes her in sections, will the parts hold?" [272]) and, in light of the function stories hold in creating identity in *Beloved*, linguistic: when Paul D assures her that "you your best thing, Sethe. You are" (273) she can only respond by questioning both affirmations. "Me? Me?" she stutters (273), doubtful not only that she is her own "best thing" but also whether she can lay claim to the ontological verb "are," a verb that, like the adjective "Beloved," lies abandoned, without a subject: an orphaned part of speech.[16]

In light of the multiple silencings and exclusions forced on Sethe, Paul D's urging for "some kind of tomorrow" with her is disquieting. Paul D

Against the Unspeakable

locates his relationship to Sethe in terms of her function in establishing his own identity and coherence: recalling Sixo's description of the Thirty-Mile Woman, Paul D thinks of Sethe, "She is a friend of my mind. She gather me, man. The pieces I am, she gather them and give them back to me in all the right order. It's good, you know, when you got a woman who is a friend of your mind" (272–73). But in light of Sethe's forced complicity and her subsequent fragmentation and exclusion from coherence, the "tomorrow" Paul D envisions takes the form of identity that is structured through and against the silencing of complicity by the unspeakable.

Hence it is not surprising that *Beloved*'s epilogue enacts a gradual forgetting and silencing in terms of a movement out of language and, specifically, of speech: "It took longer for those who had spoken to her, lived with her, fallen in love with her, to forget, until they realized they couldn't remember or repeat *a single thing she said,* and began to believe that, other than what they themselves were thinking, *she hadn't said anything at all.* So, in the end, they forgot her too" [274; emphasis mine]. The forgetting is further reiterated by the repetition of "not a story to pass on" (274–75). But the final word of the novel is posited as a gesture of naming what has been excluded from language, speaking what has been deliberately cast as unspeakable: the last word of the novel is its title, "Beloved" (275). Since her violent negotiation into language in the opening of the novel, Beloved performs complicity: brought into being by the multiple violations that Sethe endures and performs as she purchases the name on the gravestone, she is the nameless child that Sethe, like her Ma'am, "threw away" (62) in an act that justified their subjugation even as they resisted it (151). Beloved embodies "the black and angry dead" (198) that return to wreck havoc on the living and force back into speech what Sethe feels she "don't have to explain" (200); the "cursing cursed" (117) that Paul D both fears and, against his will, embraces; the young girl who moved Paul D "like a rag doll" (221), forcing him to radically revaluate his linguistic identity (220–21), and whose gaze through the ceiling drove him to "[count] Sethe's feet and [leave] without saying goodbye" (189). When this nameless "she" has been "quickly and deliberately" forgotten (274), the narrator of the epilogue speaks her name as a response to this willed silencing.

The gentle gesture of commemoration that ends the novel—"Beloved"—is, then, both the narrator's eloquent evocation of the "disremembered and unaccounted for" (274) and an equally eloquent restating of the complicity forced on the characters by Beloved's presence in the novel. As if reflecting the uneasy tension between the compulsion to speak and the equally compelling need to remain silent, the double movement of this final section (the brief paragraphs that describe a gradual process of forgetting, punctuated with the staccato "not a story to pass on") enacts a simultaneous movement away from language and toward it. The narrative traces a process of forgetting from speech ("they couldn't remember or repeat a single thing she said") to image ("Sometimes the photograph of a close friend or relative— looked at too long—shifts") to the physical world ("Down by the stream in back of 124 her footprints come and go . . . by and by all trace is gone"), and ends with a poetic disintegration into the elements of earth, wind, water: "The rest is weather. Not the breath of the disremembered and unaccounted for, but wind in the eaves, or spring ice thawing too quickly. Just weather" (275). Punctuating this narrative of forgetting is the movement from "*It* was not a story to pass on" to "*This* is not a story to pass on" and finally, "Beloved." In this movement from the unstable referent of "it" to the more immediate referent of "this" and finally into the presence of articulation, "Beloved" emerges precisely at the moment of memory's (literal) decomposition. "Beloved," then, both names the embodiment of the unspeakable who performs language's complicity with atrocity and is itself a literal performance of the inextricability of memory from forgetting, absence from presence, language from silence, the unspeakable from speech.

Call Them My People

My emphasis thus far has been on the extent to which the characters' speech and their bodies are enmeshed in complicity, so much so that slavery's survivors cannot articulate an identity, construct a community, tell a story, or remember a past without implicating themselves in the problematic ramifications of such articulations. This complicity dissolves the distinction between speech and the unspeakable by introducing agency and volition into language and its limits; speaking the unspeakable is, for the characters in the novel, a *performance* of identity, of community, of remembering, and of forgetting—a performance that culminates in the novel's final word, which is also its title. Given that *Beloved* is consistently read as itself precisely such a performance, we need to ask: if we eschew the paradoxes of presence and absence, memory and forgetting, speech and the unspeakable, what kind of readings does this texture of complicity produce?

In her widely acclaimed and oft-quoted Tanner Lecture, "Unspeakable Things Unspoken: The Afro-American Presence in American Literature," Morrison wields the unspeakable to perform a specific function for African American identity in particular, and U.S. cultural identity in general. For Morrison, race (specifically blackness) lies at the core of American cultural identity: its presence in U.S. ideology informs and determines American literature and, hence, America's national character. Describing "race" as "a virtually unspeakable thing" (3), she urges "the examination and re-interpretation of the American canon, the founding nineteenth-century works, for the 'unspeakable things unspoken'; for the ways in which the presence of Afro-Americans has shaped the choices, the language, the structure—the meaning of so much American literature" (11). Morrison never explains just what it is about race that makes it unspeakable; rather, race's absence from the Western canon is, for her, proof that race was unspeakable for writers like Melville, Hawthorne, and Poe. Thus, in a manner similar to her dismissal of any existing memorials in "no bench by the road," her statement about race's absence serves simultaneously as both the underlying assumption of, and evidence for, its unspeakability.

The phrase that lends the Tanner Lecture its title, "unspeakable things unspoken," is taken from *Beloved*'s poetic middle section, a section that Deborah Horwitz describes as "[communicating] what may at first appear to be an unintelligible experience, a story of images which the reader must grope and finally fail to figure out" (98). Critics have identified this section as a reference to the Middle Passage, and its deliberate linguistic opacity performs the same unspeakability that Morrison evoked by dedicating the novel to "sixty million and more." When the Middle Passage is the origin of African American identity,[17] the assumption of its unspeakability posits this identity as the product of an unspeakable atrocity. Race, slavery, and African American identity become unspeakable absences and silences that inform the United States' national community and its literary canon, and the ethical imperative presented by the unspeakable is further presented to the history and literature of the United States. Further, this phrase subtly situates *Beloved* (from which the phrase "unspeakable things unspoken" is drawn) as the crucible through which the unspeakable and its implications for identity are forged. Finally, describing African American identity as unspeakable enables Morrison herself to maintain a political position that cannot be interrogated or censured, just as the figure of "sixty million and more" enabled her to posit herself as ethically invested in the principle of inclusiveness over and above the notion of historical accuracy.

What are the implications of defining a national literature in terms of an explicit engagement with the unspeakable? In "'You Who Never Was There': Slavery and the New Historicism—Deconstruction and the Holocaust," Walter Benn Michaels discusses the role of memory in the construction of history. Citing Schlesinger's observation of the analogy of history and memory in the constitution of identity—memory is the core of individual identity; hence national memory is the core of national identity[18]—he expands this observation to history's identification with, and as, memory: "Without the idea of a history that is remembered or forgotten—not merely learned or unlearned—the events of the past can have only a limited relevance to the present, providing us at most with causal accounts of how things have come to be the way they are, at least with objects of antiquarian interest. It is only when it's reimagined as the fabric of our own experience that the past can become the key to our own identity" (188).

Beloved enables the construction of this collective memory. In "setting out to remember the 'disremembered,'" says Michaels, the novel "redescribes something we have never known as something we have forgotten and thus makes the historical past a part of our own experience" (187). But his concept of "redescribing" that which has not been experienced in such a way as to render it part of a collective memory is somewhat troubling when what has not been experienced is assumed to be unspeakable: just what, then, was initially described and is, now, *re*described? Was the object of the initial description presumed to be unspeakable, and if so, how is the unspeakable to be *re*described? And how is this redescription of the unspeakable supposed to enter into national memory?

Many critical readings of *Beloved* have echoed the association of psychic memory with national memory by reading the novel's structure in terms of the psychic operation of trauma. The text's repetitions, its alinearity, and its literal and figurative "circling" around the linguistically impenetrable "Middle Passage" section are presumed to reflect what Brogan identifies as "a straining toward a narrative ordering of the past that is repeatedly thwarted by the unspeakable nature of the events the telling would orga-

Against the Unspeakable

nize" (77). Thus the characters' psychic limits are performed linguistically by the novel's middle section, a section characterized by physical and psychic fragmentation ("I am going to be in pieces" [212]), syntactic dislocation ("he hurts where I sleep" [212]), and an emphasis on the limits of speech ("how can I say things which are pictures" [210]). Further, the repetition of "you are mine" reflects how Beloved, embodiment of this unspeakability, is "claimed" by the novel's characters:

Beloved
You are my sister
You are my daughter
You are my face; you are me
I have found you again; you have come back to me
You are my Beloved
You are mine
You are mine
You are mine (216)

But it is crucial to distinguish the fictional characters' traumatic experiences in Beloved from the assumption that the novel itself is an expression of a traumatized collective psyche (what black people, white people, Morrison, and her interlocutor "don't want to remember") that performs or invites identity. To forget this distinction is to conflate the characters' trauma with the rhetorical structure of trauma, or to confuse an unspeakable experience with an evocation of the unspeakable.[19] McKay, for example, writes that "Morrison faces the challenge of transforming Sethe's 'rememories' of a dreadful past into a discourse shaped by her own narrativity. For both, the question becomes: how does one, from a cluster of images (rememories), create history that represents the unspeakable and unspoken in narrative?" (15; emphasis mine). By casting the matter in this fashion, McKay effaces the many differences between Morrison's and Sethe's relation to slavery by locating both in the inaccessible realm of the "unspeakable"; more significantly, it effaces the distinction between Morrison's rhetorical construction of slavery's unspeakability, on the one hand, and Sethe's very different inability to address the traumatic events in her past, on the other.

This conflation of the characters' traumatic experiences with the author's literary rendition of these experiences is reiterated by critical readings of

Beloved that posit the novel as an invitation for all readers, white as well as black, to "claim" Beloved, to assume the burden of this traumatic memory. Yvonne Atkinson says that "Morrison is teaching the reader how to hear these unspeakable stories. . . . This process moves the reader away from the role of passive observer into the role of meaning-maker within the text" (250), and concludes that "the novel creates a place to explore and release the emotions evoked by the stories being told, and it can create a sense of community between the characters of *Beloved* and the novel's readers" (258). "'Beloved,'" states Phelan, "signals the return of the repressed. Not just ineradicably there underneath our history, she—and all those she stands for—are now produced for our contemplation and are what this narrative leaves us with" (239). Marilyn Sanders Mobley writes that "Morrison uses the trope of memory to revise the genre of the slave narrative and thereby to make the slave experience it inscribes more accessible to contemporary readers . . . by so doing, she seeks to make slavery accessible to readers for whom slavery is not a memory, but a remote historical fact to be ignored, repressed or forgotten" (191).

In the Tanner Lecture, Morrison locates her cultural specificity in her writing—specifically, the in medias res quality of her opening sentences that disorient the reader, confronting him or her with the powerful presence of what is left out. Opening *Beloved* with numerals rather than words, says Morrison, serves the purpose of making the reader feel "snatched, yanked, thrown into an environment completely foreign. . . . Snatched just as the slaves were from one place to another, from any place to another, without preparation and without defense." In order to perform this effect, she concludes, "the work of language is to get out of the way" ("Unspeakable Things" 32–33). And although critical readings of Morrison understandably offer a variety of opinions on just what determines the cultural identity of her writing, this investment in language's limits remains a crucial common denominator. For Atkinson, these limits appear as oral and nonverbal elements: "Morrison consciously writes a Black text, one that is centered in African American storytelling from within Black culture. . . . She uses in her written discourse systems from within the Black English oral tradition that facilitates the inclusion of nonverbal gestures and tonal inflections" (247). Rigney adds that Morrison's language is the "language of black and feminine discourse—semiotic, maternal, informed as much by silence as by dialogue, as much by absence as by presence" (138). "Because of their African

American origins," writes Linden Peach, "[Morrison's texts] attempt to pursue subjects and narrative possibilities which have not yet been previously realized in fiction" (2). All these critical assertions about the identity of Morrison's fiction share a common element: an emphasis on absence, exclusion, and silence. For both Morrison and her critics, what is left with language "out of the way" is precisely what marks her writing as African American, a cultural specificity that challenges the critical and historical context into which this novel enters—a context that, as Morrison emphasizes throughout "Unspeakable Things Unspoken," is an explicitly American one, informed by the problematic presence of blackness in U.S. national literature, culture, and history.

As I pointed out in the opening pages of this chapter, it is precisely this American context that effaces crucial distinctions between atrocities and elides the United States' historical responsibility for atrocities perpetrated by its citizens, on its soil, in its history. To return to the dedication and to the concern with comparative atrocities it evoked, we need to remember that the dedication to "sixty million and more" derived its effective clout *not* by appropriating the historical event of the Holocaust but rather by evoking the limits of language, of historical discourse, of numerical figures and figures of speech: the referent of "sixty million and more" (Africans? slaves? both?) is subsumed by the very challenge to reference that the figure is assumed to enact. "Speaking" this figure, treating it as referential, returns us to the issue of comparative atrocities, forcing us to address the relation of African American and Jewish American reliance on the unspeakable for the purpose of self-description.

In order to do so we need to look more closely at the figure that is so often assumed to go without saying: the six million of the Holocaust. Six million, while generally evoked as a reference to the Nazi genocide in occupied Europe, refers only to one part of that program, the "final solution" to the *Jewish* problem. Excluding other victims—Poles, Gypsies, homosexuals, real or suspected resistors to the regime, the physically and mentally ill, and many, many others—six million refers *only* to Jews. Discomfort with Morrison's dedication, then, reflects a discomfort with the appropriation not of an atrocity per se but of an atrocity figured as uniquely *Jewish*. In light of the specificity of this referent, when six million is expanded to sixty million and more, the question of appropriation and comparative atrocities reemerges.

This complex interaction of identity and the unspeakable raised by the dedication and enacted in the cultural contention it invites becomes more explicit in the epigraph: "I will call them my people, who were not my people, and her Beloved, who was not beloved (Romans 9:25)." In powerful contrast to the dedication, the epigraph is referenced by book and verse, explicitly proclaiming its New Testament origins and its alignment with Christianity. Here, too, the specificity of *Jewish* identity is effaced: "Even us, whom he hath called, *not of the Jews only, but also of the Gentiles*," reads the passage in context, "I will call them my people, which were not my people; and her beloved, which was not beloved" (Romans 9:24–25). "This is one of the major statements in the New Testament, justifying the displacement of the Jews by Christianity," writes Emily Budick. "It is also a statement frequently cited in anti-Semitic contexts" (162).

The epigraph, then, seriously qualifies the dedication's initial effect of inclusion, an effect predicated on the absence of reference and enhanced by Morrison's claim "I didn't want to leave anybody out" ("Toni Morrison's" 12). By effacing Jewish specificity in its redefinition of the "Chosen People," the epigraph reevokes the absent referent of the dedication's sixty million and more—thus, the epigraph speaks what the dedication had posited as unspeakable. Juxtaposed with the principle of inclusion that, Morrison claims, dictated the choice of sixty, as opposed to forty, million—an inclusiveness powerfully reiterated by "and more"—is a violent gesture of dispossession, an appropriation of Jewish identity and history that is made even more forceful by virtue by the historical context that informs the passage from Romans.[20] If Morrison's initial evocation of the unspeakable in "sixty million and more" invited a debate about comparative atrocities while avoiding the uncomfortable implications of actually participating in such a debate, *speaking* the unspeakable, interrogating the figure in light of its juxtaposition with the epigraph that gives the novel its name, forces these issues to resurface. The dedication, with its choice of sixty million, establishes slavery as unspeakable, and such unspeakability effectively occludes the appropriation of Jewish identity that the epigraph performs.[21]

"How can they call her," the narrator muses, "if they don't know her name?" (274). And yet the name "Beloved" forces a complicity that not only haunts the novel but encloses it. Like the epilogue, the opening pages utilize an investment with language's limits in order to perform the crucial problematic of complicity's inextricability from language, the identification of

Against the Unspeakable

memory with forgetting, and the uneasy position that this problematic forces on the novel's author, as well as on its readers and critics. As Budick puts it, "[T]he line between acknowledgement or allusion, on the one hand, and, on the other, displacement or supersessionism, may not be all that sturdy" (165). What makes that line especially tenuous is the uncomfortable fact of complicity that speaking the unspeakable reveals. When that line is invested with a strong sense of language's limits—as six or sixty million is—any act of speech is perilous, and the motivations behind choosing silence deserve our close attention.

Unspeakable Things, Unspoken

Morrison has advocated that language is a crucial political tool for address-ing injustice, but that it is also dangerous by virtue of its complicity in his-toric subjugation: "Oppressive language does more than represent violence; it is violence; does more than represent the limits of knowledge; it limits knowledge," she states in her Nobel lecture. "Sexist language, racist lan-guage, theistic language—all are typical of the policing languages of mas-tery, and cannot, do not permit new knowledge or encourage the mutual exchange of ideas" (269). But for Morrison, evoking language's limits recu-perates language from complicity, reinstating its healing force. A language that foregrounds its limits, she writes, "arcs toward the place where mean-ing may lie. . . . Language can never 'pin down' slavery, genocide, war. Nor should it yearn for the arrogance to be able to do so. Its force, its felicity is in its reach toward the ineffable" (270). Hence Morrison responds to the com-plicity of language in atrocity by evoking language's limits and investing these limits with a strong sense of ethics—to speak the unspeakable is an expression of "arrogance," a gesture away from "meaning," while gesturing toward the unspeakable and the eloquent spaces of silence is assumed to re-cuperate language from the damning implications of such alliances, imbu-ing it with (at least the possibility of) moral redemption.

Perhaps, then, it should not be surprising that critical approaches to *Be-loved* tend to emphasize the novel's challenge to language through a general emphasis on Morrison's "rendering absence present," repeated invocations of her evocative lament for the "disremembered and unaccounted for," and an emphasis on the manner in which the text renders itself unspeakable by denying its reader an affective response. Roger Sales, for example, redirects the issue from the horror of the *events* related to the manner in which their *representation* renders these events unspeakable: "[T]here are horrible images of things that happened to slaves here, no question. . . . But Morrison's art makes us gasp at these moments, then insists we *not* organize our feeling as if for protest or other action" (82; emphasis mine). Valerie Smith's claim that "the novel's reliance on paradox and indeterminacy finally undermines the authority of any single reading or interpretive posture" (353) extends this unspeakability from readers' responses to critical reading and interpretation: "[T]he novel reminds us that our critical acumen and narrative capacities notwithstanding, we can never know what they [American slaves] endured. We can never enjoy a complacent understanding of lives lived under slavery. To the extent that *Beloved* returns the slaves to themselves, the novel humbles contemporary readers before the unknown and finally unknowable horrors the slaves endured" (354). Such emphases on the text's challenge to interpretative categories and its foreclosure of a cathartic emotional response evoke the ethical imperative of the unspeakable: safeguarding the characters' suffering from the intrusive, degrading misreadings forced on them by a complicit discourse and, at the same time, safeguarding the reader from complicity in such violent misreadings.

Further, Morrison's identification of her ethnicity with what remains when language is "out of the way," and the extent to which, in the novel, "languages of mastery" so tragically situate themselves within the characters' bodies as well as within their words, shed new light on the plethora of self-conscious "apologies" or "confessions" in critical writing on *Beloved*. Jean Wyatt devotes a footnote to the discomfort her race, class, and intellectual position present, as if foregrounding her sense of guilt could, or should, safeguard her from the accusation of complicity: "As a white middle-class feminist who practices psychoanalytic theory, I come to this project burdened not only by the usual guilt about my own implication in the racist structures that Morrison uncovers but also by doubts about the suitability of psychoanalytic theory for analyzing an African American text" (485 n. 2). Phelan, identifying himself as "a privileged, white, male reader" poetically expresses his sense of the novel's inaccessibility: "Like Stamp Paid, I enter without knocking. For days I live at 124. I become Sethe. Paul D. Denver. Amy Denver; Baby Suggs; Stamp Paid. The days are intense, difficult, exhausting, rewarding. I reach to understand. Stretching, straining, marveling, I perform Morrison's world. But *Beloved* also eludes me. Like Stamp Paid on the threshold of 124,

I cannot enter. Parts of Morrison's world won't let me in . . . something, someone blocks my way. *Morrison? Me? My race? Gender?*" (225–6). Ledbetter's mea culpa–type litany of his complicity and guilt in the atrocities performed by the "narrative master plot" of a Southern white male in the United States verges on parody,[22] and in a footnote to his chapter on *Beloved* he professes himself more than willing to relinquish his entire interpretation and choose silence rather than offend: "[W]hile I do think that my reading and interpretation of these issues are responsible, I am by no means suggesting that they are right and am more than willing to remain silent in the face of understandings and approaches other than my own, in particular those of persons of an other race and/or gender" (55 n. 6).

In light of such obvious reluctance to apply conceptual criteria to a text, maintaining *Beloved*'s challenge to these criteria becomes, for the text's critics, a morally and ethically efficacious gesture. Phelan devotes his discussion of *Beloved* to an emphasis on the ethical necessity of safeguarding the limits of interpretation: "[T]he act of interpretation rests upon a desire to make texts yield up their secrets, to take possession of them. This desire to possess . . . often leads to brilliant interpretive insights, but it also blinds interpretation to its own hubris" (231). Ledbetter emphasizes "hearing silenced voices" as a crucial space in which narrative ethics can be performed (5–6). And Smith concludes her essay thus: "[B]y representing the inaccessibility of the suffering of former slaves, Morrison reveals the limits of hegemonic, authoritarian systems of knowledge. The novel challenges us to use our interpretive skills, but finally turns them back upon themselves. By representing the inexpressibility of its subject, the novel asserts and reasserts the subjectivity of the former slaves and the depth of their suffering" (354).

But this tendency to emphasize the text's unspeakability forecloses its multiple evocations of complicity. Once we posit *Beloved* beyond comprehension, interpretation, and "systems of knowledge," we lose sight of the characters' complicit actions—be they forced or chosen—a willed blindness that enables us to ignore how reading and writing about the novel posits similar pitfalls for its critics. Morrison's description of *Beloved* as a novel that "had to" exist because there was no small bench by the road—a description that posited Morrison as responsibly addressing the absence of memorials while excluding her from the painful complicity that a similar commemoration forces Sethe to perform—raises the distinction, however fragile and contingent, between the relatively safe space of fiction, on the one hand, and the more problematic space of a *response* to that fiction, on the other. While the double movement of the epilogue reflects both the need and the reluctance to speak, the imperative to forget and the violent effacement that such forgetting forces on "the girl who waited to be loved and cry shame" (274), an emphasis on language's limits establishes too easy a distance from the implications of such a problematic articulation—as my reading of the epigraph revealed. When the novel's author evokes these limits, when its critics maintain them, the painful complicities delineated in *Beloved* remain, deceptively and safely, between the covers of the book.[23]

Any account of horror reflects the problematic choice of language over silence. Stressing the limits of language, evoking the unspeakable, safeguards that account from accountability, enshrining the initial silences that needed to be broken. Silence is not an acceptable response to a history of atrocity, but neither is reiterating the paradoxes of language and silence, the unspeakable and speech, narrative and trauma, rememory and forgetting— these paradoxes merely maintain an uneasy equilibrium between two uncomfortable choices while denying the problematic implications of either. The characters in *Beloved* have no such refuge and no such privilege: they must speak the unspeakable and are forced to face the disturbing consequences of their complicit actions. Stressing the novel's and its subject's limits to language is not an ethical gesture of respect to the victims and their suffering—as *Beloved's* critics would have it—but rather, I argue, a retreat into a privileged space of silence that effectively elides the inevitable complicity that language, action, and a history of atrocity forces upon us all.

The One Word That Mattered

Earlier in this chapter I discussed how Sethe's problematic choice of "the one word that mattered" for the gravestone inscription located her own agendas, priorities, and agency at the center of her act of memorialization. "Beloved" is, indeed, not the name of Sethe's murdered baby, but an expression of her own frustrations and desires, and as I mentioned earlier, it is these frustrations and desires that come back to haunt her, both as a ghost (the nameless baby's spite) and, later, as a speaking corpse: a fecund woman whose appetite for sweet things is equally a craving for the unbearably sweet smell of rotting flesh (the man on her face whose "breath smells sweet" [210]). The one word that mattered to Sethe, then, is word become matter, as

Against the Unspeakable

Beloved's presence in the novel is a return, with a vengeance, of the body Sethe had tried to exclude, to put "out, away, over there" (163), rather than return to Schoolteacher and to Sweet Home.

Significantly, what is generally read as Sethe's attempt to save her child from the horrors of slavery is equally an attempt to save *herself*, not from the unknowable, but from what she already knows far too well:

> That anybody white could take your whole self for anything that came to mind. Not just work, kill, or maim you, but dirty you. Dirty you so bad you couldn't like yourself anymore. Dirty you so bad you forgot who you were and couldn't think it up. And though she and others lived through and got over it, she could never let it happen to her own. The best thing she was, was her children. Whites might dirty *her* all right, but not her best thing, her beautiful magical best thing—the part of her that was clean. (251)

Sethe's own sense of being wholly polluted by her experience of subjugation is somewhat alleviated by an imagination of "a part of her that was clean." Identifying her children as her own "best thing," she attempts to kill them in order to keep this part of herself unsullied. We need to keep in mind that Beloved is not (merely) the manifestation of Sethe's murdered baby, nor is she (merely) the fleshy embodiment of the inscription on the gravestone that replaces the baby's name; she is, significantly, the part of Sethe that she destroys in the shed in order to maintain an imagination of an unsullied self. Sethe is haunted, then, not by the murdered child but by herself—by her own "best thing" that she forced out of the physical world in order to maintain it. She murders her daughter not to keep her daughter's body safe but, more precisely, to maintain her own imagination of a reality that is not unbearably corrupted by physical violation: "No undreamable dreams about whether the headless, feetless torso hanging in the tree with a sign on it was her husband or Paul A; whether the bubbling-hot girls in the colored-school fire set by patriots included her daughter; whether a gang of whites invaded her daughter's private parts, soiled her daughter's thighs and threw her daughter out of the wagon. *She* might have to work the slaughterhouse yard, but not her daughter" (251).

The presence of Beloved's body in the text, though, abolishes Sethe's illusion that forcing her child's body out of the physical world could maintain its physical and psychic integrity. The scar under her chin, her association with the victims of the Middle Passage, the equally viable possibility that, before her arrival at 124, she had been "locked up by some whiteman for his own purposes" (119)—all give the lie to Sethe's illusion that murdering her daughter could keep her intact. Further, Beloved wrecks havoc on the characters in the novel, forcing each of them into a place where the distinctions between what is present and what is absent, the present and the past, the speakable and the unspeakable, dissolve. Hence, *Beloved* demonstrates how the imagination of an identity that is uncorrupted, undirtied, free from complicity excludes the crucial presence of the body in that identity. When the body returns, it returns with a vengeance, and the illusion of an uncorrupted identity that such an imagination facilitated is literally destroyed.

In chapter 3, I concluded that the speaking corpse, produced through and against the spectral, insists—albeit faintly—on the presence of the unspeakable, echoing the survivor's confrontation with the limits of language and of representation in her attempt to articulate her *experience*. The speaking corpse Beloved, the one word that mattered, adds that this insistence is also present in the survivor's attempt to articulate her *identity*. The one word that matters—both the engraving on the tombstone and the appropriation of this engraving by the girl who spells it as her name—figures the corruption of language by the corporeal. It recognizes the subject's forced complicity in her own subjugation—as Sethe assumes the responsibility of her own agency and volition as she negotiates for this word that she "got, settled for." Like the ghost, the one word that mattered violates absence with presence, the present with the past; unlike the ghost, however, it cannot be laid to rest, as the process of being forgotten by the community and the literal disintegration into "weather," the explicit denial of a living, speaking body that "clamor[s] for a kiss," is counteracted by the presence of this word that, in all senses of the term, "mattered" and—as the title of the novel suggests and as Morrison and her critics stress—matters still.

What are we to make, then, of the repeated emphases on the unspeakability of *Beloved* and the concurrent situating of the novel as a crucial element of African American identity in particular and U.S. identity in general? In this context, what I have described as the self-interested retreat into a privileged space of silence is not just an attempt by the critic to safeguard herself from complicity; it is, more precisely, an attempt to safeguard identity from the body. Positing *Beloved,* and the extreme suffering and shameful history on which the novel insists, as an unspeakable and incomprehensible element in the construction of identity—ethnic, national, or even "human"—is to render invisible the fact that those of us who assume this identity as our own are, ourselves, physical bodies. Our existence in the world is as inextricable from this past as it is inextricable from the weather on which Morrison lingers in the closing lines of the novel. To render this complicity unspeakable is to perpetuate the fiction of some untouchable realm "out, away, over there," inaccessible, uncorrupted, impervious to claim. But like the footprints in back of 124 that come and go, come and go, complicity cannot be forgotten, silenced, or effaced. Like the clamor for a kiss, it is not assuaged by its denial. Like Beloved, it will not, cannot be appeased.

On
Being
Complicit

How to speak, or how not to speak, becomes an acute
and self-conscious decision. Since we cannot get outside
of language, how do we resist imposed forms of discourse
without being contaminated by them?
—*Geoffrey Hartman*, The Fateful Question of Culture

In the course of this book I have attempted to trace some of the consequences of the assumption that atrocity, horror, trauma, and pain elude the
cognitive categories of language, representation, and thought. These cognitive categories are, indeed, both limited and limiting: language is bounded
and informed by silence; representation's relation with reality has always
been vexed; and thought, confined to what has been and can or should be, is
ill equipped to deal with the unthinkable. I have called the evocation of these
limits *the unspeakable:* "to speak" implies the presence and operation of
these cognitive categories and suggests their circumscription by the physical exigencies of the body, of her voice, of the recipients of her address—all
of which "*un*speakable," by putting these categories under erasure, simultaneously elicits and elides.

This definition of "unspeakable" is deliberately broad. If it is in the nature of cognitive categories to abstract, delimit, and exclude, and "unspeakable" names this exclusion, then all concepts, all experience, all objects, all events—everything is unspeakable. But it is precisely because the unspeakable is so inclusive that it demands additional exclusions and limits, because there are differences and distinctions among what language leaves out. In the context of atrocities like the Holocaust, American slavery, the atomic bombing of Hiroshima and Nagasaki, and the Middle Passage (keeping to events touched on in this book), the limits of these cognitive categories take on an ethical urgency. Everything may be unspeakable, but some things are more unspeakable than others. Or if they are not, perhaps they ought to be.

With this "ought," the relegation of atrocity, horror, trauma, and pain beyond the scope of comprehension simultaneously describes the limits of our access to the real *and* proscribes these limits' trespass. Rhetorical production is conflated with objective fact, a conflation anchored by this injunction: not only is atrocity unspeakable, it must remain so. This conflation, I argue, enables the masquerade of rhetorical performance (evoking the unspeakable) as ethical practice (protecting the survivors, respecting the memory of the victims, safeguarding identity, reality, or historical truth). But this ethics has another object: protecting the integrity of its practitioners. For to maintain that atrocity—any atrocity—is unspeakable does two things: it abnegates the agency required to evoke, wield, and employ cognition; and it is an active assumption of agency, establishing and maintaining cognition's limits. This conflation of agency's assumption with its abnegation, like the conflation of rhetorical production with objective fact, is informed by another ethical injunction, one directed not at the object of speech but at the speaker: don't speak the unspeakable, for to do so is to violate the integrity of historical truth, to desecrate the memory of the victims, to perpetuate the survivors' pain. Don't speak the unspeakable, for to do so may render you complicit in that very violence you so eagerly eschew.

It is this injunction, and the logic it enforces and sustains, that this book argues against. To be "against the unspeakable" is not (merely) to denounce violence, condemn atrocity, revile genocide, murder, war. It is not (again, merely) to dismiss our understandable reluctance to apply the reductive categories of cognition to such horrible events. Nor is it to deny that some events—even horrible ones—may challenge those (however faulty) methods for conveying information that are traditionally at our disposal. Indeed, such a challenge may be a source of hope if, and only if, we are not rendered passive by its presence but can assume the agency required to overcome it. I will argue that complicity is both the site of this agency and the form it assumes.

Before I can do so, however, a few words are in order about the two bodies of work (Holocaust studies and African American studies) that figure in this book, since the role of the unspeakable—and hence the implications of its eschewal—differ for each. It bears repeating that *Against the Unspeakable* is not a comparative analysis of two historical events but an interrogation of how the unspeakable operates in narratives about suffering. One of the roles that the unspeakable plays in such narratives is as a radical critique of the culture in which this narrative figures and which permitted or instigated the suffering it describes. A representation of atrocity that repeatedly and emphatically insists on representation's limits is saying something about atrocity, about representation, and about the cultural context into which this representation enters and through which it is made to signify. For each of the two bodies of work discussed here, this message is slightly different.

The alignment of political resistance with a refusal of language's potential to name, delimit, and render commensurable is well established in African American politics (think of Malcolm X) and literature (think of Ralph Ellison's *Invisible Man*). Here, language's limits serve simultaneously as a space of loss (marking the absence of language, of culture, of religion, of social and familial structures) and an articulation of presence (in and through the discourse that was imposed in order to oppress), enacting what Gates calls "the irony implicit in the attempt to posit a 'black self' in the very Western languages in which blackness itself is a figure of absence, a negation" (7). Linking the self with language's limits renders the unspeakable a crucial tool for articulating the experience of that self—her oppression and exclusion by the very language she employs. Benston describes this vexed relation to language as "a central crux of all black self-definitions" (152). For the readers of "Confessions," for the critics of *Confessions,* for Morrison, and for her readers who focus on the multiple evocations of the unspeakable in her texts, assertions of unspeakability weld the self to its experience and render both unspeakable—for the laudable purpose of empowerment and resistance.[1] The value of the unspeakable for this tradition lies in this logic: language *must* fail, its limits must be evoked, in order to open the possibility for the articulation of identities or histories hereto unconceived. To abandon the unspeakable, in this context, is to abandon a powerful instrument of political opposition and to eschew a productive vehicle for cultural identification.

For writers about the Holocaust, this refusal of reference functions less as a point of entry into an exclusionary discourse and tends rather to signal a departure from the ideologies and aesthetics of a brutal history; it is a vehement dissociation from politics (a move that is itself, of course, political) and from the self (a move that is itself, of course, self-interested). Language and culture are viewed as fundamentally contaminated not because of where, and how, they have failed but because of where, and how, they succeed. If "Hitler's regime," as Susan Gubar puts it, "depended on the deployment of elaborate rhetorical conceits and deceits (in rallies, speeches, songs, governmental documents and programs) about which artists have always been supremely conscious" (10), poetry that responds to the Holocaust is "mobilized against the forces of fascism" (13). This aesthetic and political opposition articulates a community informed by what Peter Hayes calls "a reassuring pact between asserter and audience" in which "the former, in effect, avows that '*I* cannot understand, since *I* could not have done or permitted such things,' and the latter, eager to say the same, nods in agreement" (3). Here the unspeakable does not articulate experience but marks its limits, inveighing against the transgression of these limits with urgent gestures toward ethics. To abandon the unspeakable, in this context, is to abandon the attractive position of the moral high ground.

Both by virtue of its refusal of reference and on account of the ethical weight with which this refusal has traditionally been endowed, the unspeakable evinces the ideological investment in opposition to the status quo that Jerome McGann identifies as a fundamental premise of European modernism, and one he finds "utterly inadequate as a framework for understanding contemporary artists and their work" (McGann and Drucker 207). Complicity, McGann suggests, "provides a more interesting way to think about what it is we do, and see, and read—and a more flexible way to describe the artefacts of aesthetic expression—than the modes of radical critique and oppositional aesthetics on which so much of twentieth-century criticism was premised" (219). Though the context in which McGann proffers his speculations is very different from ours, and while he does not directly discuss representations of the kinds of large-scale atrocities that are the subject of this book, the investment in opposition that both traditions evince and the alignment of this opposition with an intellectual and political agenda are most pertinent to our subject, not least because the unspeakable so powerfully enacts this opposition and atrocities like the Holocaust and American slavery more than justify it.

Abandoning the unspeakable (and the oppositional stance it performs) uncovers a number of manifestations of complicity. Here, too, important distinctions are at work. For many of the scholars I discussed in the first chapter, the object of study—the Holocaust—is unspeakable. For these scholars, to abandon the notion of the Holocaust's unspeakability is to address the complicity of contemporary culture with the presence of atrocity in its past—a somewhat conceptual or ideational structure, but one that enabled us to address the complicity of image with viewer, and the corresponding complicity of atrocity with representation in the discussion of *Schindler's List*. In this context, evoking the unspeakable works to dissociate comprehension from an atrocity presumed to be incomprehensible, essentially safeguarding the object of representation from representation itself by situating that object beyond representation's limits.

But when the object of representation is invested with historical truth, the body is figured as the guarantor of representation's verity—a figure that rests uneasily with the investment in representation's limits. Thus, in my discussions of *Night, Maus,* and *Shoah* I focused on the complicity of body with speech in the figure of the speaking corpse; turning to the vexed reception of *The Confessions of Nat Turner* I argued that the political valences of this complicity demand it be negotiated back into the realm of the unspeakable, here identified as historical truth or "the real Nat Turner." Tracing these negotiations—both within the novel and outside it—revealed patterns of flight away from a raced and gendered body. In my reading of *Beloved* I showed that this unspeakable body returns, articulating the painful manifestations of mechanisms of persecution in, and by, the persecuted. (I should remind the reader, given this final context, that complicity is often conflated with culpability or with collaboration, a conflation that the following pages will address and undo).

But if complicity, as McGann suggests, offers a productive framework for making critical judgments about contemporary works of art, the form that framework takes and the modes of its operation have yet to be determined. Does this paradigm of complicity facilitate the acquiescence to an unacceptable status quo? Is there some way to evince the ethical investment in opposition that both African American studies and Holocaust studies so rightly seek, or does opposition need to be abandoned together with the unspeakable? And to what does "complicity" apply? Does "complicity" name the relation of the object of representation to representation itself, or does it name the relation between the representing subject and the work of representation? Does it describe the position of the reader, viewer, or critic whose encounter with the subject reproduces the violence that "unspeakable" is evoked to avoid? The charge of complicity is a formidable one; extracted from McGann's suggestions about twentieth-century aesthetics and situated in the context of atrocities like slavery, the Holocaust, and Hiroshima— atrocities commonly imagined to be unspeakable—it is even more so. Weighted as the term is with implications of responsibility, guilt, and blame, "complicity" assumes the form of a criminal charge, one that elicits a judgment of innocence or guilt.[2] Any attempt, then, to follow McGann's suggestion that complicity offers a productive framework for making critical judgments about contemporary works of art needs to take into account the complex interrelation of complicity, judgment, and the unspeakable.

To begin to do so, I turn to Primo Levi's meditations on "the gray zone" in *The Drowned and the Saved.* Levi distinguishes the gray zone from the sphere of judgment, which he aligns with "the tendency, indeed, the need, to separate evil from good, to be able to take sides, to emulate Christ's gesture on Judgment Day: here the righteous, over there the reprobates" (37). Levi repeatedly cautions against judging the inhabitants of the gray zone and admonishes those who collapse the categories of perpetrator and victim,[3] raising an important distinction between complicity, collaboration, and guilt: "Collaborators who originate in the adversary camp, ex-enemies, are untrustworthy by definition: they betrayed once and they can betray again," he writes. "[T]he best way to bind them is to burden them with guilt, cover them with blood, compromise them as much as possible, thus establishing *a bond of complicity* so that they can no longer turn back" (43; emphasis mine).[4]

This initial disentanglement of complicity from collaboration and from guilt will become crucial for articulating what it means to "be complicit." As Levi begins to tease apart these concepts, what becomes clear is that complicity ensures collaboration but is not indistinguishable from it; guilt— the sense of being culpable—establishes complicity but is not identical to it.[5] I will expand on the implications of these distinctions in the following pages, but at present I want to emphasize that the distinction between complicity, collaboration, and culpability can be effectively demarcated by the possibility or impossibility of judgment: collaboration (a charge) and culpability (a verdict) are well within judgment's sphere, while to be complicit is to stand in a relation to this sphere on which judgment has yet to fall.

In a very different context, Margaret Olivia Little points out that complicity is not, itself, a judgment; rather, it names "an improper relation *to the evil* of some practice or set of attitudes" (170). Redirecting the critical gaze from the practice in question (which has already been judged and condemned) to the *relation* between an individual's actions and the practice in question, she identifies that relation as the object of our scrutiny. Identifying complicity as a relation, not a judgment, enables Little to distinguish "participating in" a system from sanctioning or sustaining it: to equate "'participating in' a system one does not endorse" with "causal reinforcement of a system" is to miss, as she puts it, "the nuance of complicity" (172), a nuance that expands the sphere of complicity to encompass a range of actions within an evil system or in relation to it. What I find most helpful about Little's observations is that she continues Levi's work: distinguishing questions about complicity from the judgment that condemns, distinguishing complicit actions within an evil system from endorsing or supporting the system and its evil, and posing complicity as a starting point, not a conclusion, for questions about ethics.

This is not to say that complicity occupies that "moral high ground" that the unspeakable so seductively supplies. To assume that one could be in any kind of relation to evil and not be touched by it is to vastly underestimate the nature of evil. But to assume absolute distinctions between evil and its other would be an equal misapprehension. This is why Levi distinguishes between "great and small complicities" (68) and why the area of the gray zone is a diverse and varied one, within which rigorous meditation is crucial (Levi 60). In *Complicity: Ethics and Law for a Collective Age*, Christopher Kutz identifies the range of reactions and responses to violence that make up complicity's "domain":

> It is an undeniable feature of our social life that people have a host of morally significant reactions when they stand in such mediated relations to harms—reactions ranging from discomfort to regret to guilt—

and that they are judged by victims and onlookers. They are often punished or compelled to make restitution and repair. These cultural and legal practices, surrounding relations of an agent to a harm that are mediated by other agents, comprise the domain of complicity. (2)

Thinking of complicity as a domain helps dissociate it from judgment and opens up the possibility of thinking about what it might mean to occupy that domain and how to function in it. To do so, we must turn our critical gaze from the violence and its evil (in which we are, as Kutz puts it, in mediated relation) to the terrain on which we stand. In other words, the question is not, What are we complicit in? but What does it mean to *be*, as the title of this chapter puts it, complicit?

To answer this question I turn to Mark Sanders's seminal work in *Complicities: The Intellectual and Apartheid*. Noting the paucity of philosophical or critical explorations of the concept, Sanders offers the etymology of "complicity" as "a folded-together-ness (*com-plic-ity*)—in human being (or the *being* of being human)" (5; emphasis mine).[6] Conceiving of complicity as a state of being enables him to articulate a theory of intellectual responsibility that is predicated on "a motivated acknowledgment of one's complicity in injustice" (8). Given this alignment of complicity with responsibility, Sanders posits complicity as the condition of possibility for productive political work: to oppose a system, you must first acknowledge your implication in it. "Opposition takes its first steps from a footing of complicity" (9).

It may bear repeating that defining complicity as a way of being does not render that being ethically viable. But what Sanders articulates so well is how, conceptually, complicity is a precondition not only for affiliation but for ethics: complicity is "the very basis for responsibly entering into, maintaining, or breaking off a given affiliation or attachment" (x). Sanders's concept of complicity, then, revises the order that Kutz's definition implies: you must *already* be in complicity's "domain" in order to be in "mediated relations to harms" and subject to "cultural and legal practices" (2).[7] This domain, constituted by complicity, is the space from which we enact our most passionate gestures of affiliation and opposition; it is, then, both the key to an assumption of identity and an ethical engagement with what that identity implies.

This figuration of complicity as affiliation and opposition in the weighty context of good and evil might be usefully addressed through William E.

Connolly's discussion of the construction of identity in *Identity/Difference*. Connolly offers an account of "[t]he consolidation of identity through the constitution of difference" and "[t]he self-reassurance through the construction of otherness" (9) by situating his discussion of the relation between identity and difference in terms of what he calls "two problems of evil" (ix). The first problem of evil, articulated by Augustine as an attempt to reconcile Christianity with Manichaeanism, evolved from the necessity to integrate the fact of evil with the belief in a benevolent, omnipotent god. As a result, Connolly writes, "[t]he indispensability of one conception of divinity, evil and will is established by defining what deviates from it as a heresy that must not be entertained as a counter-possibility" (8), essentially articulating the construction of difference as a dissociation (of a divine power) from complicity in evil. The second problem of evil is the legacy of the first: it is "the evil that flows from the attempt to establish security of identity for any individual or group by defining the other that exposes sore spots in one's identity as evil or irrational" (8). As a result, he concludes, "the definition of difference is a requirement built into the logic of identity" (9). Connolly will go on to address the challenges implicit in this dependence of identity on difference to democratic politics in the United States. For our purposes, what is important here is the extent to which identity is *complicit in* the strategies and practices of exclusion, and the subsequent challenge this complicity poses to the individual of any identity who must, Connolly emphasizes, "come to terms with one's *implication in* these strategies" (9; emphasis mine).

Connolly's account of the logic of identity reproduces Levi's account of the constitution of the gray zone. If, in the Lager, "the 'we' lost its limits," the gray zone is where community is reconstructed through a "bond of complicity" or the "foul link of imposed complicity" (Levi 38, 43, 54). For Connolly and for Levi, complicity is a structure, not a charge (like collaboration) or a verdict (like culpability); both Connolly and Levi identify the structure of complicity as the constitution of identity. While Connolly does not address the types of violence that are the subject of this book, or refer to the gray zone per se, his version of complicity as a precondition for identity is a productive one for my argument, because his implicated identity, like Sanders's, is a precondition for ethics: it is the position from which difference must be productively and creatively engaged.[8] Further: if we detach complicity from judgment, it becomes more than a simple synonym for wrong. Complicity *precedes* the charge of collaboration or of culpability; complicity is, to borrow Sanders's formulation, *the condition of possibility* for the articulation of these charges; further, it is a *necessary* one.[9] And—to return to the relation between complicity and judgment with which I opened this discussion—by virtue of being outside judgment's domain, being complicit may articulate precisely that "new mode of existence" that judgment, Gilles Deleuze argues, prevents (135).

When Hartman asks, "how do we resist imposed forms of discourse without being contaminated by them?" (*Fateful Question* 102), his assumption that resistance must be free of complicity facilitates evoking the limits of language—"how not to speak" as the only ethical oppositional practice. But it is precisely this dissociation of resistance from complicity that gives the unspeakable its power. Here, the exculpatory narrative of the unspeakable has crucial implications for the distinction between complicity (that realm of actions that are imbricated in evil but on which judgment has yet to fall) and collaboration or culpability (which designate actions in judgment's realm). According to what Kutz calls "the complicity principle," "I am accountable for what others do when I intentionally participate in the wrong they do or harm they cause" (122). Kutz's "complicity principle" proffers complicity as a logical precedent for accountability; complicity is, in fact, accountability's necessary basis—its condition of possibility. The unspeakable enables gestures toward the limits of comprehension to masquerade as accountability for wrongs or harms done by others; what I have been calling the unspeakable's ethical imperative (the assumption that to refrain from forcing suffering into speech is an ethical response to suffering) functions as a gesture toward accountability that refuses complicity as a precondition. But if complicity is the condition of possibility for accountability, accountability without complicity is not accountability at all. Evoking the unspeakable, then, is not a thoughtful response to atrocity, horror, trauma, and pain. It is an exculpatory mechanism that enables contemporary culture to literally render itself unaccountable for the atrocities that haunt its past.

This interrelation of complicity and ethics propels me to move, as Sanders and Kutz do, to Karl Jaspers's articulation, in *The Question of German Guilt*, of a community defined by those for whose actions we are "co-responsible." Jaspers offers an anatomy of guilt (criminal, political, moral, and metaphysical) that reflects a movement from the individual (the criminal, whose crimes require legal restitution) to the collective (metaphysical guilt, which reflects the recognition of "a solidarity among men as human beings that makes each co-responsible for every wrong and every injustice in the world" [32]). It is this final type of guilt that will lead Jaspers to his concept of collective guilt and the "co-responsibility" this concept implies, and to his conclusion about the implications for the individual in a political community. If "there can be no radical separation of moral and political guilt," he writes, "every enlightenment of our political consciousness proportionately burdens our conscience" (77), a conclusion that leads him to define "being German" not as "a condition" but as a "task" (79–80), the articulation of which is, significantly, the point at which "language fails" (80).

But as *Against the Unspeakable* has argued again and again, language does not fail; we do. We fail ourselves and each other when we mark as unspeakable that place beyond which we will not go lest we implicate ourselves in those very real violences we so fervently oppose. What Jaspers identifies as the limit point of language locates that space in the speaking self—specifically, the speaking self in the wake of atrocity, a self *affiliated with* the horrors of its history. And it is from this affiliation that a sense of complicity, and hence of responsibility, emerge: complicity not in the perpetration of atrocity but in the articulation of the self whose *being* is complicit—not yet a perpetrator, not quite a victim, but denied, as Levi puts it, "the solace of innocence" (53). Conceived not as a judgment or a charge but as a way of being, complicity evinces an ethical investment in opposition to the status quo that does not fall prey to the exculpatory lure of the unspeakable.

In "Portrait of Tragedy," Joseph Brodsky observes that "a thing must become unpalpable to look matchless" (87). *Against the Unspeakable* interrogates the assumption that atrocity, horror, trauma, or pain contains some quality that renders it inherently "matchless," focusing instead on why, and how, and for what reasons a thing must be made to "*look* matchless," and arguing that this incommensurability is ultimately an optical illusion. If speaking privileges the body and its capacity for speech, the unspeakable (along with its association with unbearable suffering) maintains the suffering human body under erasure. To address the implications of this erasure, to begin to undo it, is to render representation complicit with materiality, discourse with corporeality; and it is the pathological avoidance of this complicity that, I argue, compels the evocation of the unspeakable in such contexts. But complicity should not be avoided, not least because it is, as Derrida implies in "Force of Law," the only "lesson" that the unspeakable has to teach. In light of "all the collective exterminations of history," writes Derrida, "we must think, know, represent for ourselves, formalize, judge the possible complicity between all these discourses and the worst" (62–63).

In the attempt to learn this lesson, to pursue this complicity, to look this particular Gorgon in the face, *Against the Unspeakable* turns the critical gaze from the object of speech to the speaking self. For many of the scholars I discussed in the opening chapters, the object of speech—the Holocaust—is unspeakable. As we moved from representations of Holocaust testimony (representations that must account for both the body and its speech and that do so through the figure of the speaking corpse) to representations of Nat Turner's confession, the speaking subject joined the object of speech at the focus of our gaze. In this way, the progression from Holocaust studies (a body of criticism defined by its object) to African American studies (in which the subject, as well as the object, is the focus) reflects another movement: from the dichotomy of speech and silence with which this book opened to that more complex dialectic that, Barbara Johnson notes, pertains "to virtually all important investigations: the self analyzing itself, man studying man, thought thinking about thought, language speaking about language" (qtd. in Gates, "Criticism" 7). To designate *that* relationship as one of complicity is to extend complicity from a conceptual structure to a mode of being.

In my initial comments on the unspeakable I mentioned that the corporeal presence of the speaker, her body and her physical articulation, are effaced as *un*speakable welds the inability of articulation to the impossibility of communication. But I would like to end by suggesting that the unspeakable may not be, in itself, "bad." It is, as Michel Foucault says everything is, "dangerous." "If everything is dangerous," Foucault adds, "we always have something to do" (256). To be "against the unspeakable" is something to do. But merely eschewing the unspeakable as a negative force is but half the work, one step on the road toward the assumption of a being that is complicit in the conditions of its articulation and in that which it most urgently opposes. After all, the dissociation of corporeality from its rhetorical, aesthetic, and political representation which the unspeakable makes possible is not a deliberate and malevolent eradication of the suffering human body. It is, rather, a desperate gesture of self-preservation that paradoxically reifies the self out of existence. While claiming to preserve the uniqueness, sanctity, and inviolability of human suffering, the assumption of its unspeakability works to silence the suffering human body and, finally, silences us: our own corporeality, our own vulnerability, our affiliation with those whose suffering affects us most. To be against the unspeakable is to be complicit, and being complicit is, in the most literal manner imaginable, a way to re-member ourselves.

Notes

Introduction

1. A number of critics have commented on how the two texts perform similar gestures toward language's limits. For Hirsch, "*In The Shadow of No Towers,* like its predecessor *Maus* . . . performs an aesthetics of trauma: it is fragmentary, composed of small boxes that cannot contain the material, which exceeds their frames and the structure of the page" ("Collateral Damage" 1213). See Durand 114–17 for a fascinating discussion of the politics around mobilizing the Holocaust to represent September 11, 2001, including this scene from *In The Shadow of No Towers.*

2. Lang's review of Novick's *The Holocaust in American Life* is an example of this type of approach. Lang takes issue with the fact that Novick "says little . . . about the significance of the Holocaust un-constructed (that is, as fact)" (150). Given that Novick's focus is on how the historical event has been constructed in the United States and the reverberations of that construct in U.S. national and international politics, and given that the factuality of the Holocaust is not the subject of his book, it is odd that Lang should be so troubled by his neglect to address it until we remember that it is this valorization of the historical fact's "actuality" that is being expressed here, not a critical engagement with Novick's scholarship.

3. This strategy pervades Churchill's *A Little Matter of Genocide,* for example, in which the Nazi genocide is employed as a paradigm through which to view Native American history and which has, as its foreword, Colorado's poem "What Every Indian Knows": "Auschwitz ovens / burn bright / in America" (xi). Oe utilizes Holocaust imagery to concretize the horror of atomic devastation: "one whole city . . .

rendered as deadly as a huge death chamber in a Nazi concentration camp" (116). Garber and Zuckerman note that "in general, a 'holocaust' now is commonly used to connote a genocide, i.e., the systematic murder of any ethnic group. When used in this manner, the term is usually qualified so it is clear what 'holocaust' is meant; for example, 'the Armenian holocaust' or 'the British holocaust.' When the systematic elimination of the entire human race is meant, one simply shifts the qualifier from the object to the agent of destruction: i.e., 'nuclear holocaust.'" They see in this trend an important exception: "[I]n the case of 'the Jewish holocaust' . . . the qualification seems redundant" (197).

4. For a more in-depth discussion of *Holocaust Representation*, see my "Ethics."

5. While Finkelstein has attempted to delineate this context, I cannot take seriously his conviction that it is occupied and controlled solely by "the American Jewish elite" (32), especially since by "the American Jewish elite" he seems to mean straight, white (Ashkenazi), secular, professionally successful men motivated by some obscure, but apparently nefarious, pro-Zionist agenda.

6. This statement, that "this distinction [between language's limits and their rhetorical evocation] *cannot but become politicized* when what lies beyond language's limits is 'Auschwitz,'" is based on two assumptions that, since they are axiomatic to my argument, I will spell out here. First, despite its many other victims, "Auschwitz" is commonly perceived as a signifier for something that happened to Jews; it refers to suffering that is imagined as primarily, if not exclusively, Jewish. Thus to say that we are all "after Auschwitz" is to extend the category of "Jewish" to humanity, an extension that either effaces Jewish specificity or imposes some concept of "Jewish" (usually aligned with Christianity in a vision of liberal humanism) onto contemporary humanity, an imposition not all would agree with or welcome. Second, Jews, under the dubious aegis of this suffering, have knowingly or unknowingly inflicted suffering onto others—both in America, with its fraught history of relations between African Americans and Jewish Americans, and in the Middle East, as Israel's military actions in the West Bank and Gaza have come under increased, and critical, scrutiny. These assumptions pervade contemporary discourse on the Holocaust, on Jewish identity, on identity politics in the United States, on the ethics of "after Auschwitz," and on the political scenario in the Middle East. Rather than argue for or against them, I take them as a given at this point in my argument, although I hope that by the end of the book the reader will see productive ways with which to engage and ultimately revise them. Meanwhile, see Lentin, "Postmemory" 12–13, for a discussion of evocations of "Holocaust" in the political discourse around the Israeli occupation. Ezrahi's "Racism and Ethics" and Azoulay's *Death's Showcase* also provide exceptionally thoughtful accounts of these assumptions and of their operation.

7. Bennett describes Styron's first-person narrator as "a neurasthenic, Hamlet-like white intellectual in blackface" (5); Crouch, notoriously, describes Morrison's novel as "a holocaust novel in blackface" (67).

8. For Levinas, writes Newton,

"the face" captures the fact of otherness itself, and the ethical drama between persons that it instigates. Just as we ordinarily identify a person by face, the site

and emblem of selfhood, so in Levinas face signifies obligatedness itself. It isn't read so much as recognized and heard: perhaps it is best described as an annunciation. It can mean both ethical exorbitancy—"do no harm to me"—and ethical ardor—"do not turn your face from mine." Above all, it means that the self is indemnified to the other, even before freely choosing to be so. Faces that summon, faces in asymmetrical relation with one's own, faces "denuded" or exposed "in their nakedness": this is the hard figural core of Levinas's ethical philosophy (xii).
See also Levinas 194–219.

9. Michaels distinguishes slavery from the Holocaust temporally: there are, he notes, no living survivors of slavery; few living survivors of the Holocaust. But Gilman notes that "bodies have a way of being seen again and again in the past, and identity—whether that of Jews or blacks or Hispanics or women—always has to perform a perilous balancing act between self and Other" (243).

10. In this context we might also consider Gilroy's discussion, in *Against Race,* of the extent to which culture and race cannot be opposed (279–326).

11. As Gilman puts it in his discussion of "too black Jews and too white Blacks," his conclusion to *The Jew's Body,* "Once the rhetoric of 'race' is evoked, its ideological context is also present. It seems to be impossible to speak of the idea of difference, such as the difference of the Jew, without evoking this sense of the constructed difference of the body" (242).

12. In *Black Atlantic* Gilroy repeatedly gestures away from "an absurd and dangerous competition" (213) between these two atrocities and toward arguments for the Holocaust's uniqueness, which, he repeatedly reminds the reader, he accepts (213, 214).

13. An example of the hegemonic underpinnings of such evocation is provided by no less a thinker than Robert J. Lifton: "[A]mong modern genocides—recently in Cambodia, Africa, and the Indian subcontinent, as well as earlier in Turkey and the Soviet Union—the one from which we have most to learn is that of the Nazis during the fifth decade of the twentieth century. *Nazi genocide is particularly relevant to us as it was perpetrated by an advanced Western Christian nation and because it was linked with the beginnings of nuclear threat during the Second World War*" (Lifton and Markusen 9; emphasis mine).

14. "Within this discursive context," writes Yoneyama, "the downplaying of crimes against humanity at the Tokyo War Crimes Tribunal created a subtle conflation of Japanese and other Asians, for neither group was granted full membership in the category of 'humanity,' at least within the West-centric discourse of the tribunal. . . . To put it differently, remembering the atomic destruction of Hiroshima and Nagasaki as events in the history of humanity has significantly contributed to the forgetting of the history of colonialism and racism in the region" (12).

15. In a previous essay Oe proposed Hiroshima as a potential medium through which Japanese specificity may be transformed into humanity as a whole: "In the broadest context of human life and death, those of us who happened to escape the atomic holocaust must see Hiroshima as part of all Japan, and as part of all the world.

If we survivors want to atone for the 'Hiroshima' within us and to give it some positive value, then we should mobilize all efforts against nuclear arms under the maxims 'the human misery of Hiroshima' and 'the restoration of all humanity'" (107).

16. Yoneyama details the specific cultural, social, and political forces that prevailed in Japan up to and through the 1980s that resulted in "survivors' reluctance to speak" being "regarded as authentication of the experience" (88); conversely, "whenever [survivors] try to present their experiences in public, they risk their authenticity as survivors" (89). She adds that "when claims about the incommunicability of the experience shift from the individual level of coping with remembering and forgetting to universal generalizations regarding the authenticity of memory and the essential meaning of survival, they begin to repress and control heterogeneous voices and contestatory forms of memory" (89).

17. In assuming that post-Holocaust writers and post-atomic-bomb writers respond to a similar unspeakability, Treat ignores the political postwar conditions that significantly contributed to the very different challenges these atrocities posed to communication and to speech. Meditating on the differences between remembering Hiroshima and remembering the Holocaust, Sadako describes some of these challenges in a passage worth quoting at length:

> Before we can discuss atomic bomb literature in literary terms, we must note the fact that circumstances made it impossible even to read atomic bomb literature. Of the world's two great holocausts, Auschwitz was a major atrocity carried out by the enemies of the victorious Allies; Hiroshima/Nagasaki was a major atrocity carried out by the Allies. Hence works written about the Nazi war crimes were not suppressed by Occupation authorities, and from the early postwar era on, many works were written; literary analysis developed, too. In contrast, the depiction of Hiroshima/Nagasaki was forbidden by the Press Code of the Occupation Army, and survivor-writers and survivor-poets experienced the psychological pressure of censorship. . . . Thanks to censorship, Hiroshima/Nagasaki was cut off from the nation and treated as a regional catastrophe, and the true conditions of the atomic bomb were not known. Both inside and outside the literary establishment atomic bomb literature was shunned as "exaggeration that could not have existed in fact" and as "non-literature wholly dependent on its subject matter"; out of deference to the dread Occupation, works of atomic bomb literature could not be published. (86–87)

18. The emphasis on physical presence in the term can be traced to the 1957 Law Concerning Medical Care for Victims of the Atomic Bombs (Genshi Bakudan Hibakusha no Iryō nado ni Kansuru Hōritsu) that provided medical compensation for the survivors of Hiroshima and Nagasaki:

> In order to obtain the certificate, a survivor needs to provide documentation proving his or her presence at a specific location within the city between 6 and 20 August. If such documentation is unavailable, one must offer either a firsthand account or the testimony of another that can prove that the applicant was present in the city at the time of the bombing. Defined as "a type of certificate that verifies that the said individual is a survivor of the atomic bomb," it legally

authorizes the individuals' atomic bomb experiences. This institutionalized medico-legal procedure determined to a great extent the style of narrativization that atom bomb memories later took. (Yoneyama 93)

19. Lifton offers four categories of hibakusha: "those who at the time of the bomb were within the city limits of Hiroshima as then defined . . . ; those who came into the city within fourteen days and entered a designated area extending to about two thousand meters from the hypocenter; those who came into physical contact with bomb victims, through various forms of aid or disposal of bodies; and those who were *in utero* at the time, and whose mothers fit into any of the first three groups" (7). He adds that Americans tend to use the term survivor, and suggests that this term may reflect "American tendencies toward 'detoxifying' the experience" (7). Given this observation, it is especially interesting that Lifton himself returns to the term survivor in the final chapter of *Death in Life,* where he situates atomic devastation in the context of the Holocaust.

20. Such inescapably physical manifestations of identity radically challenge Treat's notion of a "contingent affinity" (xi), a concept that enables him to extend the category of hibakusha to all Japanese and ultimately to global culture, an extension that sits uneasily (which Treat does acknowledge) with his own American identity. "[A]ll Japanese were potential hibakusha since any city—as long as it was a Japanese city—could have been targeted," he writes, and he goes on to propose "that this concept of the potential hibakusha now has to extend to everyone alive today" (x–xi).

21. Sollors makes a similar move in "Holocaust and Hiroshima." Situating his discussion in the context of "the turn toward universalism" after World War II, in which "stressing ethnicity had been [perceived as] part of the problem of fascism" (57), Sollors singles out John Hersey as an exception to this assumption: Hersey's work (especially in *Hiroshima* and *The Wall,* about the atomic bomb and the Holocaust, respectively) foreshadows a concentration on the "the legacy of Hiroshima and the *univers concentrationnaire*" (60) that came to characterize much of the literary output by American ethnic prose writers. Ultimately, Sollors argues that Hersey's literary output of the period "confronted what American modernists and ethnic writers stayed away from" (59). But he has difficulty arguing for Hersey's identity as an "ethnic" writer, proffering a childhood in China (where his parents were missionaries) and describing Hersey's life story as similar to "that of an immigrant" (57). Nor does he pay any attention to the historical context that characterizes the very different atrocities he collapses under the category of "extreme," a term he does not define explicitly but which seems to refer to "unimaginable mass death" (60). My point here is that Sollors's remarkable incoherence around the concept of ethnicity is not divorced from the equally incoherent concept of atrocity—specifically, atrocity characterized as unspeakable ("unimaginable mass death")—toward which his argument is addressed.

22. Here I follow Kutz's and Sanders's theorizations of complicity and the distinction between complicity and culpability. Culpability, infused with connotations of guilt, implies that some action has been committed for which blame must be apportioned or which requires expiation. Collaboration names one such action (or

series of actions) through which one is rendered culpable. See my discussion of these terms in the final section of this book.

23. My argument, though employed in a different context, parallels Sanders's at this point, though he distinguishes between "acting-in-complicity" and "responsibility-in-complicity." "If the former involves acts subject to a system of accountability, the latter, being the place occupied by the other before whom the 'little perpetrator' is responsible, stands as the condition of possibility for any such system" (11). I will expand on this point in the concluding chapter of this book.

24. In *Ghostly Matters,* Gordon posits that ghosts and specters provide us access to "that dense site where history and subjectivity meet social life" (8). "A crucible for political mediation and historical memory" (18), the ghost signifies a "seething presence" that "[acts] on and . . . [meddles] with taken-for-granted realities" (8). For Gordon, ghosts signal the presence of the unspeakable: they emerge from the context of a failure of vocabularies, of the limits of social practices of knowledge production.

1. Thinking "After Auschwitz"

1. In *Traumatic Realism,* Rothberg makes the same point when he identifies the role of the Holocaust in "a break with the condition of modernity that constitutes the matrix of the Nazi genocide" (33). "World War II is generally thought to mark a border after which begins the institutionalization and decline of modernist art and the gradual emergence of postmodern practices. In some arguments [Rothberg specifically mentions Lyotard's *The Postmodern Condition* and *The Differend*] the Holocaust stands as a sign of this transition" (20).

2. See Hungerford 57–62, and Berger 106–33, for a discussion of Derrida's *Feu la cendre* (1987). On Derrida's references to the Holocaust, see Marks.

3. Mintz makes a similar observation in *Popular Culture:* "As the most extreme instance of evil, the camp—or to be more precise, one camp—became a metonymy for the Holocaust as a whole. To begin a statement with the words 'After Auschwitz' is not to make a specific reference but to invoke the catastrophe in its totality" (62–63).

4. The passage in its entirety reads:
Auschwitz has become the signature of an entire epoch—and it concerns all of us. Something happened there that no one could previously have thought even possible. It touched a deep level of solidarity among all who have a human face. Until then—in spite of all the quasi-natural brutalities of world history—we had simply taken the integrity of this deep layer for granted. At that point a bond of naiveté was torn to shreds—a naiveté that as such had nourished historical continuities. Auschwitz altered the conditions for the continuation of historical life contexts—and not only in Germany. (Habermas 251–52)
Friedlander quotes a section of this passage, in his own translation, in *Probing the Limits* (3).

5. For Sanyal, this "silence" is generated and wielded by a discourse of trauma, in which the historical event of the Holocaust is posited (by trauma theorists like Felman and Caruth) as a traumatic event in history, facilitating the conception of his-

tory as unspeakable. I will expand on trauma and the unspeakable, and Sanyal's critique of this discourse, later in this chapter.

6. Hungerford echoes this happy marriage of deconstruction in particular, and critical theory in general, to the unspeakable in her introduction to *The Holocaust of Texts:*

> Both historians and literary critics who write about the Holocaust . . . have found in deconstruction's emphasis on absence and unspeakability a way of understanding language that seems to mirror the absence of the millions murdered in the Nazi genocide. . . . Even critics who, like Lawrence Langer, resist the application of literary theory to accounts of the Holocaust continue to refer to suffering that stands outside of language, a concept that brings in the questions literary theory raises even though the critic does not turn to theory for answers. (14)

7. Haidu expands on the similarity to the Holocaust's unspeakability to manifestations of the sacred:

> The unspeakability of the Event, the horror which comes upon the historian as his gaze fixes on the documents of his research, enters into a tradition of the ineffability which attends appearances of the divine. The *topos* of ineffability is associated both with the experience of horror and with that of the sublime. What I wish to designate, however, precedes that distinction: the irruptions into human life of the divine as that which is awesome, that which strikes us with terror, inexplicable because of the unpredictability of its violence as well as the force of that violence. (284)

8. In this infamous speech delivered to the SS generals on October 4, 1943, Himmler eerily inscribes the Final Solution as unspeakable:

> I also want to speak to you here, in complete frankness, of a really grave chapter. Amongst ourselves, for once, it shall be said quite openly, but all the same we will never speak about it in public. Just as we did not hesitate on June 30, 1934 ["the night of the long knives"], to do our duty as we were ordered, and to stand comrades who had erred against the wall and shoot them, and we never spoke about it and we never will speak about it. It was a matter of natural tact that is alive in us, thank God, that we never talked about it amongst ourselves, that we never discussed it. Each of us shuddered and yet each of us knew clearly that the next time he would do it again if it were an order, and if it were necessary.
>
> I am referring here to the evacuation of the Jews, the extermination of the Jewish people. This is one of the things that is easily said: "The Jewish people are going to be exterminated," that's what every Party member says, "sure, it's our program, elimination of the Jews, extermination—it'll be done." And then they all come along, the 80 million worthy Germans, and each one has his one decent Jew. Of course, the others are swine, but this one, he is a first-rate Jew. Of all those who talk like that not one has seen it happen, not one has had to go through with it. Most of you men know what it is like to see 100 corpses side by side, or 500 or 1,000. To have stood fast through this and—except in cases of

human weakness—to have stayed decent that has made us hard. This is an un-written and never-to-be-written page of glory in our history, for we know how difficult it would be for us if today—under bombing raids and the hardships and deprivations of war—if we were still to have Jews in every city as secret sa-boteurs, agitators, and inciters. (qtd. in Arad, Gutman, and Margaliot 344–45) Discussing this speech and analyzing its rhetoric, Friedlander asks, "why insist on keeping it secret—not only for the duration of the war but forever?" and concludes that its emphasis on silence facilitates a larger purpose: "to insert the event into the banal course of everyday life" (*Reflections* 105).

9. Hungerford's analysis of Lang's response to the Holocaust denier Arthur Butz effectively demonstrates the transition of Butz from a historian who is mistaken to a historian who is immoral. Hungerford reads this response through her discussion of a rhetoric of personification, arguing that when representations are treated as people, misrepresentation performs the equivalent of harming a person and pro-duces a similar moral response (80–81).

10. Responding to *Eichmann in Jerusalem*, Gershom Scholem famously takes ex-ception to Arendt's "heartless, frequently almost sneering and malicious tone" (241). "The manner in which [Arendt] speak[s]," he continues, is "unimaginably inappro-priate" (242) and reveals her "lack [of] [l]ove for the Jewish people" (241). Over three decades later, a similar paradigm was in effect in one critic's claim that Novick's *The Holocaust in American Life* exposed him as "a stranger to the inner life of the Jews" who "demonstrates no feel for their habitual patterns of collective behavior" (Roskies 64); another critic asserted that "Novick writes without any awareness of Jewish peoplehood" (Raphael 535; see also my introduction, n. 2).

11. These figures appear in Hilberg, *Destruction* 767. They refer only to Jews, and they exclude Poles, Gypsies, homosexuals, the mentally ill, etc.

12. See Garber and Zuckerman for an account of the origin and evolution of this term.

13. I will return to these terms in my discussion of Lang's *Act and Idea in the Nazi Genocide* later in this chapter.

14. Weissman's choice of "Holocaust" for his study is a direct response to such cir-cumlocution, as he includes the context with the referent. "As a term," Weissman writes, "'the Holocaust' suggests not only the Jewish genocide but its Americaniza-tion, not only the event but the attempt to name or represent it" (26).

15. Haidu goes on to note that *Shoah*, too, has religious connotations: "the disas-ter is sent from God" (279). Lang would add that *Shoah* and *Churban* "are more ac-curately descriptive than 'Holocaust,' because they imply a breach or turning point in history (*and* because they reject the connotations of 'sacrifice')," but that "these ref-erences, too, have theological or at least mediating overtones, they are confined to the viewpoint of the victims, and they fail to suggest the specific role of genocide as it figured in the deeds of the Third Reich" (*Act* xxi).

16. See Ofir's "On Sanctifying" for a blistering denunciation of this sacralization, a "new religion" in which "the Holocaust is God" (198) and which is informed by these four commandments: "Thou shalt have no other holocaust before the Holo-

caust of the Jews of Europe; Thou shalt not make unto thee any graven image or any likeness; Thou shalt not take the name of the Holocaust in vain; Remember" (197).

17. Iwona Irwin-Zarecka, qtd. in Dwork and Van Pelt 365. See Dwork and Van Pelt 354–78 for a discussion of the tensions around the camp's memorial function, specifically the neglect to incorporate Birkenau into the memorial site (a neglect they describe as part of "a program of usurpation" [364]). "The Auschwitz-Birkenau State Museum presents only the main camp at Auschwitz to visitors. One can enter Birkenau, but on one's own. The standard guided tour does not include a visit to the principal site of the Judeocide, although it was there that the countless transports arrived and the four chimneys smoked. Auschwitz I alone was designated to be the permanent exhibit" (364). As reasons, they cite not only the fact that Birkenau was in ruins after the war, whereas Auschwitz was more or less intact, but also these more compelling facts: "First, the fate of the Jews did not have an important place on the national agenda of postwar Poland. And second, Auschwitz I had been established as the Germans' instrument to subjugate the *Poles* into serfdom—an enslavement the Poles rightly interpreted as the initial steps toward a 'solution' to a Polish problem." The authors conclude that "the main camp first and foremost preserved Polish—not Jewish—history" (364, 365).

18. In 1967 Emil Fackenheim established an additional, "614th Commandment" in which the survival of the Jewish people, the memory of the "martyrs" of the Holocaust, the belief and trust in God are all to be maintained, for "to abandon any of these imperatives, in response to Hitler's victory at Auschwitz, would be to hand him yet other, posthumous victories" (qtd. in Novick 199). This concept of a Nazi posthumous victory has proved resilient: in 2003 Gubar suggested that "not-writing about the Shoah would constitute a Nazi victory" (7).

19. While I agree with Hilberg's critique of Goldhagen's *Hitler's Willing Executioners* in *Critical Inquiry*, I am sympathetic to Goldhagen's contention that the Holocaust is a manifestation of an explicitly Christian anti-Semitism. In *The Destruction of the European Jews*, Hilberg, too, situates the Holocaust in the context of centuries of religious persecution (5–27).

20. L. M. Thomas echoes Brown's vision of a moral beacon, while extending this vision from Holocaust suffering (which he aligns with Jewish identity) to American slavery, producing a vision of humanity defined, strangely, by both: a "we who are black and we who are Jews." "[I]f on account of the Shoah and American slavery humanity better understands the risks that it takes when it permits acts and the kind of behavior that are readily coopted by evil, then those who have died will not have died in vain. As moral beacons, we can prevent evil from ever having a posthumous victory" ("Suffering" 210).

21. Weissman offers an excellent account of the underlying jockeying for moral prestige that informs these debates around terminology. "The act of replacing this term [Holocaust] with *the* proper name for this event (Shoah, Churban, the Event, the Tremendum, etc.) reflects a desire to get closer to the actual horror of the death camps than this now popular term allows—and to separate oneself from the masses of ordinary people who have heard of 'the Holocaust' by giving one's own

relationship to the event a special name" (24). He concludes, "The search for a more appropriate term than 'the Holocaust' is part of the contest . . . over who *really* knows the horror. . . . The fact that most writers resolve themselves to using the common-place 'Holocaust' suggests that a convincing moral-intellectual high ground has yet to be named" (25).

22. Haidu, for example, writes:

Exclusive stress on the uniqueness of the Event, combined with its sacraliza-tion, results in its disconnectedness from history. . . . The Event's uniqueness is reified; it is conceived as entirely *sui generis* and unprecedented: decontex-tualized, it therefore must escape historical comprehension. The stress on uniqueness leads, in ineluctable logic, to radical incomprehensibility. Worse, such a historical *hapax* also leads to dismissal of the event as irrelevant: if it is entirely unique and disconnected from human historicity, what can be its "rel-evance" for the perplexed, engaged in making historical and moral choices? (291)

Yehuda Bauer, though, points out, "The Holocaust, that is, the planned total annihi-lation of the Jewish people and the actual murder of close to six million of them, is a historical event; it was perpetrated by humans for human reasons, and is therefore as explicable as any other series of violent acts in recorded history" (36).

23. Both Israeli Arabs and Palestinians employ the Arabic term *Nakba*, which, like the Hebrew terms *Shoah* and *Churban*, connotes total destruction.

24. Lest my readers assume that Vital's statements are an aberration in writing about the Holocaust, let me cite Hayes's comment that Vital's argument "[provides] not only valuable correctives to hasty or superficial readings of the historical record, but also simulating models of how serious thinkers' view of the past and present can intersect in the conceptualization of the Holocaust" (8).

25. Boyarin writes,

The loss of a particular space, of a face-to-face everyday "community" of those sharing a common culture, is perhaps the smallest of three concentric registers of collective loss. A second is the loss of "tradition," of a set of lifeways passed along according to the model suggested by Tocqueville. The third is genocide, the destruction of an imagined national collective, the loss of a "people." Much as these forms of loss, especially the last, appear sacrosanct, I intend to em-phasize here, by placing them within quotation marks, that they are indeed constructions—and losing them is a construction as well. (7)

26. In *After the End* Berger defines apocalypse as unrepresentable, as "catastro-phes so overwhelming that they seem to negate the possibility of expression at the same time that they compel expression" (5). *After the End* includes an extensive dis-cussion of the Holocaust as apocalypse (59–133), symptomatically reflecting the as-sociation of the Holocaust with "saying the unsayable" and its prominence as "one of those events or objects that in some sense 'resist representation'" (xx).

27. Blanchot would agree with Budick and Iser that negativity precludes simple dichotomies of presence/absence, speaking/silence, writing/not-writing: "[W]ithout language, nothing can be shown. And to be silent is still to speak" (11).

28. "Trauma theory," writes Hungerford, "does not, as [Primo] Levi does, treat the camps as the destruction of what makes persons significant as such, but instead imagines the existential crisis that structures the Holocaust experience as the very core of both culture and personhood—that is, at the very core of our common life" (111). Hungerford is critical not only of this abstraction but of the extent to which it renders trauma transmissible, effacing crucial distinctions between survivors and their descendants, but also distinctions between survivors and nonsurvivors (her example is Binjamin Wilkomirski) and, most compellingly, survivors and perpetrators (113), a concern she shares with Leys.

29. Under the Nazis, of course, Jews were considered nonwhite. See Gilman, *The Jew's Body*, for a more extensive discussion of this issue.

30. I would extend Yael Feldman's observations about Israeli literature to this rhetoric of trauma. Feldman, writing about contemporary Israeli fiction, notes that in such literature psychoanalysis is appropriated for the purposes of ideology critique, and contends that "Freudianism is used only as a metaphor; in the final analysis, it is ideology rather than individual psychology that is the primary force behind these literary representations" (226).

31. See Hungerford 97–121 for a discussion of the extent to which Wilkomirski and Paul de Man can be seen as "traumatized."

32. Sanyal, who hints at the extent to which "trauma theory's focus on aporetic modes of knowledge and representation also assumes—too swiftly—that nonidentitiarian articulations of history and subjectivity are inherently ethical" (12), is an exception.

33. Leys's study of trauma's discursive manifestations provides important insight to the construction of "trauma" and of the "traumatic." She is quite critical of the "contemporary literary-critical fascination with the allegedly unrepresentable and unspeakable nature of trauma, especially the trauma of the Holocaust, which in effect stands in for trauma generally" (16), and identifies a retroactive temporality in trauma theory that produces the Holocaust as "*the* crucial trauma of the century" (15; emphasis in the original), "the watershed event of the modern age" which is held to "have precipitated, perhaps caused, an epistemological-ontological crisis of witnessing, a crisis manifested at the level of language itself" (268). It is worth considering, though, the extent to which the mimetic/antimimetic dichotomy that, Leys argues, structures and ultimately stymies trauma theory reflects, structurally, what Rothberg identifies as the realist/antirealist dichotomy in Holocaust studies—a dichotomy that ultimately dictates attitudes toward the Holocaust's representability.

34. LaCapra, whose writings on the Holocaust are informed by what (in a seminar at the School of Criticism and Theory in 1998) he has called a "metaphor" of trauma, notes that Caruth's work reflects an uncertainty as to whether trauma is a condition or possibility of history, or history itself, and adds that "this uncertainty may itself perhaps be seen as a symptom of posttraumatic stress in which the recognition of a crucial problem (both the prevalent role of trauma in history and trauma as a possibility that may unexpectedly happen at any time in history) is rendered in a hyperbolic fashion that seems to equate history and trauma" (*Representing* 14 n. 2).

Perceiving Caruth's work as a symptom relocates trauma from "our" relation to history to the individual critic's relation to her subject. For LaCapra, this relation takes the form of trauma, or "muted trauma," which must then be "worked through."

35. Hungerford has critiqued Caruth's abstraction of trauma (which she calls "extreme" [135]), as a move that "[makes] trauma . . . inhere in the structure of language as such," "insulat[ing] [Caruth's] analysis from . . . more concrete notions of trauma" (113). This abstraction and insulation, Hungerford continues, elides distinctions between Holocaust survivors and their descendants as well as distinctions between survivors and those who are not survivors; further, it renders trauma transmissible, a transmissibility that enabled the transformation of Bruno Dössekker into Binjamin Wilkomirski (119). Sanyal has added that Caruth's "conception of history . . . produces a potential conflation of subject positions" (11): "Transformed from fact to concept, the Holocaust becomes the matrix for a set of interchangeable traumas" (16). Both Hungerford and Sanyal refer to Leys's critique of Caruth.

36. LaCapra identifies his "basic point" as this: "[T]he deconstruction of binary oppositions need not result in a generalized conceptual blur or in the continual suspension of all judgment and practice. It should be accompanied by a careful inquiry into the status and role of resulting distinctions as well as by research into their actual historical functions, knowledge of which is crucial for even the most tentative moral and political judgments" (*Representing* 11). In other words, the "basic point" resurrects the distinction between history and other disciplines. But it is this distinction that LaCapra dismissed earlier, in favor of the distinction between victims and perpetrators: "[T]here is a sense in which less rides on the distinction between history and other disciplines than on that between perpetrators and victims in the Holocaust" (9–10). Exploring this more crucial distinction, in which he allows for "complex and ambiguous cases"—he touches on historical determinism, voluntary and involuntary collaboration, the complicity of bystanders, "dubious postwar uses of the Shoah as 'symbolic capital,'" and the assumption of collective German guilt— leads LaCapra not only to privilege "research into . . . actual historical functions" but to align the historical with a moral stance: knowledge of this historical context "is crucial for even the most tentative moral and political judgments" (10–11).

37. The study of PTSD in war veterans, for example, is predicated on the assumption that innocence is not identical with victimhood. See Leys 232 n. 3 for discussion of the expansion of "trauma" to include actions of perpetrators of atrocities (the subject is Vietnam War veterans).

38. Given that my discussion of Caruth thus far has focused on Leys's critique of her argument, I should clarify here that my own reservations about Caruth's work are predicated less on the necessity to maintain distinctions between perpetrators and victims and are more in line with what Hungerford identifies as Caruth's investment in trauma as "a kind of 'not knowing'" (114), and the implications of this alignment of trauma with the unspeakable, although Hungerford is specifically interested in the implications of Caruth's theory for language, identity, and culture: "If identity imagined in these terms [as the product of trauma] preserves one's cultural integrity in the way Caruth argues, then cultural identity has the same structure as traumatic

experience—cultural identity and trauma are incomprehensible experiences that get passed around" (117).

39. This dichotomy—and the way trauma theory threatens to collapse it—motivates Sanyal's thoughtful and rigorous critique of trauma theory in "A Soccer Match." Trauma theory, says Sanyal, reproduces the collapse of innocence and guilt that, in the concentration camp, worked as so deadly an instrument of dehumanization, and thus perpetrates its own kind of violence, suggesting that "the perpetrators, by virtue of . . . participating in the traumatic conditions of camp life, could be perceived as victims" (9). I will return to Sanyal's argument in the following section.

40. LaCapra qualifies this process of muted trauma:

This process may, in the best of cases, serve as an antidote insofar as it is related to a broader attempt to work through problems and develop a perspective that addresses certain issues (including normative issues) in social and political life. But this process may also get out of control and not only reinscribe but even intensify fragmentation and disorientation. Such a possibility threatens to occur when one identifies trauma with history or modernity and elaborates an approach that insistently remains within trauma by endlessly enacting a repetition compulsion or generating aporias. (221)

While he does advocate a responsible "working through" of trauma, his assumption of post-Holocaust culture's ability to be traumatized by the Holocaust and his implicit idea that such an ability is a reflection of post-Holocaust culture's responsible approach to the Holocaust (the attempt to understand and to empathize) are what I am critiquing here.

41. The questions genocide makes us ask, according to Lang, are "what groups can be the victims of genocide, and what aspects of such groups are the objects of the act of genocide" (Act 6).

42. Lang cites Milton's Satan in Paradise Lost—"evil, be thou my good"—noting that "historically, the figure of Satan has represented precisely this improbable conjunction: evil as a conscious and deliberate—intended—choice. We see in the phenomenon of genocide that Satan is not, after all, only a mythical figure, that also human beings can do evil voluntarily" (Act 29).

43. At this point, Lang's discussion sounds like Steiner's controversial claims about the German language. "[T]he German language was not innocent of the horrors of Nazism," writes Steiner. Asking his readers to imagine "[t]he unspeakable being said, over and over, for twelve years," he concludes, "Something will happen to it [language]. . . . Something will happen to the words" ("Hollow Miracle" 99, 100, 101). Hartman notes this similarity without addressing the problematic and controversial implications of language's complicity in Nazi evil that Steiner emphasizes (Longest Shadow 13 n. 1).

44. For Lang, the moral implications of representing evil extend beyond the language used by the Nazis to the types of representation the Holocaust undergoes in a post-Holocaust world. And although Lang is privileging literary representation in his discussion, Hartman notes that Lang's argument extends to "any Holocaust representation." Hartman writes that "there is always a decision for or against silence. In

that respect fictional elaboration is not different from history-writing or other non-fictional forms of description and commentary" (*Longest Shadow,* 3).

45. Referring to the Sonderkommandos, the Special Squads, whose position was the most acute, Levi refers to "the intrinsic horror of this human condition" which "has imposed a sort of reserve on all the testimony, so that even today it is difficult to conjure up an image of 'what it meant' to be forced to exercise this trade for months" (52–53). While I do not disagree that this condition is an intrinsically horrible one, it is not, I argue, the intrinsic horror of the condition that imposes a reserve on the testimony, but the testimonial situation itself: the exigencies of speech. Levi would probably agree. Continuing his discussion of the Sonderkommandos, he notes that "one cannot expect from men who have known such extreme destitution a deposition in the juridical sense, but something that is at once a lament, a curse, an expiation, an attempt to justify and rehabilitate oneself: a liberating outburst rather than a Medusa-faced truth" (53). Given Levi's recognition of the agency that speech implies, it is surprising that he attributes the "reserve" of the survivors' testimony to "intrinsic horror."

2. Speaking Schindler's List

1. Hartman recalls this image of the boy whose toys come alive in Spielberg's 1977 film *Close Encounters of the Third Kind,* but reads the role of childhood wonder somewhat differently.

It is the child in the adult which remains Spielberg's theme even here: the abused and disabused child. Cinema addresses that sin against the child—not only, as in *Schindler's List,* by terrifying us with pictures of a mass infanticide, but also, in general, by reviving a structural link between the adult memory and the childlike imagination. . . . The child (in us) still learns through wonder; for young people the past can never catch up with the future, with freedom, with possibility. Who can forget, in Spielberg's *Close Encounters of the Third Kind,* the boy's face, when his toys spontaneously light up, start up, come alive? That mixture of innocence and wonder, of an expectant gaze that says "I always knew you were real, you were alive" is unforgettable. Whatever our age, when we enter the cave and become "cinema animals," we also reenter a realm of possibility. Our feelings are freed—even for the sinister subject, for a film like *Schindler's List,* which reconnects them with a knowledge we had desensitized or relegated to footnotes. ("Cinema Animal" 141)

2. Lanzmann continues: "Fiction is a transgression. I deeply believe there are some things that cannot and should not be represented. . . . So the question is: in order to bear witness to what happened, should one invent a new form, or should one reconstruct? I believe I created a new form; Spielberg chose to reconstruct. The trouble is that, in a way, reconstruction is tantamount to fabricating archives" ("Why Spielberg"). Rothberg describes Lanzmann's response to *Schindler's List* as "[taking] on the role of border guard and [declaring] Spielberg's film inadequate to its subject matter. He thus protected the place of his own 'sacred' film in the canon of Holocaust representation" (224–25). Rothberg finds "similar rhetorical claims to realism

enunciated by both directors and their critics, as well as related attempts to create a mimetic correspondence between text and event, albeit with very different effects" (224).

3. See Hansen for discussion of how the classical mode of Hollywood narrative governs *Schindler's List*. The prevalence of such a narrative disturbs Gertrud Koch as well: "[Spielberg] gives us the idea that if you had been smart enough, you could have survived. The film is so pleasing because of the idea that you can be redeemed just by taking your own sovereignty back. And while it's a very nice idea, it doesn't fit the historical ends" (Hoberman 26).

4. I should clarify that while Hansen is, in this portion of her essay, describing the prevalent critical approaches to the film, she does not dissociate herself from them.

5. Hansen addresses the significance of sound in *Schindler's List,* an issue she claims is neglected in most critical discussions of the film. "The soundtrack," she notes, "is neither the seat of a superior truth (as Lanzmann seemed to claim for *Shoah*) nor merely a masked accomplice for the untruths of the image track (as assumed in summary critiques of the classical Hollywood film), but rather the material site of particular and competing aesthetic practices" (303). She goes on to point out that

temporal displacement is a function of the soundtrack, in particular an abundance of sound bridges and other forms of non-matching (such as a character's speech or reading turning into documentary-style voice-over); and there are numerous moments when the formal disjunction of sound and image tracks subtends rhetorical relations of irony and even counterpoint. This disjunctive style occurs primarily on the level of diegetic sound, in particular, speech. (The use of nondiegetic music in *Schindler's List* is indeed another matter, inasmuch as it functions more like the "glue" that traditionally covers over any discontinuity and sutures the viewer into the film). But the persistent splitting of the image track by means of displaced diegetic sound still undercuts the effect of an immediate and totalitarian grasp on reality. (304)

6. Here my reading differs from Horowitz's, who views the artificial color of the candles in the factory as an indication that the Jewish people, destroyed by the Nazis, are resurrected by Schindler. "The Jews of Kraków are emblematized by the flame of the Sabbath candles, and the extinguishing caused by the Holocaust is later reversed imagistically by the lighting of the Sabbath candles in Schindler's Czechoslovakian factory—reversed by Schindler's act of saving Jewish lives" ("But Is It" 124). While the artificial color of the candles does signify something, this moment is not as powerful a return to reality as that effected by the full color sequence at the end.

7. Schindler's collaboration with the Nazis is coyly gestured toward and away from throughout the film, even though his active participation in the systematic dispossession of Jews is rendered quite explicitly. In Schindler's discussion with Stern at the Judenrat, we learn that the factory on Lipova Street that Schindler will convert to his Deutsche Enamel Fabriken is, in fact, property stolen from a Jewish businessman: "What [Jewish business] community?" asks Stern. "Jews can no longer own businesses." He continues, "That's why the factory on Lipova Street is empty," but his

voice at this point is almost inaudible. Schindler continues to consolidate his position at the expense of dispossessed Jews as he moves into a comfortable, spacious apartment while the apartment's owners, pelted with stones and excrement, join the harried procession into the ghetto to the tune of "Good-bye Jews." His pleased surveyal of his new surroundings is contrasted with the Jewish couple's shock at the crowded slum into which they have been forced. Discussing the secret of his current financial success with his wife, Schindler says that "there has always been something missing. You can't make this thing. You can't buy this thing." His wife guesses, "Luck?" but Schindler answers, "War!" The amorphous realm of "war" is, however, a misleading, because incomplete, term: the real reason for Schindler's financial success is *the war against the Jews*, which offers him easy access to stolen property, cheap goods, and unpaid labor.

Annette Insdorf praises Spielberg for not making Schindler "transparent," referring to "the mystery of this man" and his "transcendent decency," as she applauds Spielberg's "honest acknowledgement that we cannot penetrate the mystery of this man's decisions" and grandly gestures toward "the mystery of human identity" (Hoberman 28–29). Such facile gestures reveal the extent to which an emphasis on Schindler's enigmatic nature enables critics to avoid the far more problematic fact of his active collaboration.

8. As Loshitzky puts it, "The Holocaust as memorialized by Spielberg's film has been mobilized as an educational tool in the fight against contemporary racism, reinforcing the thesis of French historian Pierre Sorlin that the historical film always interprets the past from the perspective of the present. This is most evident in the way the film has been used as a 'weapon' in the multicultural wars dividing the contemporary ethnic landscape of American society" (intro. 6).

9. Hansen, while perhaps not sharing my specific emphasis on the primacy of films for Holocaust representations in the United States in particular, does agree that the Holocaust poses specific challenges to the interaction of media and memory:

[W]hether we like it or not, the predominant vehicles of public memory *are* the media of technical re/production and mass consumption. This issue is especially exacerbated for the remembrance of the Shoah considering the specific crisis posed by the Nazis' destruction of the very basis and structures of collective remembering. (Unlike most of the "ordinary massacres" committed in the course of the German genocidal war all over Europe, the Shoah left no *communities* of survivors, widows and children, not even burial sites that would have provided a link with a more "organic" tradition of oral and collective memory.) In a significant way, even before the passing of the last survivors, the remembrance of the Shoah, to the extent that it was public and collective, has always been more dependent on mass-mediated forms of memory—on what Alison Landsberg calls "prosthetic memory." (310)

Wanda Bershen, director of the National Jewish Archives of Broadcasting at The Jewish Museum in New York, agrees with my emphasis on the specific relation between Holocaust remembrance and film in the United States: "In this country, people don't know very much history, especially of foreign countries, and have never lived through a war at home. Americans don't have occasion to pass by ruins or grave-yards or traces of a war, in daily life—as is often the case in Europe. I am always pro-gramming films about history, and often think that history is perceived as something that happens in the movies and is not very real" (Hoberman 30).

10. See Hansen for a good analysis of the comparison itself and of the cultural conversation that this comparison impedes. See also Rothberg's discussion of the two films in *Traumatic Realism* (231–37).

11. As James Young puts it, "[T]he critics all want to know of *Schindler's List:* 'Is this the last word on the Holocaust? Is this going to come to stand for all other Holocaust films?' If it does, than it is a great tragedy, especially if it wipes out 34 years of other really interesting films on the Holocaust" (Hoberman 24–25).

12. Avisar makes a similar point: "[T]he Holocaust was a terrible event of shock-ing atrocities, but ultimately good triumphed over evil, and the survivors and their families are proof of the defeat of the Nazi plan of genocide." He adds: "These are re-assuring attitudes to be sure, but they are not compatible with the unambiguous ex-istence of the evil of the architects of genocide and of the fate of the millions who perished" (56).

13. James Young says: "In the case of *Schindler's List,* I hope that the great numbers that are going to see it will have their curiosity piqued about what was lost. But I fear that they will come away sated now that they have seen the last word on the Holo-caust" (Hoberman 25).

14. Thus Avisar concludes his essay: "[A]ny truly creative and responsible treat-ment of the Holocaust cannot ignore the demanding moral aspects of the subject, which call for a consideration of the enormity of the event and the limits of its rep-resentation" (56).

15. Ken Jacobs, for example, says:
In terms of giving us an understanding of why this guy goes through whatever he goes through, the girl in the red coat, and we're put through the emotional wringer. I doubt that any critical shielding could protect us from being reached into and twisted. . . . It was crazy-making to go through that—to pick out this little girl and put us through that number. I felt really violated by that. I don't want to be tapped in that way, I don't want to be put through emotional paces in that way. (Hoberman 29)

16. Horowitz reads this scene differently, as part of the film's tendency to employ prevalent racial and sexual stereotypes. See "But Is It" 131–32 for a discussion of this scene in particular.

17. Loshitzky writes:
In both countries [Germany and Israel] the reactions (unlike those in the United States) were mixed. The film and the American director were subject to early attacks by a surprising number of both Israeli and German critics. In both countries, obviously for different reasons, both Spielberg's American-ness and Jewishness were the source of a feeling of discomfort, if not blatant hostility. For the Germans, Spielberg's Americanness was, in some cases, viewed negatively as yet more evidence of American cultural imperialism

threatening to turn Europe and Germany—as its emerging power—into "little America." Latent xenophobia and Judeophobia were disguised through criticism leveled at Hollywood's vulgarization of the Holocaust. In Israel some of the more vicious attacks on the film (for example, the one made by the historian and journalist Tom Segev) expressed latent hostility toward the American Jew who "stole our Shoah." (intro. 8)

18. For an account of Schindler's journey to virtue, see Horowitz: "We witness Schindler's spiritual metamorphosis by observing the transition in his sexual relationships. As Schindler becomes more 'good'—more authentically Schindler—he kisses chastely rather than demandingly and finally promises fidelity to his wife. Thus, Schindler proves his manhood through the enactment of Christian virtue. This further conflates the atrocity done to Jews with the eros of violence. It also, problematically, makes genocide and fornication into moral equivalents" ("But Is It" 132).

19. Rothberg, in reading this scene, notes that the gold for the ring was obtained by extracting another prisoner's tooth. "While the extraction of a prisoner's tooth might . . . constitute an index of violence and loss, here it is rendered as comedy and sentimentality and as part of the film's act of closure" (230). He reads the ceremony as homosocial ritual, one that "culminates the homeopathic 'purification rites' for Schindler, who has been partially sullied by his (opportunistic) homosocial bonds with Amon Goeth and other Nazi leaders" (230–31).

20. And this Holocaust is one that is explicitly concerned with representations of value, specifically monetary value, to such an extent that, as critics have rightly pointed out, it is a very American Holocaust. As Art Spiegelman puts it, "[T]he film is not about Jews or, arguably, even the Holocaust. . . . It's a movie about Clinton. It's about the benign aspects of capitalism—Capitalism With a Human Face. We're in Ayn Rand country: the Businessman as hero. Capitalism can give us a health care program, and it can give us a Schindler" (Hoberman 30). See also Avisar's essay for a more coherent argument about how Spielberg's film Americanizes the Holocaust.

21. In addition, we are informed by the caption that "there are fewer than 4000 Jews in Poland today. There are more than 6000 descendants of the Jews on Schindler's list." In the safe realm of memory, numbers—the right ones—do matter after all.

22. Hungerford notes that "the unnamed hand is reputed to be Spielberg's, but in its anonymity it stands in for any hand, for the reverent viewer's hand." She adds that "the hand we see is in no way marked as Jewish, and the object it places on the grave is not the stone of Jewish tradition, but the flower, associated with Christian and other religions', as well as secular American, memorial practices" (84).

23. Hence Hoberman writes that, "given our tendency to confuse the representation with the event, the act of memory with actual participation, Spielberg himself has become a heroic and representative figure" (24).

24. Bernstein makes a good point when he says, "Part of the general reluctance to think critically about *Schindler's List* arises, I suspect, because in the face of suffering on as great a scale as the Holocaust, there is a general freezing up of normal intellectual discriminations. Yet these moments of confrontation with the monstrous re-

quire more, not less, clarity and demand a greater measure, rather than an abdication, of the ability to concentrate on fundamental distinctions" (430). However, Bernstein's position does not keep him from making the very same gesture, as he concludes that "to speak about a '*Schindler's List* effect' is now perhaps more useful than to concentrate exclusively on the film," and adds that "among the most vertiginous of these effects is the way the Holocaust is currently at risk of being presented, if only in people's first exposure to the subject, chiefly as the factual 'basis' for Steven Spielberg's movie" (431).

3. The Story of My Death

1. I use this term to refer to authors, filmmakers, and scholars who did not survive the Holocaust in the sense that their bodies were not present in Nazi-occupied Europe. The significance of the body's presence or absence at the site of atrocity will emerge in my discussion of the *Fragments* controversy and the critical controversy around D. M. Thomas's *The White Hotel*. For a thoughtful discussion of the term "nonsurvivor" and its expansion to include those who were not historically present, see Weissman 4–18. Weissman prefers the term "nonwitness," which "stresses that we who were not there did not witness the Holocaust, and that the experience of listening to, reading, or viewing witness testimony is substantially unlike the experience of victimization" (20). I agree with Weissman, but I retain the term nonsurvivor in this context in order to effect a linguistic distinction between the survivor and the witness, as not all survivors can or choose to give testimony.

2. See chap. 1 for a discussion of the term "speech" and its implications for corporeality, communication, and community, all of which are effaced with "unspeakable." Hartman offers the following comments on the distinction between speech and testimony: "After the camps . . . the survivors not only testify, that is, describe the terror undergone, but *speak:* they testify to speech itself as an act of which they had been deprived and that enters once again into normal human intercourse" (*Fateful Question* 102–3; emphasis in the original).

3. Bernard-Donals, reflecting on trauma theory's contribution to theories of testimony, writes that "we cannot view testimony as a window on the past; at its most extreme—in memories of trauma—testimony marks the absence of events since they did not register on, let alone become integrated into, the victim's consciousness" (197). For more on the implications of the Holocaust as a context for trauma theory, see my discussion in chap. 1.

4. See Lappin, and Maechler. Hungerford proffers an account of how Wilkomirski "memoriz[ed] the map of Auschwitz . . . and in doing so, perhaps without intending to, he became a child survivor" (119).

5. Hungerford traces similar ground with her discussion of the rhetoric of personification that pervades Holocaust discourse. But her emphasis is on the role played by text, and on the relation between memorizing and memory. She concludes her discussion of the Wilkomirski affair by describing how, when reading is imagined to produce experience, Bruno Dössekker's reading (about the Holocaust) produced the experience to which Binjamin Wilkomirski testifies (119).

6. In the novel, Lisa Erdman, Thomas's protagonist, experiences hallucinations of falling, of burning, and testifies to pain in her breast and hip. In the penultimate chapter, she falls into the ravine at Babi Yar—not yet dead, she is kicked in the breast and hip, and her body is finally burned with the rest of the victims'. The final chapter depicts an "afterlife" in what appears to be a displaced person's camp in Palestine. Here, Lisa's pains persist but begin to fade. In the "Babi-Yar" section of the novel, Thomas borrowed liberally from Anatoli Kuznetsov's documentary novel *Babi Yar*, specifically from Kuznetsov's recounting of the testimony of Dina Pronicheva, who did survive the massacre (Dina appears as a character in Thomas's novel), a testimony that is presented by Kuznetsov as an accurate rendition of Pronicheva's story: "I wrote [the story] down myself from her words," writes Kuznetsov. "I shall give her story exactly as she told it, without adding anything" (63). But as Young has noted, Pronicheva's testimony is still mediated by Kuznetsov's authorial voice ("Holocaust Documentary Fiction" 204).

7. For Ozsvath and Satz, Thomas's novel "subsumes the horrors of the Holocaust under psychological illness and thus reduces moral and metaphysical atrocity to comprehensible human size. By doing so, it trivializes and debases the occurrence, making tawdry and cheap something that is incomprehensibly grandiose in its evil" (210). For Wirth-Nesher, Thomas withdraws from fiction at the moment of the massacre in order to make a statement on the role of fiction and its limits: "He does not go so far as to declare a temporary moratorium on fictionalizing, as others have done, because he understands how difficult it would be to fix the border between fact and fiction. But he recognizes the moral imperative to seek such a boundary and then to use fiction to impress upon us the magnitude of the loss at Babi Yar by recreating imaginatively the lives of those who died, but not their deaths" (25).

8. Similarly, Young reads *The White Hotel* through "the rhetorical trope of eyewitness," by which Thomas, referring to Kuznetsov's text, imbues his novel with testimonial authority but not authenticity, investing his novel with a "sense of the real" ("Holocaust Documentary Fiction" 213). Like Wirth-Nesher, Young focuses on the relation between texts (Thomas's and Kuznetsov's) to establish authority, assuming but not addressing the role of the body as the guarantor of testimony's status as fact. While Robertson and Tanner both argue that "the description of Babi Yar converts . . . pain into fact" (Tanner 147), they oppose that fact to fiction and valorize Thomas's novel as retaining the unspeakable: "Thomas's brutal representation of the violence at Babi Yar is unmediated by any obvious interpretive scheme; in its painstaking, literal detailing of atrocity after atrocity, it defies any facile metaphorical interpretation," writes Tanner (147). Robertson identifies "woman's discourse" with the Holocaust, and argues that both are rendered unspeakable by the male-dominated texts of the novel: "The novel shows . . . that Lisa's knowledge as woman, as analysand, and as Nazi victim is literally still unspeakable in any mainstream discourse" (477).

9. As I noted in chap. 1, "unspeakable" conjoins physical articulation, language, and community in the term "to speak." "To speak" implies the presence of a speaker, an audience to her speech (one that shares enough of the speaker's culture to be able to recognize the speaker as such, apprehend her speech, and assess its rhetorical sig-

240

nificance), a public arena in which her speech takes place (hence my choice of "to speak" over the more informal connotations of "to say"), and the assumption that such speech—by virtue of its presence, its audience, its public context—*does something* (or, just as significantly, valiantly attempts to do something and fails). Thus, the fact of speech conjoins the act of physical articulation, the performative quality of language, the space (however virtual) of a public arena, and the presence of community. While my focus has so far been on the role of language, representation, and its limits in the application of a rhetoric of the unspeakable to the Holocaust, this chapter will specifically address the role of the speaker's body, her physical articulation and presence.

10. Agamben takes this term from Primo Levi, who identifies the *Muselmänner* as those who, because they "saw the Gorgon, have not returned to tell about it or have returned mute," are "the complete witnesses, the ones whose deposition would have a general significance" (Levi 84).

11. "There can be testimony," writes Agamben, because there is "an inseparable division and non-coincidence between the inhuman and the human, the living being and the speaking being, the *Muselmann* and the survivor . . . [testimony's] authority depends not on a factual truth, a conformity between something said and a fact or between memory and what happened, but rather on the immemorial relation between the unsayable and the sayable, between the outside and the inside of language" (157–58). While Agamben explicitly dissociates himself from the notion that the Holocaust is unsayable, such formulations support LaCapra's observation, in "Approaching Limit Events," that "Agamben has a sense of the apocalyptic and a penchant for the all-or-nothing response that help to induce the figuration of Auschwitz as a radical rupture or caesura in history" (272). For an account of how such figuration contributes to a rhetoric of the unspeakable, and for additional discussion of Agamben, see chap. 1.

12. Hartman's rendition of the Adorno is slightly different: "[T]he integration of physical death into culture is to be gainsaid by theoretical considerations, not to further the idea of death as an ontologically pure essence, but for the sake of what is expressed by the stench of the corpse before it is deceptively laid out as an embalmed body" (qtd. in Hartman, *Fateful Question* 119).

13. Carroll reads Semprun's emphasis on the aesthetic in *Literature or Life* as a response to the argument that fiction, in the context of the Holocaust, is transgressive (an argument with which Fuss, who posits the Holocaust as the historical event that calls a halt to fiction, would seem to agree). "Fiction, which Semprun defines as narrative to the second degree, narrative that has been transformed and recreated as an aesthetic object, is thus for him not the enemy of memory and history but a necessary support for memory and a means of conveying the substance and paradoxical 'transparent density' of experience," writes Carroll ("Limits" 74). I read Semprun's emphasis on the aesthetic slightly differently, as an opportunity to engage with the ethical implications of the testimonial address. Semprun's concern is less with the extent to which art can do its subject justice and more with the extent to which the audience can do justice to art.

14. Langer describes a similar encounter: "She [the witness] remembers thinking that 'my family were killed' was totally inadequate, because 'killed,' she says, was a word used for 'ordinary' forms of dying. But to say matter of factly that 'My mother and brother and two sisters were gassed' as soon as they arrived at Auschwitz seemed equally unsatisfactory, because plain factuality could not convey the enormity of the event." This survivor's refusal to speak, comments Langer, "had nothing to do with the oft-repeated view that perhaps silence was the only appropriate response to such catastrophe. . . . [R]eluctance to speak," he concludes, has little to do with *preference for silence*" (*Holocaust Testimonies* 61).

15. In Holocaust testimony, writes Langer, "dying in the past and living in the present are . . . inseparable, the threat of one shadowing the future prospects of the other" (*Holocaust Testimonies* 132). Faced with these testimonies, "[w]e are forced," he writes elsewhere, "to redefine the meaning of survival" ("Pursuit of Death" 379). He concludes, "The impact on consciousness of this dilemma is a neglected but important legacy of the experience we call the Holocaust" ("Pursuit of Death" 379).

16. Avni notes that Moshe, as the emblematic Holocaust survivor, poses issues of ownership and appropriation: "It is therefore not a question of privately telling the story (to oneself, to one's editor or to one's analyst) as of having others—a whole community—*claim* it, *appropriate* it, and *react* (properly) to it" (212). But Avni, as mentioned, misses the extent to which Moshe's "story" is, more precisely, "the story of [his] death."

17. For Felman and Laub's alignment of history with Holocaust, see my discussion of *Testimony* in chap. 1.

18. While *Night* is commonly referred to as a "testimony" (Wiesel himself, in the introduction to *Night; Dawn; Day,* calls *Night* a "testimony" that is present "in all that I have written and all that I am going to write" [3]), I employ the term "novella" here in order to distinguish Wiesel's text from testimony in the juridical or historical sense. By distinguishing the story Eliezer tells (a testimony represented in the novella) from the novella itself, I attempt to avoid what Naomi Seidman, with characteristic insight, has identified as a common aspect of *Night's* reception: "[B]ecause *Night* has nearly always been received as an unmediated autobiographical account, the complexity of Wiesel's interpretive craft, his *writing*, in other words, has been very nearly invisible" (3).

19. Colin Davis, for example, writes that "Moshe's story, like *La Nuit*, does not communicate a message that is intelligible . . . rather it exposes an inadequacy within understanding, its potentially fatal failure to comprehend inassimilable data" (35), and concludes that "the essential problem of *La Nuit* derives from the tension between the formal coherence and retrospective authority of the narrative, and the subject-matter of the work" (57). For Ellen Fine, "the essence of his [Wiesel's] story—filled with unanswered political, philosophical, and theological questions— is impossible to communicate" (3). For an important exception to and critique of such readings, see Seidman.

20. Seidman offers an important comparison of *Night* with its Yiddish predecessor, *Un di velt hot geshvign* (And the World Kept Silent), which Wiesel had published

in 1956, tracing the conflicting articulations of identity the two memoirs produce. "There are two survivors," she concludes, "a Yiddish and a French—or perhaps we should say one survivor who speaks to a Jewish audience and one whose first reader is a French Catholic. . . . What remains outside this proliferating discourse on the unsayable is not what cannot be spoken but what cannot be spoken *in French*. And this is not the 'silence of the dead' but rather the scandal of the living, the scandal of Jewish rage and unwillingness to embody suffering and victimization" (8). Significantly, Seidman identifies the distinction between the two survivors in terms of the presence or the absence of the body: the image of the corpse in the mirror that closes *Night* is shattered by the narrator of *Un di velt*. "By stopping when it does, *Night* depict[s] the survivor as a witness and as an expression of silence and death, projecting the recently liberated Eliezer's death-haunted face into the postwar years when Wiesel would become a familiar figure. By contrast, the Yiddish survivor shatters that image as soon as he sees it, destroying the deathly existence the Nazis willed on him" (7). "The image that dominates the end of *Night*," she continues, "is precisely the image that Wiesel shatters at the end of his Yiddish work. And resurrects to end the French one" (8).

Implicit in Seidman's argument is the assumption that the Yiddish memoir is the "real" memoir, and the French text is the (less authentic) product of Wiesel's authorial decisions—an assumption that manifests itself in her reference to the narrator of the Yiddish memoir by the author's name (16). But I would argue that by shattering the mirror and addressing the reader, the narrator of *Un di velt* reunites body with speech. In contrast, *Night* represents testimony as silenced, utilizing the figure of the corpse to echo the role of the body as an guarantor of this representation's "truth."

21. Here Mauriac echoes Robert McAfee Brown's assertion that "[t]he descriptive term imaging the author at the book's end is that of a corpse" (pref. vi), and the general critical tendency to confuse Eliezer with Wiesel.

22. Seidman offers an extensive and insightful reading of Mauriac's foreword. "Mauriac," she notes, "in a paradoxical assertion, claims for himself the virtue of silence, presents a Christian perspective while framing it as tactfully and respectfully withheld" (11). For an additional explication of Mauriac's text, see my "Speaking Corpses."

23. To Halkin's concern that "the division into small boxes limits all utterances to the shortest and pithiest statements, ruling out nearly all verbal subtlety or complexity, while the need to fill each box with a drawing has a similar effect on the illustrations" (56), Tabachnik replies that artistic mastery can overcome the innate discrepancy between the subject matter and its representation: "[T]o someone as good as Spiegelman, the very restraint imposed by the graphic panel format becomes a challenge and an opportunity to say a lot in a little" (157). Similarly, Spiegelman stresses that his drawings are not "representations" and characterizes the animal motif as a "cipher," the purpose of which is its own undoing: "[T]o use these ciphers . . . is actually a way to allow you past the cipher" (qtd. in Witek 102).

24. "*Maus* is dominated by this absence of Anja's voice, the destruction of her diaries, her missing note," writes Hirsch (19). The loss of Anja's testimony, writes

Glejzer, is "the traumatic kernel that this text cannot put into words but cannot help but speak. It is the moment in *Maus* where the impossibility of testimony speaks over the very real testimony of Vladek or even of Artie's remembrances of his youth" (136). Huyssen reads the loss of Anja's diaries as marking the limits of mimetic approximation (78). Levine, who describes *Maus* as "a silent film about silence," identifies that silence as "of Anja first and foremost, but ultimately of everyone who perished in the Holocaust" (324). Nancy Miller writes that "the specter of [Anja's] dead body constitutes a crucial piece of the *Maus* recovery project: a son's doomed but also belated attempt to get his mother's story, a story that can neither be separated from nor fully explained by the historical event" (109).

25. My quotations from *Maus* retain the ellipses and emphases of the text. In addition, I distinguish between Spiegelman (the author, whose interviews I quote and whose graphic and textual work I analyze) and Art or Artie (the representation of Spiegelman in *Maus*).

26. The prominence accorded the missing note (the reference to the absent suicide note, not to the suicide itself, is accented by an exclamation mark) privileges the presence of text over that of bodies. When the reference to the missing note recurs in *Maus II*, Art is posited at his drawing board, head in hands, in the throes of writer's block. Again, the absence of text generates the presence of corpses. These corpses, though, are silent (*Maus II* 41).

27. McGlothlin reads the "Time Flies" section as figuring the temporal space of the "superpresent," which she says is "a place outside the movement of life, in a static space that is not the antithesis of life, but a place where life's ebb and flow do not reach" (186) and "stuck and unhinged from the conventional movement of life" (189). This temporal tension, then, generated from Art's need to "make an order," resonates with the speaking corpse generated by Vladek's need to "make an order." McGlothlin identifies the temporality of the superpresent as a space in which "the different levels of narrative, like those of temporality, are experienced simultaneously and are consequently *implicated in* each other" (194; emphasis mine).

28. See Rothberg 231–37 for a thoughtful reading of Lanzmann's inconsistent theory of representation, and for a reading of *Shoah* that illustrates surprising points of convergence with *Schindler's List*.

29. The French text actually names the experience of passivity as a ghost: "comme le passé immémorial . . . qui revient en dispersant par le retour le temps présent où il serait vécu comme revenant" (34).

30. Blanchot stresses that "absent meaning" is not "absence of meaning" or potential but lacking meaning; he also underscores the inappropriateness of the verb "to form"—as, in the writing of the disaster, "no forms hold sway" (41).

4. *Nat Turner's* Key

1. Despite certain biographical similarities, I distinguish here between Stingo (the protagonist of the novel), the mature Stingo (the novel's retrospective narrator), and Styron (the author). In doing so I differ from some of the critical work on the novel (see, e.g., Gardner) that tends to align the mature Stingo with the author Styron.

2. To argue, as Kreyling so eloquently does, that the novel advocates "speaking the unspeakable" could be more accurately parsed as arguing that the novel speaks *about* the unspeakable but maintains the ultimate inaccessibility of its subject to language—note Kreyling's description of Auschwitz as "that monolithic and inscrutable sign of the time" (199).

3. Novick explicitly links the popular miniseries with the establishment of a discourse of sacralization and unspeakability around the Holocaust in the United States (209–13).

4. This is not to say that *Sophie's Choice* did not elicit controversy. For an account of that controversy, see Vice 117–18. My point is that the controversy around the novel did not rise (or sink) to the level of controversy around *The Confessions of Nat Turner*. In a 1999 afterword to *Sophie's Choice*, Styron reflects that "unlike *The Confessions of Nat Turner . . . Sophie's Choice* was spared a bitter onslaught of criticism, though it had its detractors" (605).

5. "Virtually every aspect of Styron's approach to Nat Turner assumed a sinister aspect when seen through the eyes of his critics," writes Greenberg. "Styron, according to his critics, transformed a strong black hero into a vacillating coward; he changed a man who had died for the freedom of his people into a man who had died for the lust of a white woman; he obliterated the revolt's black roots in a strong and autonomous family and tradition, and created a new interracial and deeply perverted myth of the rebellion's origin" (*Confessions* 30–31).

6. In his account of the rebellion, Thomas R. Gray refrains from "detailing the deeds of [the rebels'] fiend-like barbarity" in order "not [to] shock the feelings of humanity, nor wound afresh the bosoms of the disconsolate sufferers" (55).

7. Greenberg adds that the public trials served the function of distancing white Virginians from the brutality of the rebellion's aftermath: "[I]t seemed inhumane to kill people without due process of law; it made Virginia look barbaric in the eyes of the rest of the world; and it destroyed the slave property of masters without the monetary compensation forthcoming when death was dispensed by a legal proceeding" (*Confessions* 20–21). The enhanced oppression to which Virginia subjugated her black population (such as the elimination of the right to trial by jury, the prohibition against black people conducting religious meetings, and, most significantly, the rejection of the Randolph proposal to abolish slavery in Virginia) is presumed to pose no such challenge to community, to comprehension, or to speech.

8. Browne situates the rebellion in a broad spectrum of events that includes Oklahoma and Beirut (328)—place-names that, like Auschwitz, stand for atrocities assumed to be unspeakable.

9. Browne distinguishes between "Gray's text," which "offers up an image of the rebel as unique, alien, mad, local, and containable," and "Turner's text," which "presents a tropological figure of universal significance, generated from within the community but ultimately destructive of it, justified if not by man then by God" (328).

10. Rushdy argues that the evocation of Gray's text by the novel's critics "had much more to do with cultural representation than with historical accuracy" (*Neo-slave Narratives* 58): the critics read "Confessions" not as a source of historical knowledge but

"for the intertextual absences and exaggerated emphases so that they can discern the significance of Styron's reading habits. None of the ten critics claims anything more for Gray's *Confessions*. They take the text seriously as Styron's primary document and they read it with an eye toward seeing what Styron systematically highlights or eliminates" (59). At the same time, however, Rushdy suggests that the novel's critics have a more historically accurate reading of "Confessions" than do Styron or his defenders. To support Bennett's explanation that the reason why Nat Turner only murdered one person was that he was the leader of the insurrection and "generals seldom kill," Rushdy, like the critics, resorts to Gray's "Confessions" for evidence. In his zeal to defend the novel's critics, then, he misses the extent to which these critics rhetorically situate Gray as a source of historical accuracy, not to claim that accuracy for themselves, but to indicate Styron's departure from it. As a result, Rushdy collapses the distinction between historical accuracy and cultural representation on which he premises his argument.

11. Rushdy's reversion to historical fact which exists only in silence reflects his investment in the unspeakable as the only reliable source of historical accuracy, though the work of interpreting these silences (work that Rushdy attributes to the novel's critics but not to its defenders) would seem to challenge his own distinction between the objective and the ideological: interpreting silences, given you have the correct capacity, will lead you, he assumes, toward a more accurate account of Nat Turner's situation in the jail cell with Gray. In this context, it is worth noting when Rushdy himself resorts to evocations of "historical fact" in order to critique Styron's novel. Commenting on Styron's account of Nat Turner masturbating in his jail cell before he is called by the executioner/God, Rushdy writes: "While masturbation is a good enough thing in itself, and an act whose representation can serve a variety of aesthetic and political purposes, it is neither what the historical Turner was doing on the eve of his execution nor a flattering representation of anyone facing death" (63). How does Rushdy know what "the historical Turner" was doing? When an unflattering representation is countered by claims for historical facticity in a critique of a discomforting aesthetics, those claims need, I suggest, to be rigorously investigated for their underlying ideological motivation.

12. Henceforth I will refer to the historical figure as Nat Turner, to Styron's character as Nat; similarly, I refer to the historical figure as Thomas Gray and to Styron's character as Gray.

13. Strategic use of language is not the sole province of Nat. In the courtroom, Nat notes that Gray's voice, "filled . . . with eloquence and authority" is "free of the sloppy patronizing half-literate white-man-to-a-nigger tones he had used in jail." This ability to shift from one language to another functions in the novel as an indicator of authority: "It was obviously he—not the prosecutor Trezevant—who was in charge of things" (83).

14. The charge of racism is, of course, a serious one, and its reverberations into the twenty-first century may account for the paucity of critical work on *The Confessions of Nat Turner*. Critics who do write about the novel are careful to evince their own ethical agendas by acknowledging this charge—by implicit affirmations of it

or respectful gestures toward it. I address these gestures in the final section of this chapter.

15. For Rushdy, Lou-Ann's transformation from victim to participant has no impact on the fact of her "actual rape" (*Neo-slave Narratives* 70), an assertion that sits uneasily, however, with his conclusion that this scene reiterates the racist stereotype of the hypersexualized African American woman who "feels violence against her body as sexual expression" (72). More productive is Ross's suggestion that this scene demonstrates "the irony of the master/slave relationship where power depends on keeping distinct the roles of master and slaves. Sexual intercourse most obviously eradicates such distinctions, altering the equation of dominance and submission, allowing the enslaved the opportunity to seize power over their masters" ("Things" 89).

16. Vanderslice writes: "Though he never commits an act of sexual aggression, the desire to do so, expressed in elaborate and violent fantasies, comes over [Nat] from time to time. These, including the ones about Margaret Whitehead, are virtually identical in action, tone, and language" (9).

17. As Nat Turner's inaccessibility becomes an expression of twentieth-century America's complex relationship with history, Greenberg seems to imply that the ethical premise of "deep humility" will result in an enhancement, and even a reproduction, of that humble self: "[O]ur search for Nat Turner repeatedly directs us down a hallway lined with endless mirrors in which we are forever destined to see little more than the reflections of our own faces" ("Name" 23). In addition to this somewhat conterintuitive calculation, Greenberg's essay subtly aligns Nat Turner's body with the American psyche, arguing that the destruction of the former results in a fracturing of the latter: "The world that dissected Nat Turner's body after he was hanged," he concludes, "may also have permanently damaged our ability to reconstruct him in our histories" (23).

18. Styron frames *The Confessions of Nat Turner* with symbols that reiterate the complex interrelation of body and text that this image of incarnation suggests: the intertwined alpha and omega, so similar to a slave brand, that precedes the novel proper, and the postscript that offers a historical account of Nat Turner's corpse ("delivered to the doctors, who skinned it and made grease of the flesh"), which is juxtaposed with the text of Revelation. We may also note the extent to which the New Testament offers itself as an eschatalogical "key" to the Old Testament; Nat's self-identification with Jesus in the final pages of the novel (which the text's eschewal of italics seems to confirm) corroborates Gray's suggestion, in the novel's opening pages, that Nat both possesses and embodies the "key" to the rebellion.

19. Swanson's formulation reiterates the interrelation of imagination and experience, whiteness and blackness, that the novel's critics identified as its foundational shortcoming. Tellingly—and given the novel's concern with Christianity, importantly—Swanson figures these distinctions in terms of a dichotomy of flesh and spirit.

20. Stewart, for example, who is careful to "endorse the righteous anger of the 'ten black writers'" (182), is equally careful to dissociate himself from the object of their anger: "Styron's personal attitudes are of no concern to me here. . . . I will repeat that

Styron's intention in writing this novel is not the issue here. . . . I have tried to critique *The Confessions of Nat Turner* by focusing on it as literary text and as social text, not on the novelist as a representative figure in the complicated matrix of American racial history" (175, 181, 182).

5. The One Word That Mattered

1. See Hilberg, *Destruction,* app. B ("Statistical Recapitulation"). See Novick 334 n. 23 for a discussion of estimates of how many Jews perished, and the implications of these estimates.

2. Curtin opens his seminal study of the Atlantic slave trade with a review of the literature and of "the numbers game" (3–15). "The principal secondary authorities and the principal textbooks," he notes, "are . . . in remarkable agreement on the general magnitude of the trade. Most begin with the statement that little is known about the subject, pass on to the suggestion that it may be impossible to make an accurate numerical estimate, and then make an estimate" (3–4). Curtin dismisses the official estimate of 15 to 20 million people enslaved in favor of Noel Deerr's estimate, in *History of Sugar,* of 11.97 million (Curtin 13, 15), which Curtin revises down to 9.566 million enslaved, adding that the human misery involved is so terrifying "that no multiplier could make it seem any worse" (87). Lovejoy rejects Curtin's figures in favor of the W. E. B. DuBois database of slaving voyages, and estimates 7.4 million people exported across the Atlantic from 1600 to 1800 (19). But these numbers refer to people exported from Africa into slavery; they include and exceed the numbers of deaths in the Middle Passage. Herbert S. Klein points out that in order to determine the number of deaths in the Middle Passage, scholars tend to calculate the difference between slaves boarded in Africa and slaves delivered to the Americas or Europe (136). This calculation, applied to the estimated statistics in Hugh Thomas's *The Slave Trade* (804–5), produces the figure of 2 million deaths in the Middle Passage. Klein proposes a different approach to understanding the mortality rate, an approach predicated on features such as sailing times, ship size, age of slaves carried, etc. (136–37). None of these numbers come close to Morrison's "sixty million," which leads me to the conclusion that "sixty million" is a rhetorical strategy and not an official account—perhaps an expression of the moral outrage that, Klein notes, the Middle Passage symbolizes for European and American writers (130–31; he does not mention Morrison specifically)—and that Thomas's reference to estimates that have "gotten wildly out of control" is a veiled reference to Morrison's dedication of *Beloved* to "sixty million and more."

3. Questioned about the historical proof for 60 million, Morrison responds: "Some historians told me 200 million died. The smallest number I got from anybody was 60 million." She proceeds to move from number to image: "There were travel accounts of people who were in the Congo—that's a wide river—saying, 'We could not get the boat through the river, it was choked with bodies.' That's like a logjam. A lot of people died. Half of them died in those ships" ("Pain" 120). Note how Morrison replaces argument with image to create an emotional effect that is designed to eclipse the unreliability of her sources and the inaccuracy of her figures.

4. L. M. Thomas addresses this issue of comparative atrocities. Unlike the Holocaust, he writes,

American Slavery was not about the mass murder of a people with extermination as its ultimate aim. . . . All the same, this does not mean that the loss of the lives of millions of black people counts for nothing. It does mean, though, that we do well to refrain from calling that loss something that it is not [i.e., a holocaust]. Whether or not the loss of slaves during the Middle Passage exceeded the number of deaths among Jews during the Holocaust, that loss was not owing to an attempt to exterminate blacks. (*Vessels* 149)

Recapitulating his discussion in "Suffering," he urges blacks and Jews to band together as "moral exemplars" with "an important role to play in society as moral beacons." Significantly, this role of "moral beacons" serves to efface the distinction between atrocities that Thomas had stressed in his discrimination between the Holocaust and American slavery: "As moral beacons," writes Thomas,

we—we who are black and we who are Jews—can both remind American society that evil is not impoverished. Neither the Shoah nor American slavery exhausts the nature of evil. . . . The Shoah and American slavery have given Jews and blacks, respectively, an extraordinary and incomparable occasion to cast some light on the ways of human beings. And I should like to think that if we fasten upon this task with all our might and soul, then we would no longer concern ourselves with the question of who has suffered the most, blacks or Jews. And when we who are black and we who are Jews have arrived at this point, then we shall become moral beacons, not only unto others but unto ourselves as well. ("Suffering" 209–10)

5. I should clarify that "the one little child who didn't make it" is a reference to *The Bluest Eye,* but in this comment Morrison is explicitly responding to Crouch's review of *Beloved*.

6. Morrison has noted that with *Beloved* she was "trying to insert this memory [of the Middle Passage] that was unbearable and unspeakable into the literature. . . . It was a silence within the race. So it's a kind of healing experience. There are certain things that are repressed because they are unthinkable, and the only way to come free of that is to go back and deal with them." Responding to this statement, Pérez-Torres reinscribes it in terms of "the interplay between absence and presence, between silence and voicing" ("Between Presence" 198 n. 2).

7. Ledbetter refers to Sethe's child as Beloved throughout his discussion of the novel, both before and after the baby's death, and Rody writes that Beloved is the murdered baby's name "because she died still unnamed" (104).

8. This is another source of critical confusion, though the distinction between funeral and burial is made quite explicit in the novel: "'They going to let you out for the burial,' [Baby Suggs] said, 'not the funeral, just the burial'" (183).

9. Stamp Paid abandons his name Joshua, after his wife Vashti is forced to sexually service her white master. Unlike the biblical Vashti, who refused to prostitute herself for the king and who was replaced by the Jewish Esther, the slave Vashti is forced to comply with her owner's demands. There is no mention of whether Vashti,

like Stamp Paid, tried to free herself of this biblical narrative by abandoning her name, only that she died. Her death may be read as a comment on the distinctions imposed by gender for the implications of unnaming, since the women in the novel (Sethe, Baby Suggs, Ella) never attempt to change their names.

10. Paul D abandons his name at one point, with the weaver lady in Delaware who "passed him off as her nephew from Syracuse simply by calling him that nephew's name" (113). But living under an assumed identity is no haven, and Paul D stays in Delaware only three years.

11. Baby Suggs uses the word unhesitatingly; the narrative voice, however, puts it in quotation marks. "Baby Suggs was all she had left of the 'husband' she claimed" (142).

12. As Wyatt puts it, "Outcast both as victim of slavery whose death is unspeakable and as preverbal infant who has not made her way into the symbolic order, Beloved remains outside language and therefore outside narrative memory" (484).

13. See Atkinson, and M. Sale on the oral tradition of Call-and-Response. Both posit this tradition in terms of a literary aesthetic that makes room for an oral aesthetic in Beloved, and both emphasize the emotional and ideological interpellation of the reader that such aesthetic performs.

14. Lawrence identifies additional echoes of slavery's discourse of appropriation in Beloved in the repetition of "mine" that Stamp Paid hears outside 124.

15. Cannibalism is widely associated with Beloved in the text, and furthers the imagination of a complicit community. As Brogan puts it, "[T]he ghost's cannibalism . . . functions as a projection of white myths about blacks, who are viewed as both self-destructive (the murder is taken as evidence of 'the cannibal life [blacks] preferred' and predatory ('their red gums ready for . . . sweet white blood')" (82).

16. For a different reading of this section, see Wyatt, who suggests that with these words Sethe is "recognizing herself in the first person singular," thus moving toward a symbolic order that excludes her relationship with Beloved, to whom Wyatt refers to as "the unspeakable." But Wyatt also concedes that these words may well be an expression of "disbelief" (484).

17. See Gilroy's Black Atlantic and the special issue of Research in African Literatures, 27.4 (1996), devoted to it (esp. Dayan) for some useful responses to this assumption.

18. For Schlesinger, says Michaels, "[m]emory is here said to constitute the core of individual identity; national memory is understood to constitute the core of national identity. Insofar, then, as individuals have a national as well as an individual identity, they must have access not only to their own memories but to the national memory; they must be able to remember not only the things that happened to them as individuals but the things that happened to them as Americans" (183).

19. See chap. 1 for additional discussion of the implications of extending an individual experience of trauma to a collective psyche.

20. Of the epigraph, Rody writes: "Suggesting that the naming function of the text be read as an offering of narrative love, the epigraph proposes a kind of history-telling that can turn estrangement into intimacy" (102). Given Rody's nuanced ap-

proach to the historiographical project of *Beloved* in her complex, luminous, and evocative essay, her inattention to the historical context of the quotation from Romans is surprising.

21. For a different reading of the dedication and the epigraph, and of the tension between black and Jewish histories in *Beloved*'s reception and text, see Emily Budick 161–67, and Gilroy, *Black Atlantic* 217–23. Budick argues that "the allusions to the Holocaust in . . . *Beloved* serve very legitimate literary purpose" (206); Gilroy sees in these allusions an opportunity to investigate modernity, rationality, science, and humanism (217).

22. Ledbetter writes:

I am a Southern white male in the United States. My narrative master plot seeks to distance me from a history of slavery and pain inflicted on African Americans, to make others complicit in its institution, and to describe all the good things which my ancestors and I did for African Americans. I am corporate white male in the United States, and my narrative master plot describes the jobs I have brought to corporate America and the money I have circulated in the economy. I do not tell of women and minorities denied jobs or given lower salaries because of race and gender. I am upper-middle-class Christian in the United States, and I like the name of God on my coins, manger scenes of Christ in the public square, and prayers in public schools. (14)

23. Commenting on the epilogue, Rody writes: "For us of course, closing the book, there is nothing but weather. The past does not exist unless we choose to hear its clamor." But for Rody, the clamor of loss that Morrison's prose evokes is, finally, "hushed" (113).

Conclusion

1. McBride's reading of Morrison's "Unspeakable Things Unspoken" exemplifies the transformation of the unspeakable from a description of the *self* (as that which language excludes) to a description of the self's *experience*. McBride defines "unspeakable" as "the sometimes seeming indefensibility of essentialist categories like race in light of much recent poststructuralist critical work (invested in social constructionism) that has placed 'race' under 'erasure'" ("Speaking" 150 n. 3). Such work, he warns, operates politically "to silence and deauthorize African American experience" (149). As a countermove, he argues for the development and employment of a "strategic essentialism" that, among other things, "empowers us to speak (through the discourses available to us) about the oppressive material and political manifestations of a racialized hegemony on our lives" (150).

2. Stoett notes that the pejorative overtones of "complicity" facilitate the apparatus of accountability. "Accusations of complicity in crimes against humanity are, to some degree, contingent on the adoption of a legal approach. Events are seen largely as 'crimes,' rather than as historical processes," an approach that has the benefit of dissuading future generations from continuing the practices in question (48). He suggests that the assumption of criminality implied by the legal approach is preferable to the broader, ideational approach, because "it enables us to be more specific

with our admonitions and, perhaps, criminal prosecution and calls for recompense" (48). I will expand on the relation between complicity and accountability in the final pages of this chapter.

3. Oddly, in discussions of Levi's gray zone this distinction tends to disappear, facilitating the common misunderstanding of the "gray zone" as a space where the victim is indistinguishable from the perpetrator. Kutz, for example, refers briefly to "what Primo Levi called 'the gray zone' of collaboration with evil" (3); Waller aligns the gray zone with the complexity of perpetrators' motives (46); Tyndall describes the gray zone as "the space where 'victims' become so demoralised that they become perpetrators in order to survive" (113). Situating "victims" but not "perpetrators" within quotation marks, Tyndall seems to be implying that in the context of the gray zone, "victim" is necessarily a contingent identity; "perpetrator" the status quo. Such an assumption is understandable—especially when the evil of perpetration is over-whelming and its manifestations ubiquitous—but it subtly reinforces the assumption that inhabitants of the gray zone are somewhat culpable, an assumption that Levi's essay passionately contests.

4. The original Italian reads as follows: "Ma i collaboratori che provengono dal campo avversario, gli ex nemici, sono infidi per essenza: hanno tradito una volta e possono tradire ancora. Non basta relegarli in compiti marginali; il modo migliore di legarli è caricarli di colpe, insanguinarli, comprometterli quanto più è possibile: così avranno contratto coi mandanti il vincolo della correità, e non potranno più tornare indietro" (30).

5. I align guilt with culpability because both are within the sphere of judgment. We may follow the logic of Freud in this context: guilt is the verdict that conscience passes on actions—real or imagined (84–85).

6. Sanders also describes complicity as "the foldedness or 'contamination' of op-positional pairs" (9)

7. Sanders distinguishes between "acting-in-complicity" (a term that refers to "acts subject to a system of accountability") and "a responsibility-in-complicity" ("the con-dition of possibility for any such system") (11). While the two cannot be dissociated, the second presupposes the first. Discussing Kutz's book, Sanders adds that "com-plicity is not merely an acting together, but is (though the two cannot be regarded as coextensive) at the same time what establishes the horizon of judgment for that act-ing" (215 n. 19).

8. Tracing a similar paradigm, Campbell and Dillon identify the political subject of violence as the articulation of violence's complicity in reason and in politics, and the embodiment of that complicity in the subject—both epistemological and onto-logical. "Precisely because the political subject of violence is . . . a reasoning subject, the complicity of reason in the violence of the modern political subject cannot be elided" (2)—a conclusion that leads them, like (and with) Connolly, to the ethical (*Political Subject* 161–78).

9. Because my argument parallels Sanders's at this point, I take this space to articulate where we converge and diverge. The context in which we situate our ar-guments is different: My sphere is a rhetoric of the unspeakable in narratives about

suffering under the Holocaust and under American slavery; Sanders's is South African writers during and after apartheid. I agree with him that "each moment of opposition or resistance depends on complicity" (10); my distinction of complicity from the work of judgment extends—productively, I think—his definition of the term. Finally, I add to Sanders the concept of "being complicit," which, I hope, enables the articulation of an ethics that is not predicated on valorizing the limits of speech—i.e., an ethics that is not predicated on the unspeakable.

Works Cited

Adorno, Theodor W. "Cultural Criticism and Society." *Prisms*. 1967. Trans. Samuel and Shierry Weber. Cambridge, Mass.: MIT P, 1981. 17–34.

———. *Negative Dialectics*. 1966. Trans. E. B. Ashton. New York: Seabury, 1973.

Agamben, Giorgio. *Homo Sacer: Sovereign Power and Bare Life*. 1995. Trans. Daniel Heller-Roazen. Stanford: Stanford UP, 1998.

———. *Remnants of Auschwitz: The Witness and the Archive*. Trans. Daniel Heller-Roazen. New York: Zone Books, 1999.

Andrews, William L. *To Tell a Free Story: The First Century of Afro-American Autobiography, 1750–1865*. Urbana: U of Illinois P, 1986.

Aptheker, Herbert. "A Note on the History." 1967. Duff and Mitchell, *Nat Turner Rebellion* 191–96.

Arad, Yitzak, Yisrael Gutman, and Abraham Margaliot, eds. *Documents on the Holocaust: Selected Sources on the Destruction of the Jews of Germany and Austria, Poland, and the Soviet Union*. Jerusalem: Yad Vashem, 1987.

Arendt, Hannah. *Eichmann in Jerusalem*. 1963. New York: Penguin, 1994.

———. *The Jew as Pariah: Jewish Identity and Politics in the Modern Age*. Ed. Ron H. Feldman. New York: Grove, 1978.

Atkinson, Yvonne. "The Black English Oral Tradition in *Beloved:* 'Listen to the spaces.'" Solomon 247–60.

Avisar, Ilan. "Holocaust Movies and the Politics of Collective Memory." Rosenfeld, *Thinking about the Holocaust* 38–58.

Avni, Ora. "Beyond Psychoanalysis: Elie Wiesel's *Night* in Historical Perspective." Kritzman 203–18.

Azoulay, Ariella. *Death's Showcase: The Power of Image in Contemporary Democracy.* Trans. Ruvik Danieli. Cambridge, Mass.: MIT Press, 2001.

Barthes, Roland. *Camera Lucida.* 1980. Trans. Richard Howard. New York: Hill and Wang, 1981.

Bartov, Omer. "Spielberg's Oskar: Hollywood Tries Evil." Loshitsky, *Spielberg's Holocaust* 41–60.

Bauer, Yehuda. "Holocaust and Genocide: Some Comparisons." Hayes 36–46.

Bell, Pearl K. "Evil and William Styron." 1979. Ross, *Critical Responses* 181–85.

Bennett, Lerone, Jr. "Nat's Last White Man." Clarke 3–16.

Benston, Kimberly W. "I yam what I am: The Topos of (Un)naming in Afro-American Literature." Gates, *Black Literature* 151–72.

Berger, James. *After the End: Representations of Post-Apocalypse.* Minneapolis: U of Minnesota P, 1999.

Bernard-Donals, Michael. "Beyond the Question of Authenticity: Witness and Testimony in the *Fragments* Controversy." Bernard-Donals and Glejzer 196–220.

Bernard-Donals, Michael, and Richard Glejzer, eds. *Witnessing the Disaster: Essays on Representation and the Holocaust.* Madison: U of Wisconsin P, 2003.

Bernstein, Michael André. "The *Schindler's List* Effect." *American Scholar* (1994): 429–32.

Bettelheim, Bruno. "The Holocaust—One Generation After." *Thinking the Unthinkable.* Ed. Roger S. Gottlieb. New York: Paulist, 1990. 373–89.

———. *Surviving and Other Essays.* 1952. New York: Vintage, 1980.

Blanchot, Maurice. *The Writing of the Disaster.* Trans. Ann Smock. Lincoln: U of Nebraska P, 1995. Trans. of *L'écriture du désastre.* Paris: Gallimard, 1980.

Bloom, Harold, ed. *Toni Morrison.* New York: Chelsea, 1990.

Boyarin, Jonathan. *Storm from Paradise.* Minneapolis: U of Minnesota P, 1992.

Brodsky, Joseph. "Portrait of Tragedy." *So Forth.* New York: Farrar, Straus and Giroux, 1996. 85–88.

Brogan, Kathleen. *Cultural Haunting: Ghosts and Ethnicity in Recent American Literature.* Charlottesville: U of Virginia P, 1998.

Brown, Cecil. "Interview with Toni Morrison." *Massachusetts Review* 36 (1995): 455–73.

Brown, Robert McAfee. "The Holocaust as a Problem in Moral Choice." Wiesel et al. 47–63.

———. Preface to the Twenty-fifth anniversary edition. Wiesel, *Night* v–vi.

Brown, Wendy. *States of Injury: Power and Freedom in Late Modernity.* Princeton: Princeton UP, 1995.

Browne, Stephen Howard. "'This Unparalleled and Inhuman Massacre': The Gothic, the Sacred, and the Meaning of Nat Turner." *Rhetoric & Public Affairs* 3.3 (2000): 309–31.

Browning, Christopher. "German Memory, Judicial Interrogation, and Historical Reconstruction: Writing Perpetrator History from Postwar Testimony." Friedlander, *Probing the Limits* 22–36.

Bryer, Jackson R., and Melvin J. Friedman. Introduction. *Papers on Language and Literature* 23.4 (1987): 419–24.

Budick, Emily Miller. *Blacks and Jews in Literary Conversation*. Cambridge: Cambridge UP, 1998.

Budick, Sanford, and Wolfgang Iser, eds. *Languages of the Unsayable*. New York: Columbia UP, 1989.

Butler, Judith. *Precarious Life: The Powers of Mourning and Violence*. New York: Verso, 2004.

Campbell, David, and Michael Dillon. "The End of Philosophy and the End of International Relations." Campbell and Dillon 1–47.

———, eds. *The Political Subject of Violence*. Manchester: Manchester UP, 1993.

Carnes, Mark C., ed. *Novel History: Historians and Novelists Confront America's Past (and Each Other)*. New York: Simon & Schuster, 2001.

Carroll, David. "The Limits of Representation and the Right to Fiction: Shame, Literature, and the Memory of the Shoah." *L'esprit créateur* 39.4 (1999): 68–79.

———. "Rephrasing the Political with Kant and Lyotard: From Aesthetic to Political Judgments." *Diacritics* 14.4 (1984): 74–88.

Caruth, Cathy. *Unclaimed Experience*. Baltimore: Johns Hopkins UP, 1996.

Churchill, Ward. *A Little Matter of Genocide: Holocaust and Denial in the Americas 1492 to the Present*. San Francisco: City Lights Books, 1997.

Clarke, John Henrik, ed. *William Styron's Nat Turner: Ten Black Writers Respond*. Boston: Beacon, 1968.

Clemons, Walter. "A Gravestone of Memories." *Newsweek* 28 Sept. 1987: 74–75.

Colorado, Pam. "What Every Indian Knows." Churchill xi.

Connolley, William E. *Identity/Difference: Democratic Negotiations of Political Paradox*. 1991. Exp. ed. Minneapolis: U of Minnesota P, 2002.

Cornell, Drucilla, Michael Rosenfeld, and David Gray Carlson, eds. *Deconstruction and the Possibility of Justice*. New York: Routledge, 1992.

Crouch, Stanley. "Aunt Medea." 1987. Solomon 64–71.

Curtin, Philip D. *The Atlantic Slave Trade: A Census*. Madison: U of Wisconsin P, 1969.

Davis, Colin. *Elie Wiesel's Secretive Texts*. Gainsville: UP of Florida, 1994.

Davis, Mary Kemp. *Nat Turner before the Bar of Judgment: Fictional Treatments of the Southampton Slave Insurrection*. Baton Rouge: Louisiana State UP, 1999.

Dayan, Joan. "Paul Gilroy's Slaves, Ships, and Routes: The Middle Passage as Metaphor." *Research in African Literatures* 27.4 (1996): 4–14.

Deleuze, Gilles. *Essays Critical and Clinical*. 1993. Trans. Daniel W. Smith and Michael A. Greco. Minneapolis: U of Minnesota P, 1997.

Derrida, Jacques. *Demeure: Fiction and Testimony*. 1998. Trans. Elizabeth Rottenberg. Stanford: Stanford UP, 2000.

———. "Force of Law." *Deconstruction and the Possibility of Justice.* Cornell, Rosenfeld, and Carlson 3–67.

———. *Specters of Marx.* 1993. Trans. Peggy Kamuf. New York: Routledge, 1994.

Des Pres, Terrence. "The Authority of Silence in Elie Wiesel's Art." *Confronting the Holocaust.* Ed. Alvin H. Rosenfeld and Irving Greenberg. Bloomington: Indiana UP, 1978. 49–57.

———. *The Survivor: An Anatomy of Life in the Death Camps.* New York: Oxford UP, 1976.

Duff, John B., and Peter M. Mitchell, eds. *The Nat Turner Rebellion: The Historical Event and the Modern Controversy.* New York: Harper & Row, 1971.

Durand, Alain-Philippe. "Beyond the Extreme: Frédéric Beigbeder's *Windows on the World.* Durand and Mandel 109–20.

Durand, Alain-Philippe, and Naomi Mandel, eds. *Novels of the Contemporary Extreme.* New York: Continuum, 2006.

Dwork, Debórah, and Robert Jan van Pelt. *Auschwitz, 1270 to the Present.* New Haven: Yale UP, 1996.

Ezrahi, Sidra DeKoven. "Racism and Ethics: Constructing Alternative History." Hornstein, Levitt, and Silberstein 118–28.

Fabricant, Daniel S. "Thomas R. Gray and William Styron: Finally, a Critical Look at the 1831 *Confessions of Nat Turner.*" *American Journal of Legal History* 37 (1993): 332–61.

Fasching, Darrell J. *The Ethical Challenge of Auschwitz and Hiroshima: Apocalypse or Utopia?* New York: SUNY P, 1993.

Feldman, Yael. "Whose Story Is It, Anyway?" Friedlander, *Probing the Limits* 223–39.

Felman, Shoshana. "After the Apocalypse: Paul de Man and the Fall to Silence." Felman and Laub 120–64.

———. "Camus' *The Fall,* or the Betrayal of the Witness." Felman and Laub 165–203.

———. "Camus' *The Plague,* or a Monument to Witnessing." Felman and Laub 93–119.

———. "The Return of the Voice: Claude Lanzmann's *Shoah.*" Felman and Laub 204–83.

Felman, Shoshana, and Dori Laub. *Testimony: Crises of Witnessing in Literature, Psychoanalysis, and History.* New York: Routledge, 1992.

Fine, Ellen. *Legacy of Night.* New York: SUNY P, 1982.

Finkelstein, Norman G. *The Holocaust Industry: Reflections on the Exploitation of Jewish Suffering.* London: Verso, 2000.

Flanzbaum, Hilene, ed. *The Americanization of the Holocaust.* Baltimore: Johns Hopkins UP, 1999.

Foucault, Michel. *Ethics Subjectivity and Truth.* Trans. Robert Hurley et al. Ed. Paul Rabinow. New York: New Press, 1997.

Freud, Sigmund. *Civilization and Its Discontents.* 1930. Trans. James Strachey. New York: Norton, 1989.

Friedlander, Saul. "The 'Final Solution': On the Unease in Historical Interpretation." Hayes 23–35.

———. *Memory, History, and the Extermination of the Jews in Europe*. Bloomington: Indiana UP, 1993.

———. *Probing the Limits of Representation: Nazism and the Final Solution*. Cambridge, Mass.: Harvard UP, 1992.

———. *Reflections of Nazism: An Essay on Kitsch and Death*. 1982. Thomas Weyr, trans. Bloomington: Indiana UP, 1993.

Friedman, Melvin J., and Irving Malin, eds. *William Styron's* The Confessions of Nat Turner: *A Critical Handbook*. Belmont, Calif.: Wadsworth, 1970.

Fuss, Diana. "Corpse Poem." *Critical Inquiry* 30 (2003): 1–30.

Garber, Zev, and Bruce Zuckerman. "Why Do We Call the Holocaust the Holocaust? An Inquiry into the Psychology of Labels." *Modern Judaism* 9.2 (1989): 197–212.

Gardner, John. "A Novel of Evil." 1979. Ross, *Critical Responses* 175–80.

Gates, Henry Louis, Jr., ed. *Black Literature and Literary Theory*. New York: Routledge, 1990.

———. "Criticism in the Jungle." *Black Literature and Literary Theory* 1–24.

Gates, Henry Louis, Jr., and Anthony Appiah, eds. *Toni Morrison: Critical Perspectives Past and Present*. New York: Amistad, 1993.

Gilman, Sander. *The Jew's Body*. New York: Routledge, 1991.

Gilroy, Paul. *Against Race: Imagining Political Culture beyond the Color Line*. Cambridge, Mass.: Harvard UP, 2003.

———. *The Black Atlantic: Modernity and Double Consciousness*. Cambridge, Mass.: Harvard UP, 1993.

Glejzer, Richard. "*Maus* and the Epistemology of Witness." Bernard-Donals and Glejzer 125–37.

Goldhagen, Daniel. *Hitler's Willing Executioners*. New York: Vintage, 1996.

Gordon, Avery F. *Ghostly Matters: Haunting and the Sociological Imagination*. Minneapolis: U of Minnesota P, 1997.

Gottlieb, Robert S., ed. *Thinking the Unthinkable: Meanings of the Holocaust*. New York: Paulist, 1990.

Gourevitch, Philip. "A Dissent on *Schindler's List*." *Commentary* 97.2 (1994): 49–52.

Gray, Thomas R. "The Confessions of Nat Turner." 1831. Greenberg, *Confessions of Nat Turner* 38–58.

Greenberg, Kenneth S., ed. *The Confessions of Nat Turner and Related Documents*. Boston: Bedford Books of St. Martin's, 1996.

———. "Epilogue: Nat Turner in Hollywood." *Nat Turner: A Slave Rebellion* 243–49.

———. "Name, Face, Body." *Nat Turner: A Slave Rebellion* 3–23.

———, ed. *Nat Turner: A Slave Rebellion in History and Memory*. New York: Oxford UP, 2003.

Gross, Seymour L., and Eileen Bender. "History, Politics and Literature: The Myth of Nat Turner." *American Quarterly* 23 (1971): 487–518.

Gubar, Susan. *Poetry after Auschwitz: Remembering What One Never Knew.* Bloomington: Indiana UP, 2003.

Habermas, Jürgen. *The New Conservatism: Cultural Criticism and the Historians' Debate.* Ed. and trans. Shierry Weber Nicholsen. Cambridge, Mass.: MIT P, 1989.

Haidu, Peter. "The Dialectics of Unspeakability: Language, Silence, and the Narratives of Desubjectification." Friedlander, *Probing the Limits* 277–99.

Halkin, Hillel. "Inhuman Comedy." *Commentary* Feb. 1992: 55–56.

Hamilton, Charles V. "Our Nat Turner and William Styron's Creation." Clarke 73–78.

Hansen, Miriam Bratu. "*Schindler's List* Is Not *Shoah:* The Second Commandment, Popular Modernism, and Public Memory." *Critical Inquiry* 22 (1996): 292–312.

Harding, Vincent. "You've Taken My Nat and Gone." Clarke 23–33.

Hartman, Geoffrey. "The Cinema Animal: On Spielberg's *Schindler's List.*" *Salmagundi* 106 (1995): 127–45.

———. *The Fateful Question of Culture.* New York: Columbia UP, 1997.

———. *The Longest Shadow.* Bloomington: Indiana UP, 1996.

———. "On Traumatic Knowledge." *New Literary History* 26.3 (1995): 537–63.

Hayes, Peter, ed. *Lessons and Legacies.* Evanston: Northwestern UP, 1991.

Hilberg, Raul. *The Destruction of the European Jews.* Chicago: Quadrangle Books, 1961.

———. "The Goldhagen Phenomenon." *Critical Inquiry* 23.4 (1997): 721–28.

Hirsch, Marianne. "Collateral Damage." Editor's Column. *PMLA* 119.5 (2004): 1209–15.

———. "Family Pictures: *Maus,* Mourning, and Post-Memory." *Discourse* 15.2 (1992): 3–29.

Hoberman, J., et al., "SCHINDLER'S LIST: Myth, Movie, and Memory." *Village Voice* 29 Mar. 1994: 24–31.

Holloway, Karla F. C. "*Beloved:* A Spiritual." McKay and Andrews 67–78.

Hornstein, Shelley, Laura Levitt, and Laurence J. Silberstein, eds. *Impossible Images: Contemporary Art after the Holocaust.* New York: NYU P, 2003.

Horowitz, Sara. "But Is It Good for the Jews? Spielberg's Schindler and the Aesthetics of Atrocity." Loshitzky, *Spielberg's Holocaust* 119–39.

———. "Review Essay: Rethinking Holocaust Testimony: The Making and Unmaking of the Witness." *Cardozo Studies in Law and Literature* 4.1 (1992): 45–68.

———. *Voicing the Void: Muteness and Memory in Holocaust Fiction.* New York: SUNY P, 1997.

Horwitz, Deborah. "Nameless Ghosts: Possession and Dispossession in *Beloved.*" Solomon 93–103.

Hungerford, Amy. *The Holocaust of Texts: Genocide, Literature, and Personification.* Chicago: U of Chicago P, 2003.

Huyssen, Andreas. "Of Mice and Mimesis: Reading Spiegelman with Adorno." *New German Critique* 81 (2000): 65–83.

Jaspers, Karl. *The Question of German Guilt.* 1947. Trans. E. B. Ashton. New York: Capricorn, 1961.

Jones, Adam, ed. *Genocide, War Crimes and the West: History and Complicity.* New York: Zed Books, 2004.

Joyner, Charles. "Styron's Choice: A Meditation on History, Literature, and Moral Imperatives." 1996. Greenberg, *Nat Turner: A Slave Rebellion* 179–213.

Keenan, Sally. "'Four Hundred Years of Silence': Myth, History and Motherhood in Toni Morrison's *Beloved.*" J. White 45–81.

Killens, John Oliver. "The Confessions of Willie Styron." Clarke 34–44.

Klein, Herbert S. *The Atlantic Slave Trade.* Cambridge: Cambridge UP, 1999.

Klein, Uri. "The Saving Grace of Humor." *Ha'aretz Mazagine* 30 Oct. 1998: 15.

Kreyling, Michael. "Speakable and Unspeakable in Styron's *Sophie's Choice.*" 1984. Ross, *Critical Responses* 187–99.

Kristeva, Julia. *Powers of Horror.* 1980. Trans. Leon S. Roudiez. New York: Columbia UP, 1982.

Kritzman, Lawrence D., ed. *Auschwitz and After: Race, Culture, and "the Jewish Question" in France.* New York: Routledge, 1995.

Kutz, Christopher. *Complicity: Ethics and Law for a Collective Age.* New York: Cambridge UP, 2000.

Kuznetsov, Anatoli. *Babi Yar: A Documentary Novel.* Trans. Jacob Guralsky. New York: Dell, 1966.

LaCapra, Dominick. "Approaching Limit Events: Siting Agamben." Bernard-Donals and Glejzer 262–304.

———. "The Personal, the Political, and the Textual: Paul de Man as Object of Transference." *History and Memory* 4.1 (1992): 5–38.

———. *Representing the Holocaust.* Ithaca: Cornell UP, 1994.

———. *Writing History, Writing Trauma.* Baltimore: Johns Hopkins UP, 2001.

Lacoue-Labarthe, Philippe, and Jean-Luc Nancy. "The Nazi Myth." *Critical Inquiry* 16.2 (1990): 291–312.

Lang, Berel. *Act and Idea in the Nazi Genocide.* Chicago: U of Chicago P, 1990.

———. *Heidegger's Silence.* Ithaca: Cornell UP, 1996.

———. *Holocaust Representation: Art within the Limits of History and Ethics.* Baltimore: Johns Hopkins UP, 2000.

———. "On Peter Novick's *The Holocaust in American Life.*" *Jewish Social Studies* 7.3 (2001): 149–80.

———, ed. *Writing and the Holocaust.* New York: Holmes and Meier, 1988.

Langer, Lawrence L., ed. *Art from the Ashes.* New York: Oxford UP, 1995.

———. *Holocaust Testimonies: The Ruins of Memory.* New Haven: Yale UP, 1991.

———. "Pursuit of Death in Holocaust Narrative." *Partisan Review* 48.3 (2001): 379–95.

Lanzmann, Claude. "Seminar with Claude Lanzmann, 11 April 1990." *Literature and the Ethical Question.* Spec. issue of *Yale French Studies* 79 (1991): 82–99.

———. *Shoah: An Oral History of the Holocaust.* Trans. A. Whitelaw and D. Bryon. New York: Pantheon, 1985.

———. "Why Spielberg Has Distorted the Truth." *Manchester Guardian* 3 Apr. 1994: 14. (Orig. pub. *Le Monde* 3 Mar. 1994.)

Lappin, Elena. "The Man with Two Heads." *Granta* 66 (1999): 61.

Laub, Dori. "Bearing Witness or the Vicissitudes of Listening." Felman and Laub 57–74.

Law, Richard G. "The Reach of Fiction: Narrative Technique in Styron's *Sophie's Choice*." 1990. Ross, *Critical Responses* 235–53.

Lawrence, David. "Fleshly Ghosts and Ghostly Flesh: The Word and the Body in *Beloved*." *Studies in American Fiction* 19.2 (1991): 189–201.

Ledbetter, Mark. *Victims and the Postmodern Narrative.* New York: St. Martin's, 1996.

Leitch, Vincent B., gen. ed. *The Norton Anthology of Theory and Criticism.* New York: Norton, 2001.

Lentin, Ronit. "Postmemory, Unsayability and the Return of the Auschwitz Code." *Re-presenting the Shoah* 1–24.

———, ed. *Re-presenting the Shoah for the 21st Century.* New York: Berghahn, 2004.

Levi, Neil, and Michael Rothberg. "General Introduction: Theory and the Holocaust." *The Holocaust* 1–27.

———, eds. *The Holocaust: Theoretical Readings.* New Brunswick: Rutgers UP, 2003.

Levi, Primo. *The Drowned and the Saved.* Trans. Raymond Rosenthal. New York: Vintage, 1989. Trans. of *I sommeri e i salvati.* Turin: Einaudi, 1986.

Levinas, Emmanuel. *Totality and Infinity.* 1961. Alphonso Lingis, trans. Pittsburgh, Dusquesne UP, 1996.

Levine, Michael G. "Necessary Stains: Spiegelman's *Maus* and the Bleeding of History." *American Imago* 59.3 (2002): 317–41.

Leys, Ruth. *Trauma: A Genealogy.* Chicago: U of Chicago P, 2000.

Lifton, Robert J. *Death in Life: Survivors of Hiroshima.* New York: Random House, 1967.

Lifton, Robert J., and Eric Markusen. *The Genocidal Mentality: Nazi Holocaust and Nuclear Threat.* New York: Basic Books, 1990.

Little, Margaret Olivia. "Cosmetic Surgery, Suspect Norms, and the Ethics of Complicity." Parens 162–76.

Loshitzky, Yosefa. "Holocaust Others: Spielberg's *Schindler's List* versus Lanzmann's *Shoah*." *Spielberg's Holocaust* 104–18.

———. Introduction to *Spielberg's Holocaust* 1–17.

———, ed. *Spielberg's Holocaust: Critical Perspectives on* Schindler's List. Bloomington: Indiana UP, 1997.

Lovejoy, Paul E. *Transformations in Slavery: A History of Slavery in Africa.* 1983. Rev. ed. Cambridge: Cambridge UP, 2000.

Lyotard, Jean-François. "Defining the Postmodern." 1986. Leitch 1612–15.

———. *The Differend: Phrases in Dispute.* 1983. Trans. Georges Van Den Abbeele. Minneapolis: U of Minnesota P, 1988.

———. "Discussions, or Phrasing 'after Auschwitz.'" Kritzman 149–79.

Maechler, Stefan. *The Wilkomirski Affair: A Study in Biographical Truth.* Trans. John E. Woods. New York: Schocken, 2001.

Mandel, Naomi. "Ethics after Auschwitz: The Holocaust in History and Representation." *Criticism* 45.4 (2003): 509–18.

———. "Speaking Corpses and Spectral Spaces: Representing Testimony after the Holocaust." *Dialectical Anthropology* 24 (2000): 357–76.

Marks, Elaine. "Cendres juives: Jews Writing in French after Auschwitz." Kritzman 35–46.

Mauriac, François. Foreword. Wiesel, *Night* vii–xi.

McBride, Dwight A. "Speaking the Unspeakable: On Toni Morrison, African American Intellectuals, and the Uses of Essentialist Rhetoric." Peterson 131–52.

———. *Why I Hate Abercrombie and Fitch: Essays on Race and Sexuality.* New York: NYU P, 2005.

McGann, Jerome, and Johanna Drucker. "Modernity and Complicity: A Dialogue." *Textual Practice* 18.2 (2004): 207–19.

McGlothlin, Erin. "No Time Like the Present: Narrative and Time in Art Spiegelman's *Maus.*" *Narrative* 11.2 (2003): 177–98.

McKay, Nellie Y. Introduction. McKay and Andrews 3–19.

McKay, Nellie Y., and William S. Andrews, eds. *Toni Morrison's* Beloved: *A Casebook.* New York: Oxford UP, 1999.

McKinley, James C., Jr. "Searching in Vain for Rwanda's Moral High Ground." *New York Times* 21 Dec. 1997: sec. 4, p. 3.

Mellard, James M. "This *Unquiet* Dust: The Problem of History in Styron's *The Confessions of Nat Turner.*" 1983. Ross, *Critical Responses* 157–72.

Michaels, Walter Benn. "'You Who Never Was There': Slavery and the New Historicism—Deconstruction and the Holocaust." Flanzbaum 161–97.

Miller, James. *The Passion of Michel Foucault.* New York: Simon & Schuster, 1993.

Miller, Nancy. *Bequest and Betrayal: Memoirs of a Parent's Death.* New York: Oxford UP, 1996.

Mintz, Alan. *Popular Culture and the Shaping of Holocaust Memory.* Seattle: U of Washington P, 2001.

Mobley, Marilyn Sanders. "A Different Remembering: Memory, History and Meaning in Toni Morrison's *Beloved.*" Bloom 189–99.

Morrison, Toni. *Beloved.* New York: Knopf, 1987.

———. "A Gravestone of Memories." Interview with Walter Clemons. *Newsweek,* 28 Sept. 1987: 74–75.

———. Interview with Cecil Brown. *Massachusetts Review* 36 (1995): 455–73.

———. Nobel Lecture. 1993. Peterson 267–73.

———. "The Pain of Being Black." Interview with Bonnie Angelo. *Time* 22 May 1989: 120–22.

———. "Toni Morrison's Beloved Country: The Writer and Her Haunting Tale of Slavery." Interview with Elizabeth Kastor. *Washington Post* 5 Oct. 1987: 1+.

————. "Unspeakable Things Unspoken: The Afro-American Presence in American Literature." Tanner Lecture. *Michigan Quarterly Review* 28.1 (1989): 1–34.

Newton, Adam Zachary. *Facing Black and Jew: Literature as Public Space in Twentieth-Century America.* Cambridge: Cambridge UP, 1999.

Novick, Peter. *The Holocaust in American Life.* New York: Houghton Mifflin, 1999.

Oe, Kenzaburo. *Hiroshima Notes.* 1965. Trans. David L. Swain and Toshi Yonezawa. New York: Grove, 1996.

Ofir, Adi. "On Sanctifying the Holocaust: An Anti-theological Treatise." 1987. Hornstein, Levitt, Silberstein 195–204.

Ozsvath, Zsuzsanna, and Martha Satz. "The Audacity of Expressing the Inexpressible: The Relation between Moral and Aesthetic Considerations in Holocaust Literature." *Judaism* 34.2 (1985): 197–210.

Parens, Erik, ed. *Enhancing Human Traits: Ethical and Social Implications.* Washington, D.C.: Georgetown UP, 1998.

Peach, Linden. *Toni Morrison.* New York: St. Martin's, 1995.

Pérez-Torres, Rafael. "Between Presence and Absence: *Beloved,* Postmodernism, and Blackness." McKay and Andrews 179–202.

————. "Knitting and Knotting the Narrative Thread—*Beloved* as Postmodern Novel." Peterson 91–110.

Peterson, Nancy, ed. *Toni Morrison: Critical and Theoretical Approaches.* Baltimore: Johns Hopkins UP, 1997.

Phelan, James. "Toward a Rhetorical Reader-Response Criticism." Peterson 225–44.

Rahv, Philip. "Through the Midst of Jerusalem." 1967. Ross, *Critical Responses* 127–32.

Raphael, Marc Lee. Rev. of *The Holocaust in American Life,* by Peter Novick. *American Historical Review* 106.2 (2001): 534–35.

Rigney, Barbara Hill. "'Breaking the Back of Words': Language, Silence and the Politics of Identity in *Beloved.*" Solomon 138–47.

Robertson, Mary F. "Hystery, Herstory, History: 'Imagining the Real' in Thomas's *The White Hotel.*" *Contemporary Literature* 25 (1984): 452–77.

Rody, Caroline. "Toni Morrison's *Beloved:* History, 'Rememory,' and a 'Clamor for a Kiss.'" *New Literary History* 7.1 (1995): 92–119.

Rosenfeld, Alvin. *A Double Dying: Reflections on Holocaust Literature.* Bloomington: Indiana UP, 1980.

————, ed. *Thinking about the Holocaust after Half a Century.* Bloomington: Indiana UP, 1997.

Roskies, David. "Group Memory." *Commentary* 108.2 (1999): 62–66.

Ross, Daniel W., ed. *The Critical Responses to William Styron.* Westport, Conn.: Greenwood, 1995.

————. "'Things I Don't Want to Find Out About': The Primal Scene in *The Confessions of Nat Turner.*" *Twentieth Century Literature* 39.1 (1993): 79–98.

Rothberg, Michael. *Traumatic Realism: The Demands of Holocaust Representation.* Minneapolis: U of Minnesota P, 2000.

Rushdy, Ashraf H. A. "Daughters Signifyin(g) History: The Example of Toni Morrison's *Beloved.*" McKay and Andrews 37–66.

———. *Neo-slave Narratives: Studies in the Social Logic of a Literary Form.* New York: Oxford UP, 1999.

Sadako, Kurihara. "The Literature of Auschwitz and Hiroshima: Thoughts on Reading Lawrence Langer's *The Holocaust and the Literary Imagination.*" Trans. Richard H. Minear. *Holocaust and Genocide Studies* 7.1 (1993): 77–106.

Sale, Maggie. "Call and Response as Critical Method: African-American Oral Traditions and *Beloved.*" *African American Review* 26.1 (1992): 41–50.

Sales, Roger. "Toni Morrison's *Beloved.*" *Massachusetts Review* 91.1 (1988): 81–86.

Sanders, Mark. *Complicities: The Intellectual and Apartheid.* Durham: Duke UP, 2002.

Sanyal, Debarati. "A Soccer Match in Auschwitz: Passing Culpability in Holocaust Criticism." *Representations* 79 (2002): 1–27.

Schindler's List. Dir. Steven Spielberg. 1993. MCA Universal, 1994.

Scholem, Gershom. "*Eichmann in Jerusalem:* Exchange of Letters between Gershom Scholem and Hannah Arendt (January, 1964)." Feldman 240–51.

Schwartz, Amy E. "*Beloved:* It's Not a Question of Who Suffered More." *Washington Post* 3 Apr. 1988: B7.

Seidman, Naomi. "Elie Wiesel and the Scandal of Jewish Rage." *Jewish Social Studies* 3.1 (1996): 1–19.

Semprun, Jorge. *Literature or Life.* 1994. Trans. Linda Coverdale. New York: Penguin, 1998.

Shoah. Dir. Claude Lanzmann. 1985. Videorecording. New Yorker Video, 1999.

Sibelman, Simon P. *Silence in the Novels of Elie Wiesel.* New York: St. Martin's, 1995.

Smith, Valerie. "'Circling the Subject': History and Narrative in *Beloved.*" Gates and Appiah 342–55.

Sollors, Werner. "Holocaust and Hiroshima: American Ethnic Prose Writers Face the Extreme." *PMLA* 118.1 (2003): 56–62.

Solomon, Barbara, ed. *Critical Essays on Toni Morrison's* Beloved. New York: Simon & Schuster, 1998.

Spiegelman, Art. *In the Shadow of No Towers.* New York: Random House, 2004.

———. *Maus: A Survivor's Tale I: My Father Bleeds History.* New York: Pantheon, 1986.

———. *Maus: A Survivor's Tale II: And Here My Troubles Began.* New York: Pantheon, 1991.

Steiner, George. "The Fire Last Time." 1967. Ross, *Critical Responses* 121–25.

———. "The Hollow Miracle." 1959. *Language and Silence* 95–109.

———. "K." 1963. *Language and Silence* 118–26.

———. *Language and Silence.* New York: Atheneum, 1967.

Stewart, Anthony. "William TurnerGrayStyron, Novelist(s): Reactivating State Power in *The Confessions of Nat Turner.*" *Studies in the Novel* 27 (1995): 169–85.

Stoett, Peter. "Shades of Complicity: Towards a Typology of Transnational Crimes against Humanity." Jones 31–55.

Styron, William. *The Confessions of Nat Turner.* 1967. New York: Vintage International, 1993.

———. "More Confessions." Carnes 220–25.

———. "Nat Turner Revisited." 1992. *The Confessions of Nat Turner* 433–55.

———. *Sophie's Choice.* 1976. New York: Random House, 1999.

———. "This Quiet Dust." 1965. *This Quiet Dust* 9–30.

———, ed. *This Quiet Dust and Other Writings.* New York: Random House, 1982.

Swanson, Roy Arthur. "William Styron's Clown Show." Friedman and Malin 149–64.

Tabachnick, Stephen E. "Of *Maus* and Memory: The Structure of Art Spiegelman's Graphic Novel of the Holocaust." *Word & Image* 9.2 (1993): 154–62.

Tanner, Laura. "Sweet Pain and Charred Bodies: Figuring Violence in *The White Hotel.*" *boundary 2* 18.2 (1991): 130–49.

Thelwell, Mike. "Back with the Wind: Mr. Styron and the Reverend Turner." Clarke 79–91.

Thomas, Hugh. *The Slave Trade: A History of the Atlantic Slave Trade, 1440–1870.* New York: Simon & Schuster, 1997.

Thomas, Laurence Mordekhai. "Suffering as a Moral Beacon: Blacks and Jews." Flanzbaum 198–210.

———. *Vessels of Evil: American Slavery and the Holocaust.* Philadelphia: Temple UP, 1993.

Treat, John Whittier. *Writing Ground Zero: Japanese Literature and the Atomic Bomb.* Chicago: U of Chicago P, 1995.

Tyndall, Andrea. "Memory, Authenticity and Replication of the Shoah in Museums: Defensive Tools of the Nation." Lentin, *Re-presenting the Shoah* 111–26.

Vanderslice, John A. "A Hidden Key to Styron's *Nat Turner?*" *Notes on Contemporary Literature* 28.3 (1998): 8–9.

Vice, Sue. *Holocaust Fiction.* New York: Routledge, 2000.

Vital, David. "After the Catastrophe: Aspects of Contemporary Jewry." Hayes 120–38.

Waller, James. *Becoming Evil: How Ordinary People Commit Genocide and Mass Killing.* New York: Oxford UP, 2002.

Weissman, Gary. *Fantasies of Witnessing: Postwar Efforts to Experience the Holocaust.* Ithaca: Cornell UP, 2004.

White, Hayden. "Historical Emplotment and the Problem of Truth." Friedlander, *Probing the Limits* 37–53.

White, Jonathan, ed. *Recasting the World: Writing after Colonialism.* Baltimore: Johns Hopkins UP, 1993.

Wiesel, Elie. "The Holocaust as Literary Inspiration." Wiesel et al. 5–19.

———. Introduction. *Night; Dawn; Day.* 1960. Trans. Stella Rodway. New York: B'nai Brith Judaica Library, 1985.

———. *Night.* 1960. Trans. Stella Rodway. Intro. François Mauriac. Twenty-fifth anniversary ed. Pref. Robert McAfee Brown. New York: Bantam, 1986.

———. "A Plea for the Dead." Langer, *Art from the Ashes* 139–48.

———. "Why I Write." *Confronting the Holocaust.* Ed. Alvin H. Rosenfeld and Irving Greenberg. Bloomington: Indiana UP, 1978. 200–206.

Wiesel, Elie, Lucy S. Dawidowicz, Dorothy Rabinowitz, and Robert McAfee Brown. *Dimensions of the Holocaust: Lectures at Northwestern University.* Evanston: Northwestern UP, 1977.

Wilkomirski, Binjamin. *Fragments: Memories of a Wartime Childhood.* 1995. Trans. Carol Brown Janeway. New York: Schocken, 1996.

Wirth-Nesher, Hana. "The Ethics of Narration in D. M. Thomas' *The White Hotel.*" *Journal of Narrative Technique* 15 (1985): 15–28.

Witek, Joseph. *Comic Books as History: The Narrative Art of Jack Jackson, Art Spiegelman, and Harvey Pekar.* Jackson: Mississippi UP, 1989.

Wyatt, Jean. "Giving Body to the Word: The Maternal Symbolic in Toni Morrison's *Beloved.*" *PMLA* 108.3 (1993): 474–88.

Yoneyama, Lisa. *Hiroshima Traces: Time, Space and the Dialectics of Memory.* Los Angeles: U of California P, 1999.

Young, James. "The Holocaust as Vicarious Past: Art Spiegelman's *Maus* and the Afterimages of History." Bernard-Donals and Glejzer 23–45.

———. "Holocaust Documentary Fiction: The Novelist as Eyewitness." Lang, *Writing and the Holocaust* 200–215.

———. *Writing and Rewriting the Holocaust.* Bloomington: Indiana UP, 1988.

Zelizer, Barbie. "Every Once in a While: *Schindler's List* and the Shaping of History." Loshitzky, *Spielberg's Holocaust* 18–40.

Index

Avni, Ora, 110–13, 242n16
Azoulay, Ariella, 222n6

Babi Yar, 103, 240n6
Babi Yar (Kuznetsov), 240n6
Barthes, Roland, 81
Bartov, Omer, 74, 78, 83, 85
Bauer, Yehuda, 44, 230n22
"Bearing Witness" (Laub), 102–3, 105
Bell, Pearl K., 133
Beloved (Morrison), 28–29, 168–207;
    dedication of, 168–71, 199–201,
    248nn2–3, 251n21; memorialization
    in, 171–76; naming and unnaming
    in, 177–85, 249n9, 250n10; speaking
    corpse in, 204–7; trauma in, 185–94;
    the unspeakable in readings of,
    201–4; and U.S. national identity,
    194–201
Benjamin, Walter, 6
Bennett, Lerone, Jr., 144, 145, 164,
    222n7
Benston, Kimberly W., 178–79, 183, 210
Berger, James, 32, 226n2, 230n26
Bernard-Donals, Michael, 102–3, 239n3;
    and Richard Glejzer, 101, 102
Bernstein, Michael André, 238n24
Bettelheim, Bruno, 20, 40, 41, 46
"Beyond the Question" (Bernard-
    Donals), 102–3
Black Atlantic, The (Gilroy), 16–17, 23,
    223n12, 250n17, 251n21
Blacks and Jews in Literary Conversation
    (Budick), 13–14, 168, 200, 251n21
Blanchot, Maurice: and the un-
    speakable, 22, 32, 48–49. *See also*
    "Instant of My Death, The"; *Writing
    of the Disaster, The*
Bluest Eye, The (Morrison), 249n5
body. *See* corporeality
Boyarin, Jonathan, 45, 230n25
Brodsky, Joseph, 218
Brogan, Kathleen, 182, 183, 185, 188,
    196, 250n15

Brown, Robert McAfee, 42, 43, 243n21
Brown, Wendy, 33–34
Browne, Stephen Howard, 139, 142, 143,
    245nn8–9
Browning, Christopher, 46, 51
Budick, Emily: on *Beloved*, 168, 200,
    251n21; *Blacks and Jews*, 13–14
Budick, Sanford, and Wolfgang Iser, 48
"But Is It Good for the Jews?"
    (Horowitz), 76–78, 80, 84–85, 97,
    235n6, 237n16, 238n18
Butler, Judith, 40
Butz, Arthur, 228n9

Camera Lucida (Barthes), 81
Campbell, David, and Michael Dillon,
    252n8
"Camus' *Fall*" (Felman), 53
"Camus' *Plague*" (Felman), 53
Carroll, David: on Lyotard, 66; on
    Semprun, 241n13
Caruth, Cathy: in Hungerford, 232n35,
    232n38; in LaCapra, 232n34; in Leys,
    55–57; on trauma, 53–54, 58
Churchill, Ward, 221n3
"Cinema Animal, The" (Hartman),
    76–78, 87
Clarke, John Henrick, 28, 135, 144
collaboration, 22, 29, 62, 64;
    distinguished from complicity,
    213–14, 216–17, 252n3; in *Schindler's
    List*, 235n7
"Collateral Damage" (Hirsch), 221n1
Colorado, Pam, 221n3
*Complicities: The Intellectual and
    Apartheid* (Sanders), 22, 215, 217,
    225n22, 226n23, 252nn6–7
complicity, 22–24, 208–10; "after
    Auschwitz" as statement about,
    64–70; and agency, 26, 86–87, 98,
    173–76; avoided, 42–44, 87–90;
    "being complicit," 64, 213, 215,
    218–20; of body with its subjugation,
    183–84, 188–93; and corporeality,

haunting, 104–5, 124–30, 132, 136–37, 226n24; in Gilroy, 23
Hayes, Peter, 211, 230n24
Heidegger, Martin, 34
Hersey, John, 225n21
hibakusha, 19–21, 224n18, 225n19
Hilberg, Raul: on Goldhagen, 229n19; on the Holocaust, 168, 228n11, 248n1; in *Shoah*, 126
Himmler, Heinrich, 227n8
Hiroshima, 17–22; and the Holocaust, 17–21, 221n3, 224n17, 225n21
Hiroshima Notes (Oe), 18, 221n3, 223n15
Hiroshima Traces (Yoneyama), 18, 223n14, 224n16, 224n18
Hirsch, Marianne: on *In the Shadow of No Towers*, 221n1; on *Maus*, 243n24
"History, Politics, and Literature" (Gross and Bender), 146–47, 165
Hitler's Willing Executioners (Goldhagen), 229n19
Holloway, Karla F. C., 169
Holocaust: appropriation, 8–11, 14, 43–44, 168–71; and the atom bomb, 17–21, 221n3, 224n17, 225n21; denial, 39, 77, 228n9; and Eurocentrism, 44–45, 51–52; and Jewish identity, 15–16, 42–45, 222n6; in the Middle East, 222n6; nuclear, 17, 222n3; sacrilization, 40–42, 75, 77, 227n7; and September 11, 2001, 1–4, 17, 221n1; and slavery, 168–71, 199, 249n4; terminology, 40–44, 222n3, 228n15, 229n21, 230n23; testimony, 100–103; in trauma theory, 49–59; as unspeakable, 5–11, 44–48. *See also* "after Auschwitz"; unspeakable, the
Holocaust (television series), 134, 167, 245n3
"Holocaust as Vicarious Past, The" (Young), 114, 115
"Holocaust Documentary Fiction" (Young), 240n8

Holocaust in American Life, The (Novick), 7–8, 9, 39, 168, 248n1
Holocaust Industry, The (Finkelstein), 10, 12, 222n5
Holocaust of Texts, The (Hungerford), 9. *See also* Hungerford, Amy
"Holocaust Others" (Loshitzky), 75
Holocaust Representation (Lang), 10, 59
Holocaust studies, 31–32, 210–12, 219
Holocaust Testimonies (Langer), 102, 108, 113, 242nn14–15
Homo Sacer (Agamben), 32
Horowitz, Sara: on *Schindler's List*, 76–78, 80, 84–85, 97, 235n6, 237n16, 238n18; on testimony, 110; on the unspeakable, 59
Horwitz, Deborah, 195
Hungerford, Amy, 7, 9, 45; on deconstruction, 227n6; on *Fragments* controversy, 231n28, 231n31, 239nn4–5; on Holocaust denial, 228n9; on *Schindler's List*, 238n22; on trauma theory, 50–53, 57, 231n28, 232n35, 232n38; "trauma without experience," 50, 101; on the unspeakable, 32, 33, 227n6
Huyssen, Andreas, 100, 114, 224n24

identity: African American, and slavery, 15–16, 144–47, 177–79, 194–201; and corporeality, 29, 132, 149–50, 158, 204–7, 223n11; cultural, and trauma, 51–55; French, and the Holocaust, 35–36; Japanese, and the atom bomb, 18–20, 224n18; Jewish, and the Holocaust, 15–16, 42–45, 199–200, 222n6; racial, as biology, 15–16, 20–22, 114, 190–91. *See also under* "after Auschwitz"
Identity/Difference (Connolley), 215–16
"Instant of my death, The" (Blanchot), 105, 106

In the Shadow of No Towers
(Spiegelman), 1–5, 9, 12, 17, 221n1
Invisible Man (Ellison), 210
Irwin-Zarecka, Iwona, 229n17

Jaspers, Karl, 22, 217–18
Jew's Body, The (Gilman), 223n9, 223n11
Johnson, Barbara, 219
Jordan, June, 147
Joyner, Charles, 147

Keenan, Sally, 188
Killens, John Oliver, 165
Klein, Herbert S., 248n2
Kreyling, Michael, 133, 245n2
Kristeva, Julia, 104–5, 106
Kritzman, Lawrence D., 35, 36, 62
Kutz, Christopher, 22, 225n22; on complicity, 214–15; complicity principle, 217; on "the gray zone," 252n3
Kuznetsov, Anatoli, 240n6, 240n8

LaCapra, Dominick: on Agamben, 241n11; on Caruth, 231n34; on deconstruction, 56, 232n36; on de Man, 50, 57; on trauma, 53–54, 233n40; "victim" in, 56, 58, 232n36
Lang, Berel: on the Holocaust, and absence, 48–49; on the Holocaust, and language, 43, 60–61; on the Holocaust, and representation, 10, 233n44; on Holocaust denial, 228n9; on Novick, 221n2; on the unspeakable, 59
Langer, Lawrence: on Semprun, 108, 242n15; on testimony, 27, 102, 108, 113, 242nn14–15; in Treat, 19; on the unspeakable, 227n6
Languages of the Unsayable (Budick and Iser), 48
Lanzmann, Claude: as narrator in *Shoah*, 123–24; on *Schindler's List*, 73, 75, 85, 234n2; on subtitles to *Shoah*, 126–28, 131; on testimony in

Shoah, 121–23, 126. See also *Shoah* (Lanzmann)
Lappin, Elena, 239n4
Laub, Dori: and Shoshana Felman, 50, 51–52, 112; on testimony, 102–3, 105
Law, Richard G., 133, 134
Lawrence, David, 250n14
Ledbetter, Mark, 203, 249n7, 251n22
Lentin, Ronit, 222n6
Levi, Neil, 6
Levi, Primo, 5, 20, 217, 218; "the gray zone," 29, 62–63, 213–14, 216, 252n3; *Muselmann* in, 241n10; on *Sonderkommandos*, 234n45
Levinas, Emmanuel, 6, 14, 109, 222n8
Levine, Michael G., 118, 119, 224n24
Leys, Ruth, 55–56, 57, 68, 231n28, 231n33, 232n35
Lifton, Robert Jay, 20–21; on *hibakusha*, 225n19; on Hiroshima and the Holocaust, 223n13
"Limits of Representation, The" (Carroll), 241n13
Literature or Life (Semprun), 104, 107–9
Little, Margaret Olivia, 214
Little Matter of Genocide, A (Churchill), 221n3
Longest Shadow, The (Hartman), 33, 233nn43–44
Loshitzky, Yosefa: on *Schindler's List*, 26, 74, 75, 77; —, in Germany and Israel, 237n17; —, in U.S. race relations, 236n8; —, U.S. reception, 90–91
Lovejoy, Paul E., 248n2
Lyotard, Jean-François, 6, 22; on Auschwitz, 32, 66, 68–69

Maechler, Stefan, 239n4
Malcolm X, 210
Marks, Elaine, 226n2
materiality. *See* corporeality
Mauriac, François, 112–13, 118
Maus (Spiegelman): complicity in, 118–21; graphic format of, 243n23;

Cultural Frames, Framing Culture

Books in this series examine both the way our culture frames our narratives and the way our narratives produce the culture that frames them. Attempting to bridge the gap between previously disparate disciplines, and combining theoretical issues with practical applications, this series invites a broad audience to read contemporary culture in a fresh and provocative way.

Nancy Martha West
Kodak and the Lens of Nostalgia

Raphael Sassower and Louis Cicotello
The Golden Avant-Garde: Idolatry, Commercialism, and Art

Margot Norris
Writing War in the Twentieth Century

Robin Blaetz
Visions of the Maid: Joan of Arc in American Film and Culture

Ellen Tremper
I'm No Angel: The Blonde in Fiction and Film

Naomi Mandel
Against the Unspeakable: Complicity, the Holocaust, and Slavery in America